SPORT&
PEACE

a sociological perspective

Brian Wilson

OXFORD
UNIVERSITY PRESS

OXFORD
UNIVERSITY PRESS

Oxford University Press is a department of the University of Oxford.
It furthers the University's objective of excellence in research, scholarship,
and education by publishing worldwide. Oxford is a registered trade mark of
Oxford University Press in the UK and in certain other countries.

Published in Canada by
Oxford University Press
8 Sampson Mews, Suite 204,
Don Mills, Ontario M3C 0H5 Canada

www.oupcanada.com

Library and Archives Canada Cataloguing in Publication

Wilson, Brian, 1969–
Sport & peace : a sociological perspective / Brian Wilson.

(Themes in Canadian sociology)
Includes bibliographical references and index.
ISBN 978-0-19-543214-5

1. Sports—Sociological aspects. 2. Peace. 3. Sports and state. I. Title.
II. Series: Themes in Canadian sociology

GV706.5.W557 2012   306.4'83   C2012-900061-2

Cover image: Ian McKinnell/Getty Images

Oxford University Press is committed to our environment.
This book is printed on paper which has been certified by the Forest Stewardship Council®.

Printed and bound in Canada.

1 2 3 4 — 15 14 13 12

Contents

Acknowledgements

There are too many people to thank for their contributions to and support during this project and the lead-up to it, but I will do my best. I would first like to thank Lorne Tepperman for kindly inviting me to be a part of Oxford University Press's 'Themes in Canadian Sociology' Series and to Nancy Reilly for her enthusiasm and early work supporting the project proposal. Immense gratitude is owed to Oxford's Peter Chambers, whose work in the development of this manuscript is greatly appreciated—as was his patience, tact, encouragement, and wisdom during the hard months of writing and revising. Amy Hick's perceptive observations and thoughtful suggestions were invaluable in the copyediting stage. I also acknowledge and appreciate the contributions of the two anonymous reviewers of this book, whose excellent recommendations helped guide revisions.

A special thanks also to Vice-Rector Dr. Amr Abdalla of the United Nations–mandated University for Peace in Ciudad Colon, Costa Rica, for his kindness and generosity in arranging my research leave time at UPEACE—a time when many of the ideas for this book were put in place. I am also indebted to my friend Sean Neeb for initially facilitating my time with Right To Play in Kampala, Uganda, as well as Dr. Lorna Reid, Dr. Rudaba Khondker, Alice Kansiime, and the many other volunteers, coaches, and program participants who were so welcoming. A similar debt is owed to Professor Mike Boit and Dr. Vincent Onywera of Kenyatta University in Nairobi, Kenya, and Professor Bill Sheel of the University of British Columbia, for facilitating the research trip to Nairobi and the Rift Valley to study `running for peace' initiatives. I also acknowledge UBC's Martha Piper Research Fund for supporting that particular project. I am also most grateful to the School of Kinesiology at the University of British Columbia—and its Director, Robert Sparks—for granting the research leave that made the background work that inspired this book possible.

I acknowledge also support from the Social Sciences and Humanities Research Council of Canada (SSHRC) that has funded my research over the years on sport, youth, activism, media, and environmental issues—research that informs many of the chapters in this book. Such support for balanced examinations of key social issues in Canada and abroad is crucial if issues around social inequality and peace-promotion are to be approached responsibly. I also acknowledge permission granted by Temple University Press for the use of material I wrote in a chapter for the forthcoming collection *Sport and Neoliberalism* (edited by David Andrews and Michael Silk). Sections of that chapter, entitled 'Growth and Nature: Reflections on Sport, Carbon Neutrality, and Ecological Modernization', appear in chapter 8 of this book.

There are many others that have made particular contributions to this book. I thank Brad Millington for his insightful and good-humoured commentary at all stages of the process and his outstanding work as the teaching assistant for the course on which this book is based. I am also grateful to Gerry Veenstra, a fellow sociologist and old friend whose enthusiasm for the project was immensely helpful and much appreciated.

My colleagues in the School of Kinesiology working in various disciplines have contributed a great deal to my thinking about doing sociological work in a multidisciplinary context. Laura Hurd Clark, Wendy Frisby, Simone Longpre, Bob Sparks, Janna Taylor, Rob VanWynsberghe, and Patricia Vertinsky deserve special mention as members of the socio-cultural group within which I work at the University of British Columbia. I am so appreciative of the encouragement and insight I have received from all.

I have also met many colleagues in the sociology of sport field and elsewhere who deserve mention and thanks. I will always be grateful to Peter Donnelly, Graham Knight, Billy Shaffir, and Phil White for the support during my years as a graduate student. Their suggestions and advice continue to guide what I do, although they (and everybody else) should feel sufficiently distant from any bad ideas contained herein, ideas that are all mine. Michael Atkinson and James Gillett as long-time friends and excellent colleagues deserve mention for similar reasons. A special thanks also to David Andrews, whose commitment to creating venues for (physical) cultural studies scholars to write and collaborate in has been immense, and whose supportive editorial work throughout my career has been helpful in so many ways. The same can be said for Jim McKay, whose mentorship to me and many others has been immensurable.

Several others deserve thanks as well for their insights and various forms of support over time, including: Ted Alexander, Mark Beauchamp, Janet Becker, Peter Berry, Sean Brayton, Ben Carrington, Peter Crocker, Simon Darnell, Will Dunlop, Dominique Falls, Meridith Griffin, Rick Gruneau, Jean Harvey, Chris Hawke, Lyndsay Hayhurst, Tim Inglis, Shannon Jette, Margaret MacNeill, Martin O'Keane, Eme Onuoha, Andre Powell, Jim Rupert, David Sanderson, Bill Sheel, James Tyer, Nicolien Van Luijk, John Waite, Cam Wilson, and Kevin Young.

I am also grateful to the students in the Sport, Peace, and Conflict class I teach at the University of British Columbia, who patiently and enthusiastically worked through the materials that became this book.

A great deal of appreciation is also owed to my Dad for his ongoing attention to anything that might aid my writing or teaching over the years and for the yearly gift of videos and news clippings. Many thanks also, of course, to Mom for her ongoing and unwavering support on all matters.

Finally, this book, quite simply, would not have been produced without the encouragement, patience, and love of Desiree Sattler—thank you.

Preface

In the opening chapter of his international bestseller, *How Soccer Explains the World: An Unlikely Theory of Globalization*, journalist Frank Foer reflects on time he spent with supporters of the notorious Serbian football club, Red Star Belgrade. Foer describes their well-earned reputation for using intimidation tactics to 'police' Red Star players who are not performing to an acceptable standard, and their frequent attacks on supporters of rival teams who are caught in the wrong place at the wrong time. Most startling is Foer's account of the key role that these supporters—actively recruited by the Serbian government—played in the paramilitary offensive against the Croatian people and army during the Balkan Wars of the 1990s. As Foer put it, 'Red Star fans would become Milosovic's shock troops, the most active agents of ethnic cleansing' (2004, p. 13).

Foer's depiction would seem to sit strangely beside portrayals of sport in the work of international non-governmental organizations (NGOs) like Right To Play and Shoe4Africa. These organizations are well known for their use of sport as a tool to support development efforts and conflict transformation in war-torn and/or poverty-stricken regions of Africa, the Middle East, and elsewhere. It is not uncommon to see media stories that describe how these sorts of groups use recreational sporting events as forums to educate about HIV prevention, to rehabilitate and (re)integrate child soldiers, and to bring together groups that have been in conflict—offering 'neutral' settings where empathy can be developed and positive relationships built.

In this book, these types of seemingly contradictory portrayals are linked through an exploration of sport's complex and multi-layered relationship with peace. Certainly, as Foer recognizes in his book, not all soccer fans are violent, and sport supporters of all backgrounds may collectively stand for a variety of peace-related issues. An example of this emerged in coverage of recent protests in Egypt:

Last Thursday, the Egyptian Soccer Federation announced that they would be suspending all league games throughout the country in an effort to keep the soccer clubs from congregating. Clearly this was a case of too little, too late. Even without games, the football fan associations have been front and center organizing everything from the neighborhood committees that have been providing security for residents, to direct confrontation with the state police . . . The involvement of the clubs has signaled more than just the intervention of sports fans. The soccer clubs' entry into the political struggle also means the entry of the poor, the disenfranchised, and the mass of young people in Egypt for whom soccer was their only outlet. (Zirin, 2011)

At the same time, I will use existing research and writing by sociologists to help explain the role of sport in peace, war, and violence—and to demonstrate why it is necessary to understand the social and cultural contexts within which sport-related conflicts take place before attempting to make sense of these conflicts. I use various theoretical lenses to further this book's exploration of, among other topics, international sport for development and peace groups like Right To Play—and the reasons that even these groups have attracted some well-founded criticism.

Of course, this look at the sport–peace relationship leads to questions and topics that extend well beyond international development and soccer-related conflict. For example, and recognizing that recent Nobel Peace Prize winners include environmentalists like Al Gore and Wangari Muta Maathai, I will consider debates about the potentially negative environmental impacts of maintaining sporting venues like golf courses and ski hills, and hosting major sporting events like the Olympics, and critically examine responses by sport managers and others to these issues. I will also encourage reflection on how sport can be a forum for educating about environmental issues, and ponder how the creation of cross-border 'peace parks' might promote reconciliation and intercultural relationships through environmental recreation.

I will recognize how sport has for years been used in diplomatic efforts, noting the various meanings and consequences of cultural exchanges like the oft-celebrated 1972 Canada–USSR hockey series, and public diplomacy efforts associated with the Beijing Olympics and the FIFA World Cup in post-apartheid South Africa. I acknowledge also the role that sport has played and continues to play as a forum for protest against (for example) the use of native mascots by sport teams, or against forms of economic globalization commonly associated with the overseas sweatshops of Nike and other athletic apparel companies.

This journey into sport's relationship with peace is also intended to inspire thinking about how physical education and other styles of pedagogy through sport can perpetuate violent attitudes among boys and men who are commonly socialized within misogynist and homophobic sporting cultures—or, conversely, how physical education and sporting contexts can be forums that enable reconciliation between conflicting groups. I will similarly consider how the sport–peace linkage is relevant to thinking about how sport media may perpetuate forms of cultural violence through the stereotyping of particular ethnic or racial groups and how more progressive sport commentary and coverage is possible in the form of what I call sport-for-peace journalism.

In the end, what will become clear is that while debates persist about *how* sport is related to peace, it is unquestionable that sport and peace are integrally linked. They are linked in the work of practitioners interested in using sport to deal with social problems, and for sporting event promoters and corporate executives hoping to align themselves (and their brands) with the feel-good stories that often emerge from sport-for-peace work. With these trends in mind—and for better and worse—it should be no surprise that linkages between sport and peace are becoming part of the popular imagination.

. . .

This book is ultimately driven by the well-founded assumption that hope for positive changes in society comes, first, from identifying and understanding social problems that exist in society—and identifying viable solutions and alternatives. The arguments underlying this book are therefore grounded in a sociologically informed understanding of the ways that sport has become better than it was (e.g., for many women and girls, for youth interested in alternative, non-competitive sport)—and an awareness of sport-related social problems that continue to emerge and exist. For example, the battle to promote access to sport and physical activity for those with limited economic resources is ongoing. As well, corporate groups are increasingly influencing the decisions of those responsible for dealing with sport-related social and environmental problems—a trend that has led many sociologists to question whether democratic principles are being undermined as those motivated ultimately by profits are taking the lead on some of the key issues of our time.

In my investigation of these issues I am guided by what Henry Giroux (2007) has called an 'educated hope', the idea that by understanding and identifying injustices in and around sport we are not only better positioned to create change—we are also emboldened to do so. I am similarly inspired by the challenge set out by sport journalist Dave Zirin (2008)—who has urged members of the sociology of sport community to 'break out of the academic ghetto', to 'eschew excessively coded and obscure language', and to 'fight to become part of the general discourse of sports conversation, both on campuses and in the broader sports world' (p. 28). Responding to this, I spend the following chapters featuring the work of many sociologists of sport who are already 'off the bench'.

. . .

I have organized this book into four main parts. Part 1, Introduction to the Study of Sport, Sociology, and Peace, includes an introductory chapter that outlines the value of critical and sociological thinking about sport and peace and offers definitions of key terms. Chapter 2—Theory, Sport, and Peace:

Tools and Lenses for Seeing Sport in Context—is intended to equip readers with tools for 'seeing' the sport and peace relationship from a variety of perspectives. I discuss a range of sociological theories that commonly influence researchers who study sport and demonstrate how it is that the opinions we hold about sport can often be traced back to the theoretical lenses through which we prefer to look. This chapter offers a platform upon which all the subsequent chapters in the book rest, because a proper understanding of various sociological theories is crucial if we are to make sense of the sport–peace relationship. It is also the chapter where I advance an argument for privileging critically oriented theories because they help us see and ask questions about the inequalities that exist in and around sport, and ways these inequalities are perpetuated–fundamental questions for those of us concerned with promoting positive forms of peace.

With this background, I proceed to Part 2, Exploring the New and Old Politics of Sport and Peace, which includes chapters 3 and 4. Chapter 3—Sport, Diplomacy, and Nationalism—discusses what Lincoln Allison (2005) refers to as an 'old politics of sport', which in this case means an examination of ways that governments use sport as part of their efforts to promote nationalism and unity. This also means exploring sport's role in foreign policy, and especially how sport is used to gain prestige and recognition in the international community.

In chapter 4—Sport, Global Politics, and Peace—I focus on what Allison (2005) describes as a 'global politics of sport'. To do this, I define and discuss the term 'neo-liberalism'—a term that is central to contemporary discussions about sport-related politics, and one that will draw our attention to ways that the policies and ideologies that influence government and corporate decision-making trickle down to the lives of those in and around sport. I then examine the term 'globalization', another concept commonly used to help sociologists explain how it is that sport-related politics have become not only global in scope, but also heavily influenced by transnational corporations. The term 'corporate nationalism' is similarly introduced here to help us see and understand some implications of nation–corporation linkages. Chapter 4 concludes with a broader look at the complex relationships between globalization, peace, and sport, with particular attention to what Thomas Friedman (2000) called the 'Golden Arches Theory of Conflict Prevention'.

While chapters 3 and 4 identify many sport-related social problems that can be traced back to political decisions made 'from above', chapters 5 and 6 consider ways that grassroots activists, educators, and scholars respond to some of these problems 'from below'. These chapters make up Part 3 of the book, Peace Activism, Peace Education, and a Sporting Praxis. In chapter 5, I examine the possibilities for peace promotion within and through sport, focusing on sport-related social movements and social change. The chapter features work by sociologists who examine the relevance of sport subcultures that promote and embody anti-competitive and pro-community values, and considers the extent to which these groups undermine, challenge, and/or offer alternatives to dominant sport culture. The chapter also includes an overview of research on sport-related social movements—movements that explicitly attempt to incite social change through, for example, organized lobbying and protest against the use of mascots and mascot names such as 'Indians', 'Redskins', and 'Braves' that are considered degrading by many aboriginal groups and others. As a whole, the chapter highlights the range of sport-related activities that might be considered activist and resistant, and considers whether and how these activities make a difference in the lives of activists and in the broader structures and political entities that are often the target of protest.

The discussion about strategies for proactively addressing problems that exist within and around sport continues in chapter 6—Pursuing Praxis: Peace Education, Critical Pedagogy, and the Sociology of Sport. The focus here is on how forms of peace education—and particular forms known as 'critical pedagogy' especially—can be used to raise awareness about ways that sport is enabling and constraining. I discuss specific strategies that have been used to facilitate forms of sport-related praxis, featuring a series of short case studies that explore the utility of creative film and writing about sport and social inequality, community-based 'action research' focused around barriers to accessing recreation and sport, values-based peace-building physical activity and programs, and anti-violence education led by athletes.

In Part 4—Key Topics and Pressing Concerns in Sport and Peace: International Development, the Environment, and Media—I discuss sport's relationship with international development, environmental issues, and the media. Although any number of topics could have been chosen for this section, these stood out for me because they are at the centre of so many contemporary discussions and debates about the relationship between sport and peace. For example, chapter 7—Reflections on Intervention and Imperialism in the Sport for (International) Development and Peace Industry—follows up on issues that have emerged as the United Nations and sport for development and peace (SDP) groups like Right To Play have brought attention to (and advocated for) sport-driven development efforts in countries of the Global South (i.e., 'developing' countries). In this context, I address critical questions about the work of and pressures on NGOs in an era when these organizations are increasingly required to fill gaps left by government. Debates and issues around the 'development' concept are also explored, as are strategies and theories of peace-building and conflict resolution that underlie the work of Right To Play and organizations like the Mathare Youth Sport Association (based in Nairobi, Kenya) and Football 4 Peace (run out of the University of Brighton in the UK). Football 4 Peace, and especially the work of sociologist-activist John Sugden, who is one of the program's leaders, is featured here as a way of showcasing how Sugden and his colleagues use a sociological imagination to inform their efforts to enable conflict transformation and intercultural under-standing for Jewish and Arab children and youth in Israel.

Chapter 8—Sport, the Environment, and Peace: Debates and Myths about Carbon-Neutral Sport—also focuses on one of the key peace-related issues of our time. That the United Nations Development Program (UNDP) and the International Olympic Committee host the biennial World Conference on Sport and Environment—a conference that brings together sport-related cor-porations, mega-event organizers, NGOs, and others interested in minimizing sport's impacts on the environment—is evidence of the issue's relevance for major international governing bodies. Of course, the work of these powerful groups is not immune to critique, as I will show in this chapter. In fact, I spend much of the chapter outlining ways that sport has been critiqued for its impact on the environment and discussing how sport-related organizations and cor-porations respond to these critiques. With the latter point in mind, I outline why claims by sport-related organizations and mega-event organizers to be carbon neutral might not be as progressive and unproblematic as they seem. In this context, I introduce Schnaiberg and Gould's (2000) 'treadmill of pro-duction' metaphor as a way of outlining how consumer societies are designed in ways that put the natural environment at risk. This chapter also explains how natural environments can be platforms for peace-building—drawing on emerging research on the role that peace parks can play in conflict resolution.

The final chapter in this section, chapter 9—Towards a Sport-for-Peace Journalism? Problems and Possibilities in Sport Media—was chosen in re-sponse to ongoing concerns expressed by sociologists and others about ways that sport-related media are consistently implicated in the promotion of violence, war, and militarism. The chapter speaks to this issue through an overview of research on sport media's links with violence/war/military, and discussion of how particular ideological positions and inequalities are rein-forced though these connections. With these issues in mind, I then challenge researchers, journalists, and others to contemplate the possibility of a sport-for-peace journalism.

Finally, chapter 10—Six Summary Arguments and a Minor Utopian Vi-sion—concludes the discussion and book. In this chapter I examine the key arguments and observations that underlie the book's various chapters, sum-marize suggestions for social change drawn from the work of key theorists and practitioners that appear throughout the text, and consider ways to pursue a more peaceful and peace-promoting sport in the future.

• • •

Decisions about what topics to feature and how to feature them are for any book necessarily selective and guided by the preferences and experiences of the author. This book is no exception.

For example, my choices were partially guided by a series of impactful sport and peace–related experiences I had during a research leave I took in 2007—a leave granted by the University of British Columbia where I work. I spent the early part of the year at the United Nations–mandated University for Peace (UPEACE) in Ciudad Colon, Costa Rica, where I was exposed to a curriculum that is based entirely around the study of peace—with streams for postgraduate students interested in peace education, environmental security and peace, international peace studies, gender and peace, international law and human rights, and 'media, peace, and conflict', among other topics. I was especially struck by the emphasis on 'peace and the environment' and 'peace and media', and spent time thinking about how a peace studies–influenced approach to these topics might be informative for sociologists of sport—thinking that led to the development of chapters 8 and 9.

My research leave also took me to Kampala, Uganda, where I had the opportunity to attend the East African meetings of Right To Play, and visit Right To Play program sites around the city. I should state here that my writing about the sport for development and peace industry in this book includes a set of critiques of work done by organizations like Right To Play, and especially of a system that requires such organizations to compete with other humanitarian groups for funding and survival—a system where international development agencies sometimes play an uncomfortably prominent role in local communities. At the same time that I understand and agree with many of these critiques, I should also be clear that these visits to the Right To Play sites in Uganda opened my mind to the inspiring on-the-ground work that is being done in many areas, and the role that international sport for development and peace NGOs can play in promoting community and health. In a similar way, recent research I conducted in the Rift Valley of Kenya—which included interviews with high-profile distance runners who organized and were featured at 'run for peace' events intended to bring together warring tribes following Kenya's post-election violence in late 2007—highlighted the key role that sport and respected athletes can play in reconciliation efforts. These thoughts are reflected in chapter 7's discussion of the pros and cons of sport-related international development work and chapter 6's exploration of sport-related social movements.

The final leg of my leave took me to Beijing, China, to attend the pre-Olympic World Conference on Sport and the Environment, co-organized by the Beijing Olympic Organizing Committee (BOCOG) and the United Nations Development Programme. The conference included a trip around Beijing's cutting-edge event venues where tour guides highlighted the astonishing progress—driven by innovation and new technologies—that had been made on environmental issues in the soon-to-be Olympic city (e.g., venues designed to collect rain water and conserve energy). I noted other remarkable (and at times troubling) pro-environment initiatives that were taking place—from razing areas of the city to plant trees, to the banning of polluting taxis from the roads.

In fact, the one-minded focus on innovation and technology, and the apparent lack of reflection on whether mega–sporting events like the Olympics might be a bad idea (i.e., that they might, under some circumstances, do more harm than good; that they might negatively impact more vulnerable groups while benefiting more wealthy groups) inspired chapter 8's critical examination of the dominant 'ecological modernist' approach to dealing with environmental problems—the approach that guides the work of recent Olympic Organizing Committees and many other sport-related organizations and corporations.

Of course, my choice of topics for this book was ultimately informed by research and writing I have been doing for several years in areas related to sport and social movements, youth culture and recreation, social inequality and mass media, and the environment. In chapter 6 I refer to previous studies I have conducted on the importance of new media in the formation and functioning of contemporary sport-related social movements (Wilson, 2002; Wilson, 2007a), while in chapters 6 and 7 I draw on research I conducted with Lyndsay Hayhurst amd Wendy Frisby, where we demonstrate how forms of sport-for-peace activism are ironic in the sense that practitioners are often attempting to resolve sport-related problems in ways that inadvertently perpetuate these same problems (Wilson and Hayhurst, 2009; cf. Hayhurst, Wilson, and Frisby, 2010). Chapter 8's discussion of sport and environmental issues—and especially the critical look at claims about carbon neutrality by those in sport-related industries—is based on studies I am conducting with Brad Millington on ways that sport organizations and corporations are responding to concerns about the environment (Millington and Wilson, 2010b; Wilson, in press; Wilson and Millington, in press). Chapter 9's call for a sport-for-peace journalism is similarly based on a study I am conducting with Dominique Falls that considers how the principles of peace journalism proposed by Galtung (1998), Hackett (2007), Lynch and McGoldrick (2005), and others might be relevant for sport media. This same chapter was influenced by my research with Bob Sparks and others on ways that various forms of inequality and violence are perpetuated through mass media (Wilson, 1997; Wilson and Sparks, 1999; Millington and Wilson, 2010a). My arguments about the value of sport for underserved youth are similarly informed by studies I conducted with Phil White on the 'tolerance rules' youth develop in recreational drop-in centres that target diverse sub-groups of low income young people (Wilson et al., 2001; Wilson and White, 2001, 2003).

All this to say, this book offers a necessarily partial, selective, and in many ways personal view of sport and peace. I am up-front about this partiality and selectivity in hopes of inspiring an honest, open, but certainly evidence-driven conversation about a complex and controversial topic of immense contemporary relevance.

PART I

Introduction to the Study of Sport, Sociology, and Peace

1

Critiquing Sport, Transforming Sport: An Introduction to the Study of Sport, Sociology, and Peace

Questions to Consider

- Should we question the widely accepted idea that sport promotes peace?
- How can using a 'sociological imagination' help us understand how sport can be used to promote and/or undermine peace?
- How does the critical study of sport leave us in a better position to make informed recommendations for changing sport for the better?
- What are useful definitions for the terms 'peace' and 'sport', and why might these terms be considered 'floating signifiers'?

Introduction: The Many Sides of Sport

I am a sociologist with a particular interest in the contributions that sport makes to society—as well as the problems that are embedded in and reinforced by **sport**. When conducting research on these topics, it is not difficult to find high profile and popular examples of ways that sport is 'a force for good'. Consider the recent film *Invictus*, which depicts Nelson Mandela's famous use of rugby to unite a post-apartheid South Africa, or the work of celebrity athletes like NBA star Steve Nash, whose charitable foundation supports projects for underserved children. Media coverage surrounding the Vancouver 2010 Olympics also highlighted ways that sport connects people within and across nations—while coverage of the subsequent Paralympics provoked discussion about sport's role in combating discrimination against persons with disabilities.

Although it is difficult to pinpoint all the ways that sport is considered valuable for society, former United Nations Secretary General Kofi Annan encapsulated many of these in the following quotation—a quotation widely referred to in promotional materials for sport-related humanitarian groups:

> People in every nation love sport. Its values—fitness, fair play, teamwork, and the pursuit of excellence—are universal. At its best, it brings people together, no matter what their origin, background, religious beliefs or economic status. And when young people participate in sports or have access to physical education, they can

build up their health and self-esteem, use their talents to the fullest, learn the ideals of teamwork and tolerance, and be drawn away from the dangers of drugs and crime. That is why the United Nations is turning more and more often to the world of sport for help in our work for peace and our efforts to achieve the Millennium Development Goals. (United Nations, 2004)

In fact, and although the recent Vancouver Olympics and Paralympics—and subsequently the FIFA World Cup held in South Africa—raised the profile of a number of sport–peace linkages, publicity around the sorts of benefits Annan refers to has been at a peak since the United Nations International Year of Physical Education and Sport (IYSPE) in 2005. For example, the Canada-based sport for development and peace (SDP) organization Right To Play frequently receives attention for their work in African refugee camps, aiding in post-conflict reconciliation by bringing together rival groups in friendly sporting competitions. Peace-promoting exhibition sporting events are similarly lauded for their positive impacts on social cohesion within and among societies. A high profile example of this an example featured in IYSPE promotional materials—was a 2004 soccer match between Brazil and Haiti in Port-au-Prince, a match intended to support humanitarian and anti-violence efforts in the region by improving the morale of the Haitian people and encouraging armed factions in Haiti to hand in their guns. Sport programs in North American inner cities, such as 'midnight basketball' programs and Boys and Girls Clubs that 'get youth off the streets' into safer recreation-driven environments—where they are exposed to positive adult role models who teach social values through sport—are also celebrated for their role in reducing youth crime and gang involvement.

The examples described above and others like them rightly inspire some educators, youth workers, conflict resolution experts, international development workers, and others to consider ways that sport could support their objectives. *The problem, however, with these types of all upside portrayals of sport is that they are, at best, partial and somewhat deceiving, and at worst, dangerously one-sided and simplistic.* That is to say, just as there is evidence to stand behind the view that sport supports peace-building and social development, there is also an abundance of research demonstrating how social inequalities and various social problems are inherent to and perpetuated by sport.

Why is this absence of critique a problem? Why should social issues associated with sport receive fair attention? Consider the kinds of problems that are, at times, underplayed, and the potential consequences of being overly focused on sport's positive contributions. For example, forms of abuse, violence, and exploitation are known to take place in sports for youth and children when the behaviours of influential and revered adult coaches go unchecked or unchallenged. The notorious case of Canadian minor league hockey coach Graham James and his abuse of adolescent boys who played on his teams (including former NHLer Sheldon Kennedy, who is now a dedicated advocate for groups that fight child abuse) is one of many instances that can be found across a range of sports (Donnelly, 2006). In a related way, the competition and performance orientation that has come to dominate youth involvement in North American sports means that values like tolerance, personal development, kindness, and 'playing for fun' may be de-emphasized in favour of those associated with winning, such as dominating opponents and 'playing through pain' (Young, 2004).

Issues raised about Own the Podium—the funding program intended to support Canada's elite athletes in the lead-up to the Vancouver 2010 Olympics—are similarly relevant here. For example, scholars like Peter Donnelly (2009/2010) argue that the Olympic-related vision of promoting peace through friendly competition is undermined when a host nation designs a program that is symbolically and literally intended to support the domination of opponents. Moreover, by promoting the influx of more and more money into developing faster and stronger athletes with superior equipment, one can begin to see the Olympics as an athletic 'arms race'—where nations with fewer resources and/or less interest in investing in elite sports are disadvantaged (see Donnelly, 2009/2010). The tragic death of a luger from Georgia in a practice run leading up to the Vancouver Games—on a track developed to allow for the fastest runs, especially for the Canadian athletes who had privileged access to the track for training—raises further questions about the tendency to promote and invest in 'faster, higher, stronger' versions of sport.

Of course, these issues are subject to debate, as proponents of higher levels of athlete funding understandably describe the financial hardships that many athletes experience in the years leading up to major sport events. To be clear though, these are *political* debates about the best ways for government to invest money—since the evidence that speaks to the actual impact of success in elite-level sport on the everyday lives of Canadians is largely anecdotal, with a recent study conducted in the Netherlands suggesting that increases in 'national pride' and the 'stimulation of social cohesion' following athletic success are only temporary in that country (van Hilvoorde, Elling, and Stokvis, 2010).

Even the often-lauded 'sport for development and peace' interventions are not immune to critiques—the same sorts of critiques that are commonly levelled at international NGO work more generally. For example, some argue that aid recipients are not always well positioned to take ownership of the (sport-related) projects initiated by aid providers—leading some critics to question whether SDP programs are another form of neo-imperialism (Giulianotti, 2006).

Speaking more generally, critics of sport's positioning in North American culture and in other contexts argue that people are socialized to be passive and dedicated *consumers* of spectator sport (not necessarily good citizens who are brought together by sporting events). Other researchers in the sociology of sport field show that gender- and race-related stereotypes tend to be reinforced through and within physical education classes and sport-related media (Millington and Wilson, 2010a).

Finally, and as I write this chapter in the aftermath of the Vancouver 2010 Olympics—a Games promoted as 'carbon neutral' and guided by concerns for environmental issues more generally—it is worth noting that some scholars reasonably argue that *not* hosting a sporting mega-event like the Olympics is the best thing that a city could do for the environment, suggesting that the environmental benefits that the Olympics leverage could be achieved in other ways for far less money. In his keynote presentation at a 2008 sociology of sport conference entitled Remember to Resist held at the University of Toronto—a conference featuring the work of athlete-activists and sport scholars concerned with inequality and civil rights—Harry Edwards, renowned sociologist of sport and Professor Emeritus from the University of California, Berkeley, offered the following solution: hold the Olympics in 'set' locations, but allow different cities to 'host' the Games in these set locations. Such a strategy would, according to Edwards, save cities from the collateral damage commonly associated with preparation for these events, while also allowing these 'hosts' to promote themselves (e.g., as tourist locations) in other ways. Sociologists Jay Coakley and Peter Donnelly (2009) offer a similar suggestion, indicating that having 'multiple hosts' for a single Games would allow several nations/cities to use *existing* facilities in running a portion of the events—thus attaining the cultural and economic benefits that are sometimes associated with the Games, without having to develop 'massive and highly specialized facilities that may never be regularly used or filled to capacity' (p. 438; cf. Kidd, 2009/2010).

Critiquing Sport, Transforming Sport

With this background, the upcoming chapters will be guided by the well-founded assumption that while sport unquestionably plays a role in many positive social developments, it is in and through sport that many social problems and inequalities are reflected and reproduced. To be clear—by looking at these various sides of sport I am not intending to distract from sport's value as an appreciated and revered form of contemporary culture, or to undermine the experiences of those who take pleasure in it. On the contrary, the point is that balanced and critical thinking about sport's role in society is crucial if its full potential is to be approached. In other words, *putting sport under a critical lens is good for sport.*

With this in mind, it is important to think through what it means to 'put sport under a critical lens', and how this book might contribute to a socially conscious approach to sport. Although I engage these questions throughout the upcoming chapters, it is worth stating up-front that the key arguments I make throughout this book are all, in one form or another, guided by my use of what C. Wright Mills (1959) called a '**sociological imagination**'. What this means (following Mills) is that to understand social problems, it is crucial to *pay attention to the (historical) contexts within which these problems take place*. For example, to bring a sociological imagination to the opening ceremonies of the Vancouver 2010 Olympics—and specifically the representation of aboriginal groups in those ceremonies—would require knowledge of, among other contextual information: a history of race relations in Canada; a history of spectacular, mass-mediated representations of nations and nationalism at opening ceremonies of Olympic Games; knowledge of ways that stereotypes about certain racial groups are perpetuated through their portrayals within mediated spectacles; and an understanding of ways that major sporting events may act as forums for promoting social change and challenging existing power structures and stereotypes. Using this and other contextual information (such as pre-existing studies on aboriginal issues and sport) one can begin to consider the broader relevance and implications of these events, how they are packaged for spectators and viewers, and how particular perspectives and versions of history are selectively promoted (and hidden) through sport spectacles, like opening ceremonies.

Mills also highlights the need to 'imagine' *relationships between the problems experienced by individuals, and the structural explanations for these problems—* what he calls 'the public issues of social structure' (1959, p. 8). For example, a young person living in poverty in Canada may have difficulty accessing physical activity spaces in recreation centres. This would appear to be an 'individual problem' for an analyst who does not account for or uncover any contextual information—an analyst who *only* considers how this individual attempts to manoeuvre around the barriers that exist for him or her in the existing system. Analysts who also pay attention to the structural level, however, would recognize that decision-makers at Canadian recreation centres are increasingly required to reduce the amount of funding that is directed towards services that are 'unprofitable' because of government cutbacks to these sorts of programs (Donnelly and Coakley, 2002; Frisby et al., 2005). A sociological imagination can help us begin to consider how the policies and ideologies associated with these government cuts impact the day-to-day experiences of those who use (or do not use) these recreational services, as well as those employed by Canada's recreation centres. It can also alert us to ways the economic, cultural, and political developments taking place on a global level may impact the decision-making of politicians who are tasked with maintaining relationships with—and sometimes aligning their policy objectives with—political leaders in other countries. For example, one can begin to imagine how a collective move by politicians from many countries toward the use of market-driven approaches to dealing with social problems may, in fact, 'trickle down' to and negatively impact the young person living in poverty.

Sociologists of sport interested in understanding all kinds of inequalities will also use their sociological imagination to help explain, for example, why it is that some groups are perpetually marginalized in and around sport, how certain stereotypes are reinforced though sport media, how various forms of media might also be used to challenge problematic depictions, and how hosting mega–sporting events like the Olympics might be enabling for some and constraining for others. To engage these questions, sociologists use various 'lenses' that have been developed to highlight the complex reasons that inequalities are often exacerbated and perpetuated, and how actions seemingly intended to reduce inequalities may, in fact, reinforce these same inequalities.

Other theories/lenses will help us identify and make sense of instances where sport has been useful as a forum to, for example, support intercultural understanding and conflict transformation. Research conducted in places like post-apartheid South Africa, Israel, and Bosnia and Herzegovina have shown how sport and physical education settings can be powerful contexts for this sort of peace-building work (Gasser and Levinsen, 2006; Keim, 2003; Sugden, 2006). Further research focused around peace-building at national and international levels has also been conducted to show the role sport can play in breaking down sometimes long-standing political barriers.

Many of these topics will bring us to literature within the broad area known as **peace studies**. Peace studies is an interdisciplinary, social science–based academic field that draws from research in disciplines like sociology, environmental studies, international relations and political science, anthropology, psychology, theology, health studies, and other fields. While the field grew in the 1980s in response to Cold War–related international issues like preventing nuclear destruction, the 1990s saw an increased emphasis on domestic issues related to structural, domestic, and civil violence (Harris, Fisk, and Rank, 1998).

Like all fields, peace studies has not been immune to critique and controversy. For example, and despite the efforts of peace studies scholars like Fuller (2004), who have been vigilant in their efforts to highlight the experiences, perspectives, and peace-promoting potential of marginalized groups, a long-standing concern is that research in the field has been overly focused on state-level power relations, and has therefore inadvertently privileged state-driven (i.e., hierarchical or 'top-down') solutions to conflicts and violence. This tension between top-down and bottom-up approaches to attaining peace remains today, although researchers are increasingly conceptualizing ways that these approaches might be integrated, or used in complementary ways (Richmond, 2007).

Broadly speaking then, peace studies, while not an entirely unified field, remains concerned with better understanding why armed conflicts take place, exploring and devising responses to stop human rights violations, and promoting various ways of thinking about how to create and maintain more peaceful societies. Peace studies texts, like the *Handbook of Peace and Conflict Studies* edited by Webel and Galtung (2007), *Peace and Conflict Studies* by Barash and Webel (2002), *Peace and Conflict Studies: An Introduction* by Jeong (2000), and *The Transformation of Peace* by Richmond (2007) include work on topics ranging from conflict mediation and resolution, to strategies for using the arts to promote peace, to techniques for journalists interested reporting the news without glorifying conflict, to the important and sometimes controversial role of human rights legislations in peace promotion. In this book, research in these and other areas will inform discussions about, for example, methods for resolving conflict through sport, the practice of peace education through sport, and ways to promote novel and progressive understandings of conflict through sport journalism.

In highlighting research focused around the use of sport in peace promotion alongside research that alerts us to social problems associated with sport, the goal is to both *understand* sport-related social problems and their origins, and with this information *offer suggestions for change* that are beneficial for various social groups (i.e., not just the most powerful groups). Mills's sociological imagination is pertinent in this context too, since envisioning large-scale social change—and understanding how the contexts we exist within are always influenced by and also constituted through our social and cultural practices—is difficult without sensitivity to progressions that have been made over time and in other settings (Slack, 1996). Ann Hall and her colleagues, in their foundational text *Sport in Canadian Society*, describe this well:

> Very often we feel we have no impact on the structures of our society. However, despite the temptation to conceive of 'the system' as having a logic and momentum of its own, social institutions are composed of what people do. . . . Social structures, in other words, are not natural; they are historical creations. They are not immutable, but rather manifest the collective practices of men and women who make them up. It is also important to remember that the very people who change social structures are themselves products of these structures. Indeed, it is only by realizing the extent to which we are ourselves shaped by social institutions that we can begin to appreciate the complexity of social change. (Hall et al., 1991, p. 23)

It is also important to recognize at the outset of this exploration of sport and peace, following John Sugden of the University of Brighton, that 'we sociologists are usually much better at identifying problems than we are at finding solutions . . .' (Sugden, 2007, p. 175). Sugden's point will be an ever-present reminder of the need to make links between 'understanding sport' and 'changing sport'.

Of course, in placing critically oriented theories alongside research focused on uncovering ways that sport can be used to promote peace, some frictions and contradictions will emerge. For example, those who emphasize the contributions sport can make to society and those focused on the social problems around sport often come to the table with different assumptions and inclinations. Those who are committed to demonstrating how sport can support the maintenance or creation of social order and cohesion may not be as sensitive to the subtle but important ways that inequalities continue to be perpetuated in society—or how existing systems may need to be challenged or rethought if problematic cycles are to be interrupted. In the same way, those focused on identifying and explaining reasons for various social problems related to sport may have less to say about concrete strategies for change.

The assumption underlying this book is that a constructive tension can exist between these perspectives, and that a synthesis of research and theory that speaks to both of these ways of thinking is not only possible, but crucial. In fact, scholars like theorist-activist Paulo Freire—in his use of the term 'praxis' to explain how practical action and reflection are imperative if transformation is to be attained—have attempted to move past the tension by envisioning a more integrated approach. In a related way, Jutila, Pehkonen, and Väyrynen (2008) explored the possibility of what they call a 'critical peace research', that begins to deal with some of the tensions outlined above. In the upcoming chapters, these and related attempts to bridge critically oriented perspectives on sport with an understanding of the contributions that sport can make to peace building are explored.

Linking Sport and Peace

By approaching the study of sport in this way I am responding to the unprecedented attention that the sport–peace linkage has received in recent years. This attention is at least partially attributable to the awareness-raising campaigns that took place in the years leading up to and following the United Nations International Year of Sport and Physical Education in 2005. It is also associated with the rise to prominence of international sport for development and peace NGO Right To Play mentioned earlier. The NGO, which originated as an Olympic legacy program following the 1994 Lillehammer Games—led by Norwegian speed skating legend Johann Olav Koss and actively endorsed by athletes and celebrities like Wayne Gretzky, Silken Laumann, Lance Armstrong, Matt Damon, and Tim Robbins—is frequently in the public eye for its work using sport in areas of conflict and poverty (especially in 'developing' countries) and to promote health education and reconciliation among groups that have been at war. This linkage of sport, peace, and celebrity is especially pertinent as we begin to think about the processes through which the 'brands' of groups like Right To Play have attained widespread exposure and recognition.

Right To Play's success and the United Nations' decision to feature sport in its International Year program inspired the emergence of many other SDP NGOs around the world. As Levermore and Beacom note in the 2009 book *Sport and International Development*, there are currently 255 SDP projects currently listed on the International Platform on Sport and Development website, 93 per cent of which were formed from the year 2000 onwards, and 28 per cent from 2006–09. Multinational corporations like Nike, leagues like the National Basketball Association (NBA), and organizations like the Fédération Internationale de Football Association (i.e., FIFA, the international governing body for football/soccer) are also on-board, actively associating themselves with SDP work, often as part of social responsibility programs that feature their celebrity athlete representatives.

It should come as no surprise in this context that during the Vancouver 2010 Olympics the University of British Columbia (UBC) hosted a well-publicized speaker series focused on sport and peace that featured, among others, academic-activist and leader in the SDP movement Bruce Kidd, Right To Play's Olav Koss, and renowned Canadian diplomat and political commentator Stephen Lewis—who talked about the potential and power of sport for positive social change. It may be slightly more surprising that leading up to the Games the University hosted another speaker series—a series focused largely around human rights violations associated with the Olympics, corruption and the International Olympic Committee, the negative environmental impacts of the Games, indigenous land issues and the Games, and propaganda in the marketing of the Olympic dream. This other series entitled The Olympic Games in Myth and Reality featured (among others): University of Toronto professor and author of *Olympic Industry Resistance: Challenging Olympic Power and Propaganda*, Helen Lenskyj; UBC professor Chris Shaw who authored *Five Ring Circus: Myths and Realities of the Olympic Games*; investigative reporter Andrew Jennings who authored *The Great Olympic Swindle*; Laura Track, a Vancouver-based lawyer who spoke about how the Olympics impact the poor and homeless; and indigenous activists like Lindsay Bomberry, Angela Sterritt, and Dustin Johnson who spoke about the environmental and social issues that are raised by hosting the Olympics on indigenous lands.

Clearly, something unique is happening that is inspiring a range of people to think about sport and peace from a variety of perspectives—and some sociologists of sport to begin writing about and focusing research on the topic. In fact, the theme of the North American Society for the Sociology of Sport (NASSS) Conference in 2008 in Denver, Colorado—one of the main gatherings for sociologists interested in sport and social issues—was Sport and Peace/Social (In)Justice. The edited collection from Levermore and Beacom (2009) referred to above is a foundational collection of essays examining facets of sport and international development, a key topic commonly associated with the sport and peace area. A set of papers by scholars from the University of Toronto who contributed to a document entitled *Report for the Sport for Development and Peace International Working Group* is also unique because of the direct links that are made between sport, sociology, and the 'peace' concept (Donnelly, 2007; Larkin, 2007; Kidd, 2007; Parnes, 2007; Zackus,

2007). Other examples of research and writing that explicitly make these links include: Sugden's (2006, 2010a; Sugden and Wallis, 2007) research on the Football 4 Peace program that is designed to break down barriers between Israeli youth from conflicting areas, Keim's (2003) study of the role physical education classes played in the process of integration in a post-apartheid South African school, Darnell's (2010a, 2010b) study of the experiences of volunteer interns working with sport for development and peace NGOs, Hayhurst's (2009, Hayhurst and Frisby, 2010) work on negotiations between government and NGOs around policies to support sport for development, McCardle and Giulianotti's (2006) collection of essays on sport and human rights, and Armstrong and Giulianotti's (2004) edited book on soccer's (i.e., football's) role in 'conflict, conciliation and community' in various regions of Africa.

Of course, other sociologists of sport have been doing work pertinent to the peace studies field for many years but have been less explicit about ways that their work connects with the peace concept. For example, there is a wealth of research that examines the role of sport in:

- international relations (e.g., scholars have studied the role sport plays in Canadian foreign policy and as part of diplomatic relations),
- national politics (e.g., researchers have examined the importance of soccer in negotiations amongst rival groups in Ireland),
- social movements (e.g., sociologists have studied protests against the use of native mascots for sport teams),
- race and ethnicity studies (e.g., the threats to traditional aboriginal sporting festivals in Canada have been studied, as has the role of sport in raising awareness about the historical mistreatment of aboriginal groups in Australia),
- gender studies (e.g., the ways gender-based inequalities are reinforced in and through physical education classes has been studied), and
- media studies (many sociologists of sport specialize in the study of ways that social inequalities are reinforced in and through sport media; others examine representations of and the role of war and military in broadcasts of sport events).

There is also a growing number of studies that speak to relationships between environmental issues and sport—such as Wheeler and Nauright's (2006) examination of the environmental impact of golf, and Stolle-McAllister's (2004) study of an anti-golf protest group.

'Sport' and 'Peace' as Floating Signifiers

Although the terms 'sport' and 'peace' may inspire familiar (often positive) images and meanings, like those outlined in the introduction to this chapter, to examine links between the two is far from straightforward. This is because the meanings attributed to these concepts—which are considered stable and obvious by many commentators—are actually quite variable and ambiguous. In fact, I demonstrate throughout this book that the concepts 'sport' and 'peace' are what French anthropologist Claude Lévi-Strauss (1987) referred to as 'floating signifiers'. That is to say, the terms have different meanings and refer to different things depending on the social and historical contexts within which they exist—and the backgrounds and dispositions of those who are making sense of them. This is not to suggest that the words do not mean anything. On the contrary, the idea is that the meanings of words like these are 'relatively anchored', having particular meanings, in particular contexts, for particular audiences (cf. Cowie, 1977; Hall, 1985; McKay, 1995).

'Peace', for example, has variably been associated with acts of violence in the name of peace, with a 'lack of war' but the acceptance of various social injustices, and with being a pacifist—a label sometimes linked with 'being cowardly' or 'unwilling to fight for what is right' (Cortright, 2008, p. 1). In his famous treatise *The Art of War*, Sun Tzu (2002) noted how a goal of war is to create 'peace on the terms of the victor', a perspective that unflatteringly links peace with forms of colonization. Cortright (2008) highlights the historically negative associations between peace and Cold War politics, referring in particular to 'Moscow sponsored ersatz "peace councils"' of the era (p. 6). Even before the Cold War, the term was viewed suspiciously by people like late nineteenth- and early twentieth-century philanthropist Andrew Carnegie, who 'lavishly funded programs to prevent war and advance international cooperat[ion]' but remained 'uncomfortable with the word peace and wanted to leave it out of the title of the international endowment he left as his legacy' (Cortright, 2008, p. 6).

Of course, and despite these reservations, peace was and is commonly linked with ideas about inner tranquility, a harmony between governments, civil order and safety, and a state where justice, equity, and equality are pursued and observed (Webel, 2007). At the same time, according to the *Oxford English Dictionary*, to be 'at peace' can also mean 'dead'—and to 'hold one's peace' means to 'remain silent'. As Charles Webel points out in the introduction to the *Handbook of Peace and Conflict Studies*, peace can refer to something that is both 'inside and outside' the individual, both 'positive and negative', and 'present and absent'.

Following Webel's idea, Johan Galtung, one of the founders of the peace studies field, attempted to anchor the term for practical purposes by specifying 'negative' and 'positive' peace. **Negative peace** means only an 'absence of war', while **positive peace** refers to situations where various forms of equality and equity—related to economic, social, cultural, and political rights—have been approached. Jeong (2000) elaborates on these ideas in his description of negative peace as the absence of 'direct violence', meaning the absence of physical and verbal/psychological abuse or intimidation. Positive peace, in his context, refers to 'the removal of structural violence beyond the absence of direct violence', with structural violence referring to poverty, discrimination, and denial of economic, social, and political equality, and situations where 'a sense of autonomy and freedom' is denied (Jeong, 2000, pp. 24–25).

The term 'sport' is similarly ambiguous. In fact, authors like Andrews (2006) suggest that because the meaning of sport is so malleable—and dependent on the social and historical context within which it exists—that to offer a stable definition is to deny the term's contingent features. Sport, for example, has taken on a particular set of meanings in an era where athlete icons like Yao Ming, David Beckham, and LeBron James have attained global recognition, where many cities strive to host celebrity mass entertainment spectacles like the Olympic Games, and where sport for many young people has become based around organized and adult-led activities. The term 'sport' in these instances is associated with global capitalism, individualism, competition, celebrity, mass entertainment, violence, and spectatorship.

Sport is also associated with various forms of social development—including international development work that is conducted in areas of conflict or poverty in various regions of the world, and development work in the inner cities of Western countries (a.k.a., countries of the 'Global North') where sport programs are considered tools for enhancing life skills among underserved youth. Sport refers also to unstructured and expressive play and youth-driven alternative sport activities like skateboarding. In such contexts sport is associated with human movement, play, community, teamwork, safety, resistance, and pleasure.

One of the reasons that the meaning of sport 'floats' is that it is a 'social practice'—which is to say, sport emerges, evolves, and is 'made' and 'remade' by (and because of) the actions of people (Gruneau, 1983). These people share sport experiences and collectively alter and impact the meaning of the sport experience on an ongoing basis. In the same way, the institutions people create and are a part of shape these sport-related experiences and their meanings—they are 'influenced by and influential upon the broader social context' (Giulianotti, 1999, p. xv). Because institutions and group perspectives evolve and change over time—and are distinct across geographic regions, and for different social and cultural groups—what counts as sport also changes over time, and according to context.

Coakley and Donnelly (2009) counterpoise this contingent understanding of sport against a more traditional definition, where sports are described as 'institutionalized, competitive activities that involve rigorous physical exertion or the use of relatively complex physical skills by participants motivated by internal and external rewards' (p. 4). Sport in this context is distinct from 'play', which is 'an expressive activity done for its own sake'. It is also distinct from 'dramatic spectacle', which is 'a performance that is intended to entertain an audience' (p. 5). This more stable definition helps anchor the meaning of sport and related terms in the current historical moment—although, and as Coakley and Donnelly themselves acknowledge, such a definition is limited because it cannot possibly represent the variety of meanings sport is assigned in other contexts.

With this background, we can begin to see how linking 'sport' and 'peace' is not entirely straightforward. To say that 'sport promotes peace' then begs many questions, including: What type of sport promotes peace?; Does it always promote peace?; What kind of peace does it promote?; Does sport promote peace for everybody?; and under what circumstances is sport most likely to promote peace? Throughout this book I will both acknowledge the messiness and uncertainty of the sport–peace linkage, and at the same time identify moments and spaces where a 'sport and peace' relationship is relatively anchored, where a particular form of sport may (or may not) contribute to a particular form of peace.

Addressing Social Inequality: The Underlying Theme

You may have noticed by now that I am not featuring separate chapters on sport's relationship with gender, 'race' and ethnicity, or social class—concepts that are necessarily highlighted in any comprehensive sociology of sport text. This should not be taken to mean that these key concepts are not absolutely central to this book. On the contrary, *concerns about the various forms of social inequality and social division that are inherent to the study of concepts such as 'sport' and 'peace' are pivotal to and underlie* all *chapters in this book*. Consider the following arguments that will be encountered in upcoming chapters:

- When governments put pressure on leaders/administrators in community recreation centres to deliver sport and recreation in an economically self-sufficient way (instead of seeing recreation programs as services deserving subsidization), lower-income groups that are unable to pay fees —or are required to 'prove poverty' in order to gain access at a discount (a process which itself discourages participation)—are negatively impacted (Frisby et al., 2007).
- Despite the best efforts of sport for development and peace organizations to be inclusive in their programming, girls and women commonly participate at lower rates due to cultural and social barriers. These same barriers prevent the girls and women who do participate from attaining the status and connections that many boys and men accrue in the same contexts.
- Relationships between international sport for development and peace organizations and local communities in regions of the Global South (e.g., in poverty-stricken areas of some regions in Africa) are sometimes post-colonial. That is to say, there is evidence that some organizations impose

Western values through their sport for development work, thus undermining local cultural traditions.

Other, more hopeful, examples include:

- There is evidence that, under particular conditions, sport programs may be spaces for underserved youth (e.g., youth from low-income families, those living in dangerous neighbourhoods) to feel safe and be involved in values-based sport programming intended to promote self-confidence and more compassionate relationships with peers and the community. These programs, under ideal circumstances, are spaces where youth learn about 'possible futures' and develop 'hope of making positive things happen in their lives' (Coakley, 2002, p. 28).
- High-status athletes can be key figures in anti-violence education programs, raising awareness about and inspiring reflection on ways that people can intervene in social situations where forms of bullying and sexual abuse often go unchecked and unchallenged. These sorts of interventions and attempts to change cultures of abuse and violence require heightened awareness of ways that norms around gender relations present barriers to change.
- There is evidence that friendly sport events and exchanges can provide opportunities for the development of the types of empathy and intercultural understanding that are required for effective conflict transformation. This has been shown to be effective for addressing conflicts between ethnic groups in divided societies.

This is just a small sample of instances where social divisions and inequalities associated with class, gender, and race/ethnicity (and in other instances, disability and age) are at the centre of, and inseparable from, upcoming discussions of sport and peace. In fact, to study issues related to 'positive peace'—as I do in this book—requires a focus on these social inequalities and social divisions. The critical theories that are referred to in the next chapter and elaborated on through this book will aid our understanding of these various inequalities and the explanations for them.

Looking Ahead: A Warning and an Opportunity

As an undergraduate student at McMaster University in Hamilton, Ontario, I sat alongside nearly 200 others in my introductory sociology of sport class as our instructors offered the following warning—'after this class, you will never see sport the same way again.' At the time I felt a little disappointed. I had enjoyed sport as a competitive and recreational athlete for as long as I could remember—and had entered a Kinesiology program (known as

Physical Education at the time) with the goal of pursuing my passion for sport and physical activity. Why did I need to see sport differently? Why did I need to see sport critically?

I realize now that I misinterpreted the 'warning' to mean that thinking differently about sport, thinking critically, would somehow impact my ability to enjoy my various engagements with sport, to be a sport supporter. In fact, my instructors, Peter Donnelly and Phil White, were suggesting that we do quite the opposite. Their goal was (and is) to challenge themselves and others to consider how the taken-for-granted beliefs we have about sport may, in fact, have negative consequences—and how we all might use this knowledge to strive for a more responsible and 'peaceful' sport.

These days I offer the same warning to those who take the sociology of sport classes that I teach. While many are at first skeptical about the idea that critiquing sport can lead to a better sport—as I was in the first class I took—it is from these same students that inspiring and innovative ideas for creating a more peaceful sport emerge. Students taking the Sport, Peace, and Conflict course that this book is based on create their own 'sport for peace' groups and design projects intended to, for example: raise awareness about and combat human trafficking at sporting mega-events; encourage young people to consider the impacts of sport on the environment; respond to negative and overly simplistic depictions of transgendered athletes in mass media; provoke thinking about how new media might be used to network organizations committed to sport and peace; bring attention to ways that sport can be used to address problems associated with homelessness; and use friendly sporting competitions as forums to educate about various forms of violence. Each of these student-driven projects is based on the idea that responsible action requires understanding—and that sociology can help.

It is with the optimism and hope generated by these students that I have put together a book intended to promote balanced and critical thinking about sport—and positive, peace-promoting social changes within and through sport.

Discussion Questions

1. What are the dangers of overemphasizing the benefits of sport? Why is it so common to see one-sided portrayals of sport?

2. Consider some of the associations between sport and peace. Why is the peace concept valuable for those studying sport? Have your views on the meaning of sport changed over time? How and why?

3. How can a sociological imagination inspire balanced and critical thinking about sport?

Suggested Readings

Cortright, D. (2008). What is peace? In D. Cortright (Author), *Peace: A history of movements and ideas* (pp. 1–21) New York: Cambridge.

Eitzen, S. (2003). Sport is healthy, sport is destructive. In S. Eitzen (Author), *Fair and foul: Beyond the myths and paradoxes of sport* (pp. 59–78). New York, NY: Rowman & Littlefield Publishers. An excellent overview of the various paradoxes that exist within and around sport.

Kidd, B. (2007). Peace, sport and development. In *Report for the Sport for Development and Peace International Working Group (SDP IWG) Secretariat* (pp. 158–194). University of Toronto, Faculty of Physical Education and Health. This article, and the four others that are also included in the Report, offers a succinct introduction to the sport for development and peace area.

Leistyna, P. (2005). Introduction: Revitalizing the dialogue: Theory, coalition-building and social change. In P. Leistyna (Ed.), *Cultural studies: From theory to practice* (pp. 1–15). Malden, MA: Blackwell. A thoughtful introduction to thinking about connecting theory and practice using cultural studies-influenced principles.

Relevant Websites

United Nations Sport for Development and Peace
www.un.org/wcm/content/site/sport
> This site includes information on the variety of ways that the United Nations is engaging peace-promotion within and through sport.

TRANSCEND International: An International Conflict Resolution Network
www.transcend.org
> Founded by peace studies pioneer Johan Galtung, TRANSCEND is an Internet platform intended to support education, research, and information dissemination around peace-building and nonviolence.

Peace and Collaborative Development Network
www.internationalpeaceandconflict.org
> According to the site's homepage, the Peace and Collaborative Development Network is a 'free professional networking site (with over 19,200 members from around the world) to foster dialogue and sharing of resources in international development, conflict resolution, gender mainstreaming, human rights, social entrepreneurship and related fields.'

Key Terms

negative peace refers broadly to situations where there is an 'absence of war' and absence of direct forms of violence, including physical and psychological abuse.

peace studies Peace studies is an interdisciplinary, social science–based academic field that is focused on research in disciplines like sociology, environmental studies, international relations and political science, anthropology, psychology, theology, health studies, and other fields. The field grew in the 1980s in response to Cold War–related issues like preventing nuclear destruction. This emphasis on international relations was replaced by a concern with domestic issues related to structural, domestic, and civil violence through the 1990s (Harris, Fisk, and Rank, 1998). Broadly speaking, peace studies is concerned with better understanding why armed conflicts take place, exploring and devising responses to stop human rights violations, and promoting thinking about how to create and maintain more peaceful societies.

positive peace refers to situations where various forms of equality and equity— related to economic, social, cultural, and political rights—have been approached. Put another way, it refers to 'the removal of structural violence beyond the absence of direct violence', with structural violence referring to poverty, discrimination, and denial of economic, social, and political equality—to situations where 'a sense of autonomy and freedom' is denied (Jeong, 2000, pp. 24–25).

sociological imagination A way of seeing and interpreting the social world that is sensitive to, among other factors, people's everyday activities, experiences, and biographies—and ways the situations in which people find themselves (and the social problems they face) can be understood and explained through 'imagining' their relationships with and interconnections to the social structures and institutions of societies, processes operating at macro-levels, and the (historical) contexts within which these problems take place.

sport Sport is a social practice (i.e., something that people 'do') and a social institution (something that frames and impacts people's lives). While many authors argue that what 'counts' as sport is malleable and changeable because it is made and remade by people, others note the stable features of sport—it is generally agreed to be competitive, and to 'involve rigorous physical exertion or the use of relatively complex physical skills by participants motivated by internal and external rewards' (Coakley and Donnelly, 2009, p. 4). It is distinguished from non-competitive, expressive forms of 'play' and entertainment-focused 'dramatic spectacle'.

2 Theory, Sport, and Peace: Tools and Lenses for Seeing Sport in Context

Questions to Consider

- ⚙ How are our understandings of and opinions about sport's relationship with peace influenced by the theoretical lenses through which we usually look?
- ⚙ How can critical sociological theories help us understand the ways that existing forms of social inequality are perpetuated?
- ⚙ Why is a 'contextual cultural studies' approach to thinking about sport and peace useful? How might theories drawn from critical sociology and those grounded in peace studies be used together, and what tensions exist between critical and functionalist views of sport?

Introduction: Difference Lenses, Different Interpretations

In her 2006 book *Pink Ribbons Inc.*, Queen's University professor Samantha King makes the controversial claim that the Susan G. Komen Race for the Cure—the largest 5k running series in the US, a series created to raise money for breast cancer research and awareness around the health issue—may not be as positive and beneficial for society as we are led to believe. How could King come to make such a claim? What could she possibly argue that would convince readers that an event like Race for the Cure—or other philanthropic, physical activity–based initiatives, like the Avon Walk for Breast Cancer or the Paddle for the Cure rowing event—deserve criticism? What does this have to do with sport and peace?

In this chapter I demonstrate how the perspective one has on an event like Race for the Cure—or the view one has on the Olympic Games, 'sport for peace' international development organizations like Right To Play, the building of a new sport stadium, or the use of native symbols and mascots in sport (like the Washington Redskins or the Atlanta Braves)—is related to the types of questions we ask about these sport-related phenomena, the assumptions that underlie these questions, and the level at which the social processes we are observing exist. Put another way, our views on and interpretations of various aspects of sport—and sport's potential to promote peace—are influenced by the theoretical lenses we prefer to look through.

Although there are various ways we can define theory, I like this lens metaphor because it foregrounds the idea that a sociological theory is a tool that helps us see the world in different ways, helping illuminate particular features of the social and cultural world, and inspiring questions about these features. Some theories—what are often called '**critical theories**'—are useful for highlighting some of the mechanisms through which different forms of social inequality are perpetuated, a central concern for those interested in the sport–peace relationship. For example, particular versions of critical theory, like feminist theories, are helpful for highlighting the processes that underlie, and the taken-for-granted features of, gender-based inequalities. While feminist theories, and other theories that inspire questions related to race (e.g., critical race theory, postcolonial theories), and class (e.g., versions of Marxism) differ in many respects, the authors that use them often share an understanding of the underlying *processes* through which inequalities of all kinds are perpetuated. These processes are highlighted in the work of renowned philosophers like Antonio Gramsci and Michel Foucault, who in their own distinct ways described how and why it is that oppressed groups continue to be oppressed, and how more powerful and more vulnerable groups are both active and complicit in this relationship. Without understanding these processes, according to critical theorists, these inequalities will continue to persist as we will be in no position to respond to or challenge a system that favours some and is oppressive for others, or to support well-reasoned and strategic social justice initiatives. Here is the value of using tools like critical theories—tools used routinely throughout this book—for assessments of sport's role in peace promotion, and its relationship to forms of conflict, violence, and social exclusion.

Other theories, while offering less critically oriented visions of how society works, are used by some sociologists to explain the existence of social problems, the reasons that people engage within human group life in the ways they do, and the patterns of activity that emerge when we look closely at these engagements. Such theories can also be useful for highlighting the meanings that people give to their experiences within these systems, and are therefore helpful for those interested in understanding how people's perspectives (on the value of the Olympics, for example) relate to the choices they make. **Symbolic interactionist theory** is an excellent example of a theory that guides this sort of thinking and related research.

Functionalist theory—which was the dominant approach to studying sport and society for many years—inspires a similarly uncritical understanding of sport's role in society. That is to say, although the theory is used by sociologists who query how sport can contribute to society and the types of problems that need to be resolved for sport's potential to be optimized, it is not as useful as critical theories for challenging the basic assumptions underlying systems of social and power relations—a problem it shares with symbolic interactionism. So, although symbolic interactionism and functionalism are commonly used to highlight how existing systems can better support those who are excluded or oppressed, they cannot help us 'see' the processes that support the often unintended perpetuation of inequalities, processes that operate in ways we might find quite surprising and disconcerting. I elaborate on the value of and problems with these different theories, below, when discussing Samantha King's study of Race for the Cure, a study so powerful in its implications that it inspired an acclaimed documentary film also called *Pink Ribbons, Inc.*, released in 2011 at the Toronto International Film Festival.

It is important to note here that sociological theories like these do not emerge from nowhere. That is to say—and although the term 'theory' is commonly defined in opposition to 'practice' or 'the real world'—the idea here is that theories are based on people's observations of and experiences in the real world. For example, when studies consistently show (for example) that women and girls, and those from less wealthy families, and those in First Nations communities, are less likely to be involved in particular sport- and recreation-related activities, it would make sense to pay attention to the possibility that these patterns exist in other contexts. As we shall see, the theories that developed from these sorts of observations can also help us ask excellent questions, and in turn, help us see the most pertinent information about the issue of concern.

Seeing Sport Up Close and In Context: Race for the Cure and Why Theory is Important

To begin this discussion of how different theories help us 'see' different aspects of social and cultural phenomena—let's consider what Race for the Cure and related events look like through a sociological lens that magnifies the micrological (i.e., the 'micro') level of social life, the level associated with the everyday experiences and perspectives of people. On this level, according to many researchers, there would appear to be few problems with a physical activity–based event that is designed to promote awareness about and raise money for an important health and social issue. There is some research that speaks to the benefits of awareness-raising campaigns when it comes to increasing the public's sensitivity to an issue (Barr, 2003). There is other evidence that the sense of community that people may experience when they are involved in these sorts of events and activities has great benefits. For example, female breast cancer survivors interviewed in a study by Unruh and Elvin (2004) described the social support and self-confidence they gained through their involvement in dragon boating.

Interpretive Sociology, Symbolic Interactionism, and Their Limits

These sorts of benefits are highlighted by researchers conducting studies that explore questions like 'What meanings do cancer survivors give to involvements in cancer runs?', 'How do people respond to awareness-raising campaigns?', and 'What sorts of bonds and networks are created through physical activity–based challenges?' These types of questions have guided the research of micro or **interpretive sociologists** of sport for years, sociologists who offer key insights into: group dynamics and social cohesion in and around sport-related activities and teams; the role of sport and physical activity in identity development; and the social and cultural aspects of human group life generally (Donnelly, 2000; Prus, 1996). Interpretive sociologists commonly use what is known as a symbolic interactionist theory. Those who prefer this approach tend to focus on the meanings people give to their activities, ways these meanings arise from and are negotiated with others, and ways that these negotiated meanings (in turn) influence people's actions (Blumer, 1969). Sociologists of sport who adopt this theoretical lens commonly explore micro-level power relations through studies of status hierarchies within and around sport teams and organizations, and research ways that certain people and sub-groups come to be included or excluded in sport-related contexts—and on the positive, negative, and ambivalent experiences of sport participants more broadly (Atkinson, 2000; Beal, 2002; Donnelly, 2000; Donnelly and Young, 1988; Wilson and White, 2003).

While much can be gained by focusing on this level of social life, if the only lens that a sociologist uses is one that magnifies individual perceptions and small group dynamics, then entire sets of social and cultural processes operating at and across other levels are overlooked (Donnelly and Young, 1988). Why is this important, and how could this be a problem? I return here to Samantha King's examination of Race for the Cure—which includes a focus on processes operating at a macro level (and their relationships with processes operating at other levels)—to help answer these questions.

King points out that events like Race for the Cure take place at a moment in history—a moment which (arguably) began in the 1970s and continues to this day—where corporations, non-profit organizations, and donating individuals are increasingly relied upon to deal with many social concerns that had, to differing degrees, previously been the responsibility of governments. A problem with this newer system, according to King, is that corporations begin to have a great deal of influence when it comes to deciding which causes are supported and which are not. While the contributions made by these businesses can be impressive, in this system—what is commonly labelled a 'neo-liberal' system—citizens begin to have less and less say about what social issues are deemed worthy of attention at any given time. That is to say, people are put in a position to express their support for particular initiatives by *consuming* the products of corporations that are doing the (philanthropic) work that is meaningful to them (i.e., by supporting sponsors of philanthropic sport events; by purchasing products with a pink ribbon label on them, symbolizing the company's support of breast cancer awareness and research), instead of voting for politicians who make like-minded decisions, or through other voluntary acts of citizenship that are not based around consumption. Even donating directly to non-profit organizations is not outside the influence of corporations who have ongoing relationships with and commonly sponsor the work of groups like Right To Play or UNICEF—or in King's case, the Susan G. Komen Race for the Cure organization.

While the argument King makes is not meant to undermine or dismiss the research showing the benefits of physical activity–based philanthropic events and the positive meanings people commonly assign to them (there are obviously immense and various benefits to such activities)—she is clear in her suggestion that the meaning and practice of citizenship in democratic countries is altered when the people we vote for (and can 'vote out') are no longer our primary decision-makers and representatives around many key social and health issues. The critique here, then, is of the *process* through which particular social and health issues are funded and given priority, and the heightened role of corporations (concerned ultimately and by mandate with profit for shareholders) and thus consumers (who have varying levels of income through which they can make their voices heard) in this sort of decision-making. The idea that we should have to consume at all in order to make our voices heard on social issues is also worth considering, a point I return to in chapter 8's discussion of environmental issues and sport.

Another potential implication is that corporations may influence *how* the funds donated to breast cancer research are spent—and thus influence the type of work that cancer researchers are most likely to do. With this in mind, the film *Pink Ribbons, Inc.* is based around the argument that the focus of corporate sponsors on 'raising awareness' about breast cancer and on 'curing' cancer has meant that the actual causes of breast cancer (i.e., the factors that help us explain why some people are more likely to develop breast cancer) are understudied, as health promoters and researchers are compelled to pursue these other well-funded goals. It is also notable here that problems like skin cancer and heart disease, which lead to far more deaths for women, receive far less attention from corporations, and thus consumers. The main point here is that corporate donors are having an uncomfortably large influence on a response to an important public health issue—and on decisions about which issues should be pursued.

The Need for Context and the Critical Cultural Studies Imperative

I would like to bring the focus here to the way that King conducted her analysis. Consider how, by paying attention to the social processes that operate on a broader or macro level (and considering interrelationships between micro, meso, and macro levels), King was able to demonstrate how an event that some researchers have shown to be beneficial and empowering for its many participants can also, at the same time, be seen as an event that perpetuates and represents a corporate-driven approach to dealing with societal issues—an approach that has been heavily critiqued by sociologists of sport and others. Put another way, King was able to demonstrate through the use of what has been termed a '**critical cultural studies**' approach that *social life is complex, multifaceted, multilayered, and laden with contradictions*— and that attempts to break problematic cycles and move toward long-term social change require attention to various social processes that exist across multiple levels of social life.

The term 'critical cultural studies' is used for a few reasons. First, the approach is guided by the use of any number of critical theories—theories that highlight (in different ways, depending on the theory) how power operates in and around a given subject, and how inequalities are maintained and exacerbated in sometimes taken-for-granted ways. The cultural studies part of the term refers to the field of cultural studies. Later in this chapter I offer more detail on this history and key characteristics of the field, but suffice it to say here that those working in the field are, generally speaking, concerned with identifying how various contexts (i.e., historical, political, social, cultural, geographical, and economic contexts) can help us understand how what is happening on one level (e.g., the experience of attending a Race for the Cure event) is connected to what is happening at other levels (at the levels where neo-liberal social policy is developed and enacted—where profit-driven businesses become influential players in responses to important social and health-related problems). Following this, those working in cultural studies are intent on using the results of the 'contextual analyses' they conduct—like the one King conducted that demonstrated how Race for the Cure is both enabling and problematic—as the basis for commenting on ways that sport-related social problems might be addressed.

The critical cultural studies approach is used by many sociologists of sport concerned with power relations, social inequality, and peace-promotion. For this reason I elaborate later in this chapter and throughout this book on the various critical theories used by cultural studies scholars, and strategies offered by these scholars for linking theory with practice.

The Questions We Ask and the Theories We Use

So, 'what you see' in and around sport—and the claims made about sport's contributions to society—depend, in part, on the 'magnification' of your analytic lens. If we take a close-up and particularistic view of sport (e.g., looking at the experiences of people in a sport group) we may see sport quite differently than if we are looking at sport from a distance—at the broader social and political context within which sport takes place. In a similar way, if we only ask questions about ways that sport can contribute to effective social development efforts, then we will again see sport differently than if we are concerned with ways that sport may reflect and reproduce the inequalities of society at large.

Functionalism and Critics

As I noted in the first chapter, it is most common to hear questions and comments about ways that sport can and does contribute to society. Although it might not be explicitly identified, these sorts of questions and comments are informed by a theoretical perspective. That is to say, these questions and comments are based on a set of (often taken-for-granted) assumptions about sport's potential as both a socializing institution and practice, and a related set of assumptions about the characteristics of well-functioning societies more generally. These assumptions include:

- society is an organized system of parts—like a living organism—held together because people hold similar values and have ties to one another, and because major institutions of society (family, media, religion, government) complement one another;
- when people and institutions are well-integrated, society is at its healthiest—it is socially stable;
- sport—along with media, education, family, and religion—is an excellent vehicle for promoting the values that are so fundamental to well-integrated societies because of its potential as a tool for 'mold[ing] good citizens . . . by teaching discipline, teamwork, and self-confidence' (Crossman, 2003, p. 9);
- in espousing these values, sport can play a role in minimizing deviance and maintaining social stability.

For those familiar with the major theories that sociologists have used over the years to understand social phenomena, you will recognize that the questions and assumptions mentioned above are guided by the functionalist perspective mentioned earlier in this chapter

Proponents of a functionalist perspective are commonly critiqued by sociologists of sport who are concerned with issues around inequality and power relations. A main reason for this is that the kinds of questions that tend to guide functionalist-oriented thinking—such as 'How can sport be used to maintain social order?', 'How can sport be used to eliminate problems that upset the social order?', or 'What values can sport teach that will support the creation of cohesive and moral communities?'—are driven by the often unquestioned assumption that the social order we are seeking to foster and maintain is one that is beneficial for everyone.

Critics of this perspective point to evidence showing that marginalized groups (e.g., those with fewer economic, social, and cultural resources) remain disadvantaged over time, despite efforts to tinker with existing systems and implement programs targeting these groups. Put simply, *the existing social order favours some groups and marginalizes others*. These critics also emphasize that attempts to keep the current system running smoothly will not break cycles of inequality. The reason for this is that the current system is structured according to a set of values and ideologies that will always position certain groups—often the same groups—at a disadvantage to others.

To demonstrate this idea, I refer to the widespread use of sport programs (e.g., midnight basketball programs, or sport programs in Boys and Girls Clubs) to support youth living in inner city areas where poverty is widespread—areas commonly associated with gang violence, drug use, and other social problems. These sorts of programs are functionalist in the sense that they are not designed to change the complex *systemic* problems that are at the base of poverty and related social problems. Instead, they are intended to address the individual problems experienced by these youth, using sport to 'get kids off the streets'—giving young people alternatives to the destructive activities referred to above while exposing them to role model leaders that sometimes work in these programs. Sport in this context is commonly associated with the development of 'character' through attempts to teach proper values—all with an eye to moulding these youth into contributing members within the (existing) social system. Coakley (2002) offers a pointed critique of this approach:

> . . . [attempts to] 'fix' the character and lifestyle defects of certain young people in inner cities is problematic because it does not focus attention on the need for social justice, or on rebuilding strong community-based institutions, or on reestablishing the resource base of the communities where these young people live, or on politicizing and then empowering these young people to be effective change agents working on behalf of their communities. (p. 16)

The point here is this: if the only questions that are asked by researchers and commentators are related to the ways that sport can be used to eliminate deviance and maintain social order, then problems inherent to the existing social order—problems that continue to re-emerge, with no end in sight—are not being addressed. Moreover, the argument that 'sport builds character' that underlies these kinds of sporting initiatives has been justifiably questioned by researchers like Miracle and Rees (1994) and Eitzen (2003) who show that sport can just as easily be used to teach values associated with extreme individualism (e.g., 'winning at all costs') and the acceptance and perpetuation of various form of sport-related violence—values that many would see as undermining the building of character. Ultimately then, and as with the Race for the Cure example, the point here is not to dismiss the value of sport programs for underserved youth, but to highlight why this type of solution to a set of poverty-related social problems is limited.

Coakley and Donnelly (2009) outline other critiques of functionalism in their text *Sports in Society: Issues and Controversies*, pointing out, for example, that functionalists tend to overestimate the contributions of sport and understate sport's negative effects. Coakley and Donnelly also note that the functionalist assumption that 'the needs of all groups in a society are the same' is limiting for those interested in understanding conflicts between groups with disparate interests and backgrounds, or the ability of sport to bring together culturally distinct nations or people while remaining respectful of cultural differences between groups (cf. van Hilvoorde, Elling, and Stokvis, 2010; Wilson, 2006a). This is not to suggest that sport cannot be extremely useful in breaking down barriers between groups or providing a forum of intercultural understanding and conflict transformation. Rather, that in order for sport to be useful in this regard, analysts and practitioners must be sensitive to questions about ways that sport may perpetuate inequality, or how it may act as a forum where conflicts are ignited or exacerbated.

So, as you might suspect, the functionalist perspective is often appealing to those who have had largely positive experiences with sport because its emphasis on sport's benefits is both hopeful and familiar. The perspective is also appealing for groups with a vested interest in maintaining the status quo—those who might feel threatened or undermined by radical changes to the system. As Coakley and Donnelly (2009) suggest:

> People in positions of power in society also favour functionalist theory because it is based on the assumption that society is organized for the equal benefit of all people and therefore should not be changed in any dramatic ways. The notion that the system operates effectively in its present form is comforting to people with power because it discourages changes that might jeopardize their privilege and influence. (p. 31)

Sport, Cultural Studies, and Hegemony

Fortunately, sociologists of sport have for many years been acutely aware of these problems with functionalism, and responded by developing and adapting approaches to studying sport that are sensitive to the reasons why social inequalities are perpetuated, and to ways that sociologists of sport can contribute to positive social change. Although a variety of strategies have been used to take on these topics—strategies to be explored throughout the upcoming chapters—the field of cultural studies has been especially influential for critically oriented sport scholars. Having introduced the central tenets of cultural studies in my earlier discussion of Samantha King's research, I elaborate below on key ideas that have underscored research in the field, and some relationships between cultural studies and peace studies. I begin, however, with some background information about the field.

Cultural studies refers in its broadest sense to work conducted across a range of fields focused around aspects of contemporary culture—with consideration given to anything from the consumption of media to the usage of language, the symbolic meaning of music or clothing, or the role of sport in society. As noted earlier, though, many sociologists of sport and others who 'do' cultural studies research emphasize how being a cultural studies scholar means being concerned with 'context' and 'intervention' (Leistyna, 2005). These sociologists have been particularly influenced by a (more critical) strain of cultural studies that emerged in the 1960s at the University of Birmingham, England, at the Centre for Contemporary Cultural Studies (CCCS). The work of the CCCS was in many respects a response to a concern that scholars and others were not effectively accounting for ways that cultural forms like sport and music are integral to the maintenance of and challenging of existing power relations (Carrington and McDonald, 2009).

In their attempts to explain how it is that power relationships persist and how these relationships are challenged and sometimes changed, CCCS members were guided by the work of early twentieth-century Italian social theorist and activist Antonio Gramsci (1971)—and especially by his writing on the concept of **hegemony**. Hegemony refers to a process whereby dominant groups (e.g., ruling classes) maintain their dominance by generating 'consent' for their authority amongst less powerful or subordinate groups, or as Joll (1977) put it, it is when the dominant group 'has succeeded in persuading other classes of society to accept its moral, political and cultural values' (p. 99). So, in an effective hegemonic system, dominant or ruling groups do not have to rely on coercive techniques to maintain authority.

A preferred strategy for generating consent is to control and influence the distribution of ideas in a society, using education, media, and other 'superstructural' forms to promote certain ways of thinking such that existing sets of power relationships and hierarchies seem natural and unchangeable (cf., Althusser, 1971). For example, if the curricula for history classes in Canadian high schools deemphasizes the study of aboriginal cultures, then this would contribute to a view of aboriginal histories (and, in turn, aboriginal issues) as less important, less worthy of attention than other histories and issues. A similar argument on a completely different topic has been made about kinesiology programs in North American universities where curricula are commonly dominated by natural sciences courses, and where there is sometimes only a small selection of social sciences and humanities courses. In these instances, the idea that the social sciences and humanities are 'less important' than the natural sciences would be implicitly promoted. This and related issues have been central to the struggle for recognition among sociologists of sport who work in kinesiology departments for many years (Gill, 2007; Silk, Bush, and Andrews, 2010; Vertinsky, 2009).

From these examples you can see how a system of power relations that privileges the interests of some groups over others may be unquestioned, taken-for-granted, and seen to be unchangeable—despite the fact that these systems are not based on any kind of immutable truths about, for example, aboriginal cultures or the kinesiology discipline. Rather, they reflect the systemic ways that particular social and organizational hierarchies are maintained.

More than simply promoting a set of ideas, however, in an effectively functioning hegemonic system, groups with less power are drawn into accepting the current/dominant mode of power relations. In order to maintain this acceptance, so the theory goes, dominant groups need to make ongoing concessions—concessions that allow subordinate groups to 'feel better' about their social position without actually changing the system that sustains the privilege and power of the dominant group. Sociologist Ann Hall (1996; 2007) refers to this process in her work on women and sport, where she describes how small concessions were made to women in the early twentieth century (e.g., allowing access to new sports, changing some clothing restrictions for sporting women) that in no way undermined the patriarchal power structure—which is to say, women were still lower status and without significant decision-making power in the new areas of sport to which they were 'granted' access (cf., Vertinsky, 1994).

Gramsci also described how consent is maintained when less powerful groups develop an emotional attachment (what Gramsci called 'feeling-passion') to existing systems of power relations, such that these groups feel an affectively driven commitment to defending the system. The mobilization of emotion around spectator sports like men's hockey—and the use, for example, of nostalgic images associated with great Canadian victories over the years—is an excellent case in point. For example, Canadian successes in international competitions are commonly held up as exemplars of ways that sport 'brings together a nation'—where courageous performances of elite players can be re-lived by young people on the rinks and ponds around the country. Some critics have argued, however, that this sort of emotional, nostalgic, mythical (i.e., 'partially true') view of hockey and its unassailable place in Canadian culture is the reason that many social problems associated with the game have been overlooked or ignored (Gruneau and Whitson, 1993; Robinson, 1998; Wilson, 2006a). Consider, for instance, the tolerance or ignorance of various forms of violence in and around the game (e.g., incidents of child molestation and abuse that have occurred in junior hockey), and the reality that professional hockey is a business as well as a civic institution (as ardent fans in Winnipeg and Quebec who lost their National Hockey League franchises to more lucrative markets will tell you). More recently, one might see attempts to garner support for the controversial Own the Podium program in the immediate aftermath of Olympic successes as an attempt to use the emotion of medal-winning performances as a way of generating uncritical support for a particular perspective on sport. To be clear, my goal here is not to diminish the Own the Podium program or attempts to support athletes so much as it is to show how emotion can be used to attain support for—to manufacture consent for—one particular view of a sport or program.

Although the hegemony concept is particularly helpful for sociologists intent on explaining how power structures are maintained and perpetuated, the concept is also useful for thinking through the impacts of various forms of social resistance. I am referring here to questions commonly raised by Gramsci-inspired scholars, questions like 'Do the efforts of sport-related social movement groups, such as groups that fight against the marginalization of women and girls in sport, or against the use of aboriginal mascots by sport teams, actually lead to substantial changes in the dominant sport system?', and 'Could the changes that have taken place be viewed as concessions intended to placate these subordinate and resistant groups, rather than meaningful changes to the underlying power structure?' These questions—which I pursue in some depth in chapter 5's discussion of sport, activism, and social change—are essential for sociologists of sport because they speak to ways that sport and other forms of culture are objects of and arenas where struggle and tension around social issues take place, where consent is secured and/or overturned.

Michel Foucault and Critiques of Hegemony

Hegemony, like all concepts, has its limitations and problems. It has been critiqued because it is sometimes associated with the assumption that those with power are always intentionally manipulating less powerful groups (Moores, 1993). Of course, there is evidence that influential segments of society—such as the advertisers and public relations experts who are mandated to 'sell' particular products and/or ideas—are purposively promoting certain ways of thinking. However, many theorists convincingly argue that dominant ways of thinking become pervasive in and circulated through our culture through complex processes that are less about the direct manipulation of less powerful groups by more powerful groups.

In fact, renowned social theorist Michel Foucault (1980, 1990) argued that existing power relations are maintained because the 'materials of social and cultural life' that people work with, within, and around (e.g., the spaces we move within, the language we use, the various media messages we encounter, the ways that we are governed) collectively reflect and support certain ways of thinking and acting. Put another way, the 'discourses' (to use Foucault's term) that permeate all facets of our lived experiences work together to regulate our conduct. In this way, power is something, according to Foucault, that circulates within and through a diffuse system of messages and practices, becoming embodied and embedded in our taken-for-granted way of living. Although some groups are advantaged and others disadvantaged in this process, Foucault suggests that the relations of power that support these inequalities operate more subtly, systemically, and in a more decentralized fashion than Gramsci and many of his followers suggest. Markula and Pringle (2006), in their book *Foucault, Sport, and Exercise*, use the sport of rugby—which has a privileged positioning in the nationalist discourse of New Zealand—as a way of demonstrating Foucault's vision of power:

> Rugby union within New Zealand, for example, is typically known as the country's national sport, yet the 'power' source of this nationalistic discourse is somewhat unidentifiable; it is everywhere and nowhere in particular, circulating in a dispersed fashion through multiple networks of social relations in a manner that simultaneously helps produce rugby's dominance. (p. 37)

Scholars like Jette (2009) and Norman (2009) have also used Foucault's work to demonstrate how various discourses about 'fatness' and the body (discourses supported through messages from healthcare professionals, in the mass media, in government reports, through education) have led to an extremely body-conscious North American culture—a culture where condescending portrayals and treatments of those considered overweight often go unquestioned or unchallenged, and where excessive and obsessive self-monitoring body practices (e.g., looking in mirrors and standing on scales) are commonplace (cf., Markula and Pringle, 2006). Although Gramsci-influenced scholars might see this situation as being related to the strategic creation of insecurities in our society (e.g., by advertisers) to support the promotion and sale of consumer items meant for 'body-improvement', sociologists guided by Foucault's work would focus more on ways that messages about the body have become woven into the fabric of our society over history, and that the exploitation of certain groups is less intentional than it is historical. That is to say, the problems and inequalities outlined by scholars like Norman and Jette, when viewed though a 'Foucaultian' lens, would seem to be based around a set of assumptions and social practices that have become part of our culture over time.

Others suggest that the hegemony concept is too often used to describe the power of one group over another, without adequate consideration of the 'agency' of individuals who resist in symbolic ways, and the political importance of their activities (e.g., Beal, 1995; de Certeau, 1984). In fact, authors like Duncombe (1997) argue that activities like skateboarding or surfing, that might be dismissed by some as trivial or apolitical, are precursors to 'counter-hegemonic' actions that will change (and have changed) some of the values associated with 'mainstream' sport (Wilson, 2006b; see also chapter 5). Those who observe the distinct culture associated with snowboarding, a previously stigmatized sport that is now a popular Olympic event, will be aware of this.

Still other scholars, like Richard Day (2005), have concerns that the hegemony concept cannot help sociologists visualize social life without hegemonic forms of power, since the successful overthrow of one hegemonic group is often seen to result only in the rise of another hegemonic regime.

An Underlying Problem and a Way Forward

Day's critique of hegemony and others like it are important because they speak to the fundamental problem with making assessments about what 'counts' as a peace-promoting practice, and what counts as a practice that compromises attempts to make positive social changes (i.e., a practice that inadvertently reinforces the extant hegemonic power structure). How are sociologists able to tell whether a friendly match between countries is disseminating propaganda (remember the battle of ideologies that underlay the renowned 1972 Canada–USSR hockey series), or a genuine attempt to build bridges between these countries? Can events intended to promote healing in divided societies also reinforce these same divisions?

Of course, the problem here is that we can never know for sure what actions will lead to particular consequences. There are no guarantees that actions intended to promote peace will not sometimes, in some ways, lead to undesirable outcomes. What we can do, however, is use concepts that allow us to see contradictions and problems, and to thoroughly study the contexts and historical circumstances within which these actions take place along with the meanings that people give to their actions—all the while remaining reflexive about our own ability to effectively interpret and potentially intervene. With all of its flaws, this sort of rigour is at the core of a cultural studies approach to studying sport and physical culture—the approach I privilege in this book.

With this in mind, and recognizing that looking through other theoretical lenses will always reveal other ways of describing and making sense of social phenomena, hegemony remains one of the key concepts for sociologists interested in power relationships and social processes that underlie inequality. In the sociology of sport and cultural studies fields, the hegemony concept is especially popular amongst those studying sport and masculine hierarchies (Bairner, 2009a; Pringle, 2005), as the concept speaks to ways that conforming to ideals associated with what it means to be a 'real man' (what is commonly termed a hegemonic masculine identity) may, in fact, reinforce some of the social problems associated with men's participation in sport. These problems include violence by male athletes toward other men, women, and themselves (referring here to high rates of injury in hypermasculine sports) (cf., Messner 2005; White and Young, 2006).

Critical Theories and Contextual Cultural Studies

The hegemony concept that is featured within a Gramscian cultural studies approach more generally—which took hold in the sociology of sport in the mid-1980s and into the 1990s with the work of Hargreaves (1986), Donnelly (1996), Messner and Sabo (1990), Young and White (1995), Tomlinson (1999), McKay (1986), Whitson (1984), and others (cf., Carrington and MacDonald, 2009; Rowe, 2004)—is just one of many concepts that came to be adopted by sociologists of sport working in a cultural studies tradition into the 1990s and up to the present. In introductory sociology of sport textbooks (like Coakley and Donnelly, 2009), the terms 'critical theory', 'critical feminist theory', 'conflict theory', and 'social reproduction theory' are commonly used to summarize theories that are all, in their own way, used to highlight ways that unequal power relations are reinforced and perpetuated. In fact, and as David Andrews (2002) acknowledges, the growth of cultural studies has been 'characterized by multiple theoretical influences, research methods, and sites of analysis' (p. 111). With this in mind, I will be exploring throughout the upcoming chapters the work of influential authors in these various traditions who offer strategies for conceptualizing power relations—like the work of Foucault mentioned earlier, Pierre Bourdieu (chapter 7), Allan Schnaiberg (chapter 8), Paulo Freire (chapter 6), and others. In doing so, I will be elaborating on the relevance of different theories not only for the sociology of sport field, but also for those concerned with peace-promotion.

Although the work of these theorists differs in many important ways, sociologists of sport who are influenced by these various ways of understanding power tend to agree—above all—on the importance of being mindful of: (a) the contexts within which cultural practices and forms exist; and (b) ways that people who engage with these practices (e.g., through sport participation or sport spectatorship) are part of creating and re-creating the contexts or social conditions within which these practices take place. That is to say, although there are different ways of seeing how existing power relations are sometimes perpetuated and reinforced—and seeing interconnections between the structural conditions people live within and the cultural practices of these same people—all theories in the cultural studies tradition require attention to the relevant historical, political, economic, technological, and social contexts.

Andrews (2002) and others working in this tradition draw on the important work of Larry Grossberg (1997), who used the term 'radical contextualism' as a way of describing this approach to the study of culture and power (following Hall, 1986). This approach helps sociologists 'see' relationships between sport-related social practices and the contexts they take place within, while remaining cognizant of their own inability to know 'for sure' (i.e., to guarantee) what these relationships will look like in the future (Hall, 1986). Put simply, cultural studies scholars recognize that although social life is complex, multifaceted, multilayered, and laden with contradictions, there is value in connecting 'contexts and practices' as a way of seeing through the clutter.

It is important to keep in mind here that what Andrews and others (drawing on Grossberg) are really offering is a more developed strategy for doing what C. Wright Mills was arguing for in his call for scholars to use a sociological imagination. Of course, making the sorts of linkages that Andrews, Grossberg, and Mills are alluding to requires: (a) knowledge of various forms of power relations; (b) background research on the various contexts sport takes place within; and (c) some work getting used to seeing through 'sociological multi-focals' (cf., Kemple and Mawani, 2009). With this in mind, the upcoming chapters are designed to provide background knowledge about the various contexts of sporting practices and insight into ways we might 'see' how power operates in and around these contexts. In doing so, the hope is that we become more practised and skilled in the use of different theoretical lenses, and thus continue to develop our sociological imaginations.

Making a Difference In and Through Sport

Developing and honing a sociological imagination is more than an academic exercise for many sport scholars influenced by the cultural studies field. These scholars argue that being committed to the critical study of sport means a commitment *to promoting more inclusive sporting cultures, to identifying ways that sport is implicated in the perpetuation of social inequalities, and to using sport as a forum for positive social change.* With this in mind, Andrews and Giardina (2008) have challenged sociologists of sport to embrace a 'cultural studies that matters'.

Central to this approach is the use of 'critical pedagogy' (see chapter 6), which in this context means providing students and citizens alike with access to information and tools (i.e., theories) for seeing sport from various perspectives— information and tools that may enable social justice–inspired interventions into and around sport. This approach also supports the creation and maintenance of stronger democracies, where citizen engagement is informed by an understanding of who benefits and who does not in the existing political systems.

Sport, Constructive Tensions, and Critical Peace Studies

It is not a stretch to see how this sort of commitment is well aligned with the pursuit of 'positive peace', at least as it has been described by Johan Galtung (1998) and those influenced by him. In fact, and as we will begin to explore in upcoming chapters, the field of peace studies—which includes a wealth of research on topics like conflict transformation, peace-building, and negotiation—has a great deal to offer sociologists of sport intent on making recommendations for change based on studies of power and inequality. That is to say, those working in this field (especially practitioners who do conflict resolution work) are beginning to pay attention to ways that shared cultural activities (like playing sport) may be part of the peace-building process.

Although much of this work would have been from a functionalist perspective, this does not mean that this knowledge is unhelpful, or that it cannot be understood in other ways, from other perspectives. On the contrary, what this does is challenge researchers as well as practitioners to ask more questions—to consider how the value and benefits of sport can coexist with questions about the problems with sport. Put another way, in order to address many sport-related social problems and make tangible improvements to sport programs intended to promote peace, analysts and practitioners must look to the constructive tensions that exist between different perspectives, tensions that provide the lifeblood for what some have termed the '**critical peace studies**' approach to conflict transformation (Jutila, Pehkonen, and Väyrynen, 2008).

This is also pertinent in light of concerns expressed by Giulianotti (2005) and Morgan (1993, 2004) that critical sociologists could benefit from greater attention to ways that existing systems can be improved using more 'normative' strategies, as well as more revolutionary ones (Leistyna, 2005). With this in mind, the upcoming chapters will include 'shifts' between discussions about ways that dominant sport structures are (and could be) challenged and altered, and ways that existing research and theory can be drawn on to aid those involved in sport-related peace-building efforts.

Discussion Questions

1. What is meant by contextual cultural studies? What is the relationship between critical theory (or theories) and contextual cultural studies?

2. How might a contextual cultural studies approach help us think through relationships between sport and peace?

3. What contradictions around sport are revealed when you think about relationships of power across the different levels of analysis?

4. What might a constructive tension between different theoretical perspectives look like? How might a 'multi-perspective' approach aid attempts to deal with social problems around sport? What barriers would you likely encounter?

Suggested Readings

Andrews, D. & M. Giardina. (2008). Sport without guarantees: Towards a cultural studies that matters. *Cultural Studies ↔ Critical Methodologies*, 8(4), 395–422. An excellent discussion of what it means to be guided by a cultural studies sensibility in the study of sport.

Carrington, B. & McDonald, I. (2009). *Marxism, cultural studies and sport.* New York: Routledge. An intriguing set of essays on relationships between cultural studies and Marxist thought.

Giulianotti, R. (2005). *Sport: A critical sociology.* Cambridge: Polity. A helpful overview of key sociological theories that are most commonly used to guide studies of and commentaries on sport.

Markula, P. & Pringle, R. (2006). *Foucault, sport and exercise: Power, knowledge and transforming the self.* London: Routledge. A focused examination of ways that Michel Foucault's work is pertinent to the study of sport and exercise.

Rowe, D. (2004). Antonio Gramsci: Sport, hegemony and the national-popular. In R. Giulianotti (Ed.), *Sport and modern social theorists* (pp. 97–110). New York: Palgrave MacMillan. A reflection on the relevance of Antonio Gramsci's work for the sociology of sport.

Relevant Websites

Cultural Studies Central
www.culturalstudies.net
> A website with a wealth of information about cultural studies and recent publications in the field.

International Gramsci Society
www.internationalgramscisociety.org
> This is the website for a 'non-profit organization whose aim is to facilitate the communication and exchange of information among the very large number of individuals from around the world who are interested in the life and work of Antonio Gramsci.'

Michel Fourcault
www.michel-foucault.com
> According the website's introduction page, this site 'provides a variety of resources relating to the work of the famous French philosopher [Michel Foucault] who lived from 1926 to 1984.'

National Film Board
www.nfb.ca/film/pink_ribbons_inc_clip
> This is the National Film Board of Canada website that features the documentary film *Pink Ribbons, Inc.* This film was inspired by Samantha King's contextual cultural studies analysis of Race for the Cure, published in the book also named *Pink Ribbons, Inc.*

Key Terms

critical cultural studies Cultural studies refers in its broadest sense to work conducted across a range of fields focused around aspects of contemporary culture—with consideration given to anything from the consumption of media, to the usage of language, to the symbolic meanings of music or clothing, to the role of sport in various societies. Many sociologists emphasize that being a 'cultural studies scholar' means being concerned with 'context' and 'intervention'. Those who do cultural studies–influenced work are generally concerned with explaining how it is that particular inequalities persist and how these relationships might be changed.

critical peace studies An approach to peace-promotion that is sensitive to ways that unequal power relations are sometimes perpetuated through attempts to, for example, transform or prevent conflict or promote intercultural understanding. The term is used in this book to highlight how peace-promoting interventions (typically underscored by functionalist assumptions) can be guided by a sociological imagination.

critical theories Theories that highlight (in different ways, depending on the theory) how power operates in social life, and how inequalities are maintained and exacerbated in sometimes taken-for-granted ways. These same theories, in their own ways, help researchers explore how the sets of ideas and beliefs that that we use to govern our own behaviours—ideas and beliefs that may, in fact, reinforce the very inequalities people are hoping to overcome—are adopted and taken for granted.

functionalist theory A sociological perspective that is based on the assumption that society is an organized system of parts held together because people hold similar values and have ties to one another, and because major institutions of society (family, media, religion, government) complement one another. Proponents of the theory argue that when people and institutions are well-integrated, society is at its 'healthiest'—it is 'socially stable'.

hegemony A theory of power relations, commonly associated with the work of scholar-activist Antonio Gramsci, who described ways that unequal relations of power are maintained because 'consent' is garnered from groups with less power.

interpretive sociology Interpretive sociology refers to a collection of sociological perspectives (including symbolic interactionism, dramaturgy, ethnomethodology, phenomenology, existential sociology) that have as their primary concern the actions and meanings people give to their everyday experiences and the social world around them.

symbolic interactionist theory Those who use this interpretive sociological theory focus on the meanings people give to their activities, ways these meanings arise from and are negotiated with others, and ways that these negotiated meanings (in turn) influence people's actions (Blumer, 1969).

PART II

Exploring the New and Old Politics of Sport and Peace

3 Sport, Diplomacy, and Nationalism

Questions to Consider

- ⊛ How can sport be used to unite and divide countries?
- ⊛ How can sport be used to advance government objectives through 'public diplomacy' and 'serious diplomacy'?
- ⊛ What are the complex and contradictory relationships that sport has with peace-promotion at a macro-political level?

Introduction: An 'Old' Politics of Sport

The Clint Eastwood–directed film *Invictus* (2009) and John Carlin's book *Playing the Enemy: Nelson Mandela and the Game That Changed a Nation* (2008) offer poignant illustrations of sport's power to unite an otherwise divided society. The film and book detail Nelson Mandela's attempts to promote healing and community in post-apartheid South Africa through his support of the national rugby team during their historic run to the 1995 World Cup championship. In *Playing the Enemy*, Carlin is particularly attentive to Mandela's strategic efforts to foster peace through sport, including Mandela's decision to argue for maintaining, and to himself wear, the national team uniform—a uniform with symbolic links to the apartheid years. Mandela's view was that changing the *meaning* of the uniform—instead of changing the uniform itself—would be a more effective means of transforming thinking and behaviour in South Africa. His reasoning was that a uniform change would only serve to marginalize those who were current supporters of the team, thus reinforcing old societal divisions.

In light of arguments made in chapters 1 and 2, it may come as no surprise that optimistic portrayals of sport's role in supporting diplomatic efforts and peace-building—like the ones provided in *Invictus* and *Playing the Enemy*—inspire a range of questions and concerns for sociologists who strive to promote more balanced and contextualized portrayals of sport. Bairner and Sugden (2000), for example, suggest that what sport actually does for nations, and for peace-building especially, is far more complex and ambiguous than many portrayals of the 1995 Rugby World Cup in South Africa would imply. For instance, the use of a phrase like 'the power of sport to promote peace', a phrase that we might hear in discussions about the 1995 World Cup, or an event like the Vancouver 2010 Olympics, or the NGO Right To Play, offers a deceiving image of sport as a 'social agent'—an agent that 'acts on' people, and makes positive changes in the world. Of course, sport does not inherently do anything positive (or negative)—it is people like Nobel Peace Prize winner Mandela who use sport as a tool for peace, or someone like Adolf Hitler who employed sport to promote extreme and terrifying forms of nationalism.

This chapter explores many of the sociological themes and complexities raised in this introductory discussion of Mandela, sport, and peace. The focus in this context is on what Lincoln Allison (2005), a long-time specialist in sport and international relations, refers to as an '**old politics of sport**'. This is somewhat distinct from a '**global politics of sport**', which will be discussed in the next chapter. Those who study an old politics of sport focus on ways that nations and their governments use sport as part of their efforts to promote nationalism and unity. This also means exploring sport's role in foreign policy, which means considering (for example) how sport is used to attain prestige and recognition in the international community.

If you are thinking that these topics do not seem particularly 'old', you are of course correct. There are many current examples of sport's use by governments to support nation-building and international diplomacy efforts, including in Canada. The Own the Podium Olympic excellence program referred to earlier is an example of a program designed to heighten Canada's prestige level on the world stage, and to promote nationalist sentiments amongst Canadians by inspiring a collective pride in their athletes' successes. In a not-unrelated way, sport scholars have also shown how sport is commonly used to generate consent for military initiatives and war efforts (Falcous and Silk, 2005).

To examine an 'old' politics of sport means placing the nation state at the centre of analysis. This differs from the newer or 'global' politics of sport, where nations are thought to share the stage more evenly with transnational corporations (like Nike) and global non-governmental organizations (like the IOC, FIFA, or the World Anti-Doping Association)—and often compete with one another within the agendas set by these entities (Allison, 2005, p. 1–2). Put another way, the study of the global politics of sport refers to research that recognizes and places greater emphasis on the role of sport-related transnational corporations and international NGOs and their heightened importance (alongside nations) on the world stage.

Although there is a temporal component here—since focusing on 'the nation' is especially popular in studies of sport and diplomacy during the Cold War, and at other moments when transnational corporations and organizations were less influential—most sociologists who study this evolution from an 'old' to a 'global' politics of sport would agree that this change is ongoing, and without a distinct beginning or end point. So, to study the old politics of sport is to peer through a lens that illuminates particular features of sport-related diplomacy and international relations. When we see the old and the global together—as we do in the next chapter—an increasingly contextualized picture of sport and politics will begin to emerge.

As a final introductory point, I should note that although the focus of this chapter is on politics and sport, in fact, all chapters of this book examine political aspects of sport. That is to say, the term **politics**, as it is used by sociologists, refers broadly to the 'processes through which power is gained and used in social life' (Coakley and Donnelly, 2009, p. 419)—a definition that pertains to topics like social movements, international development, and the environment. Coakley and Donnelly also provide a somewhat narrower definition of politics—'the processes and procedures of making decisions that affect collections of people, from small groups to societies' (2009, p. 419). This particular definition is useful for guiding the current chapter's examination of sport, nationalism, diplomacy, and foreign policy—and next chapter's look at neo-liberalism, globalization, democracy, and sport.

Introducing and Contesting the 'Nation'

Although it is common to talk about sport's value as a tool for nation-building, the concept of the 'nation' is itself contested by those who see nothing natural or immutable about the practice of dividing the world up with legal borders. For example, sport scholars like Silk et al. (2005) remind us that the modern, diplomatic, sovereign state is a relatively recent phenomenon—with the idea of a 'sovereign state' emerging in the Holy Roman Empire with the signing of treaties now referred to as the Peace of Westphalia, in 1648. As Silk et al. (2005) put it, 'this covenant instantiated the very idea of the sovereign state—and indeed that of an international community of states—through a mutual agreement as to the common independence of state formations' (p. 5). Of course, even this agreement did not mean that all people in the world began living as or seeing themselves to be members of formally and geographically circumscribed nations. Robert Jackson claims, for example, that 'when we speak of the "state" in sub-Saharan Africa, we are creating an illusion' (quoted in Levermore, 2004, p. 26).

With this background, and remembering arguments and theories from the previous chapter, it will come as no surprise that there are various (sometimes conflicting) approaches to understanding the role of sport in supporting nation-building and promoting nationalism. Below, I outline some of these different approaches, and in doing so highlight topics commonly studied by sociologists interested in sport, politics, and the nation state.

Sport and Nation-Building in Divided Societies

As I note in the introduction to this chapter, Nelson Mandela's use of sport in his efforts to unite a post-apartheid South Africa raised important questions for sociologists about relationships between sport and peace-building. To explore these sorts of questions, authors in Sugden and Bairner's (2000) edited collection *Sport in Divided Societies* took an in-depth look at the role of sport in various politically and socially splintered regions around the world. Included in the collection is an examination of sport's political, social, and cultural positioning in the Canadian province of Quebec; a study of sport and politics in states of the former Soviet Union; a look at divisions around sport in Northern Ireland; research on the politics of 'cricket nationalism' in India; an exploration of sport's role in and around apartheid in South Africa; as well as chapters on sport and societal divisions in Belgium, Switzerland, Germany, and Yemen.

In the book's introductory essay, Sugden and Bairner argue that because sport is a 'contested terrain' where struggles between various groups are reflected, reinforced, and reproduced, it only makes sense that sport should be seen for its capacity to both 'promote unity' and 'reinforce divisions'. Supporting this view, Jean Harvey (2000) argues in his chapter 'Sport and Québec Nationalism: Civic or Ethnic Identity' that while sport is commonly used by the Canadian government to promote a distinctly Canadian national identity, sport is also (often at the same time) used in Quebec to advance a similarly distinct Québécois nationalism. In this context, Harvey describes how sport has been implicated in the promotion of French–English divisions in Canada around major sporting events—noting how leaders in Quebec's separatist movement have highlighted Quebec's medal count as compared to the rest of Canada (Quebec commonly does very well in this comparison, especially in winter sports).

Moreover, and in the face of common arguments about hockey's role in uniting Canadians, the infamous 'Richard Riot' of 1955 exemplify how historical divisions between French and English Canada can also be exacerbated through sport. The riot—which took place on the streets of Montreal following a smoke bomb–inspired evacuation of the Montreal Forum arena—was a response to the suspension of French Canadian hockey hero and Montreal Canadiens player Maurice 'Rocket' Richard for his part in a melee with another player and a referee. According to many French Canadians and the French Canadian press, the suspension of Richard—who was known to be a regular victim of extremely physical on-ice play—was 'the typical French Canadian unfairly treated by his English boss', in this case Clarence Campbell, the commissioner of the National Hockey League (Harvey, 2000, p. 34).

Harvey's finding that sport plays an ambiguous and contradictory role in a 'divided' Canada—and especially his suggestion that to understand the role of

BOX 3.1 ❄ INDIGENOUS GROUPS AND SPORT IN DIVIDED SOCIETIES

Studies on indigenous groups are especially pertinent to thinking about sport in divided societies. University of Windsor professor Vicky Paraschak (1997), in her study of the Northern Games in Canada (which feature traditional Inuit activities) and the Arctic Winter Games (which consist of activities associated with major national and international sport competitions) came to conclusions akin to those reached by Jean Harvey in his work on sport and Quebec. For example, Paraschak described how sport was used by the Canadian government to encourage forms of cultural integration and assimilation—and how aboriginal groups, at the same time, adopted sport as a tool to promote their own distinct cultural identities (cf., Forsyth and Wamsley, 2006).

In the Australian context, sociologists Toni Bruce and Christopher Hallinan (2001; cf., Bruce and Wensing, 2009) explored controversies around 400 metre runner, Olympic gold medalist, and aboriginal Australian Cathy Freeman. Freeman is especially well known for displaying Australia's aboriginal flag—and sometimes the Australian flag and the aboriginal flag together (she did this after her gold medal at the Sydney Olympic Games)—during her post-race victory laps. Although Freeman was viewed by some as a symbol of a more united Australia, responses to her desire to foreground her aboriginal heritage led some to see her actions as divisive. Bruce and Hallinan note that although Freeman was viewed by some aboriginal Australian leaders as an important figure for raising awareness about race-related inequalities, historical forms of racism, and the difficult living conditions of many indigenous peoples around the world—she was touted by others as a symbol of what indigenous people could do if 'properly motivated'; a sentiment that often carries the underlying insinuation that individual-level factors like 'laziness' and 'lack of motivation' are the main reasons for the problems experienced by indigenous peoples.

Of course, critical sociologists take issue with such an interpretation, noting that opportunities for athletic excellence among many aboriginal groups are limited by structural factors (e.g., lack of access to the financial and social resources needed to succeed in sport) and because of overt or subtle forms of racism. That is to say, success at sport and social mobility more generally is about far more than simply being motivated—and to offer overly simplistic links between 'success' and 'motivation' sets the stage for unfounded critiques of and stereotypes about unsuccessful (aboriginal) athletes.

At a recent forum on social inclusion held at the University of British Columbia during the Vancouver 2010 Games—which featured aboriginal Canadian water polo player and former Olympian Waneek Horn-Miller—similar issues around barriers to sport participation for indigenous Canadians were taken up. Horn-Miller talked about ongoing challenges associated with being an aboriginal athlete and the stereotypes she faced when dealing with coaches. Although she ultimately excelled at a team sport, she indicated that in her early years as an athlete, she participated mainly in sports measured by time (e.g., swimming or track and field) and not sports requiring a subjective assessment of ability (e.g., team sports where athletes are chosen based on coaches' perceptions). This allowed her to avoid barriers to access that would have been unavoidable if she encountered coaches whose behaviours and decisions were guided by negative stereotypes about 'undisciplined' aboriginal Canadians. Horn-Miller's experience should inspire questions about the extent to which sport does, in fact, 'unite Canadians'—and the ways in which sport simply reflects and possibly reinforces existing divisions and inequalities.

sport in society one must be sensitive to the specific social and cultural context within which it exists—is akin to results and arguments in Tamir Sorek's (2007) book-long study entitled *Arab Soccer in a Jewish State: The Integrative Enclave*. In his book, Sorek notes that sport plays multiple and ambiguous roles in Israel, although the nature of this ambiguity is of course quite different in Israel as compared to Canada. For example, and unlike the situation in Canada, Sorek notes that despite the deep and ongoing divisions that define Arab–Jewish relations in the Israeli context, soccer has seemingly taken on a *less* political character than one might expect. Sorek explains:

> . . . despite the significant place that Arab men in Israel give to soccer in particular, soccer is far from being a site for political resistance or explicit national identification. One does not see Palestinian flags in the bleachers of Arab soccer teams; the songs, cheers, and swearing are largely taken from the verbal repertoire of Israeli soccer supporters as a whole, and mostly lack a national-based uniqueness. Outbreaks of violence are no more common at games between Arabs and Jews than at other games. In addition, the Arab soccer stars who play in Israel's leagues seek to downplay their national identity, instead emphasizing their professional identity. Even though the ethno-national cleavage constitutes the deepest chasm in Israeli society, and even though the Palestinian citizens have developed diverse forms of political national process, these processes have only rarely and marginally diffused into the soccer bleachers, where the integrative discourse still prevails. . . . At the same time, it is noteworthy that this integrative discourse is not translated into a tangible change of the discriminatory character of the state. (2007, p. 9)

Although Sorek's study is obviously relevant to thinking about sport and politics in divided societies, his work also offers an excellent example of how, depending on the theoretical lens one adopts, findings can be interpreted any number of ways. For instance, Sorek's finding could be taken to suggest that sport is surprisingly apolitical in Israel, and for this reason sport spaces might be well used for the promotion of reconciliation and integration efforts in this context. This view of sport aligns well with an uncritical, functionalist approach to thinking about the role sport plays, and could play, in a divided Israel. With this perspective in mind, Sorek does argue that soccer has great potential as a tool for integration.

From another perspective—a critical perspective—Sorek 'sees' how, by promoting soccer as an apolitical cultural practice in Israel, 'soccer may play a conservative political role that legitimizes the political, social, and economic inferiority of the Arabs in Israel'. This is a role that Sorek suggests 'is a major component in the political function that soccer serves in Israel' (pp. 9–10). With this interpretation in mind, it may come as no surprise that Sorek employs Antonio Gramsci's hegemony concept in his analysis to help him explain how sport may also help generate consent for extant relations of power. Sorek's suggestion (noted above) that 'the integrative discourse [around sport] is not translated into a tangible change of the discriminatory character of the state' is fundamental to his argument that while sport would appear to be a progressive and unifying influence, it may do little to alter existing problems and inequalities. Put simply, sport may not be associated with a significant counter-hegemonic movement in Israel.

Finally, and returning to the South Africa example—the most prominent instance of sporting success in uniting an extremely divided society—it is worth highlighting Bairner and Sugden's (2000) point that although various sport-related progressions have been made around reconciliation in the post-apartheid context, much is left to be done. As they put it:

> South Africans of different colours are still likely to be involved in separate sporting experiences, either by playing different sports or by playing for teams that do not reflect the country's cultural and racial mix. On the other hand, the situation is much better than it was and sport may yet achieve what some have already claimed for it. Even if it does so, however, there is little room for complacent reflection on the integrative capacity of sport. (pp. 9–10)

Although Bairner and Sugden published this passage in the year 2000, it remains relevant today. In fact, as South Africa hosted the 2010 FIFA World Cup—an opportunity owed in part to Nelson Mandela's support for South Africa's bid for the event—discussions about progress around human rights and reconciliation efforts in post-apartheid South Africa were especially vigorous. Reflecting on these issues, F.W. de Klerk, the former president of South

Africa who collaborated with Mandela on peace-building work in the 1990s (de Klerk and Mandela shared the Nobel Peace Prize) was quoted as follows:

> The new South Africa with all these big problems is a much better place than it would have been had we not taken the initiatives we did in the early 1990s. . . . We are back in the international community; we play a positive good role on the problematic continent of Africa. So life is good *but not for the poor* [italics added]. (quoted in CNN, 2010)

Reflecting on Sport, Unity, and Community

By noting these complexities and contradictions, my intent is not to dismiss the real ways that sport does bring people together. There is a wealth of research, in addition to the work outlined above on South Africa, that speaks to the shared feeling of belonging that sport can sometimes inspire (cf., Allison, 2000, 2008; Bairner, 2001; Cronin and Mayall, 1998). Still, and while acknowledging the important contributions sport can make here, an ongoing concern expressed by critical sociologists of sport is that the role sport actually plays in promoting unity within countries and communities is frequently overstated. That is to say, evidence supporting the view that sport brings people together is only sometimes accompanied by a thorough discussion of research findings that directly contradict the 'sport builds community' thesis, or about the complex ways that terms like 'unity' and 'community' can be understood.

For example, commentators seldom differentiate between the *types* of connections sport enables. In an excellent essay on sport and community, Ingham and McDonald (2003) address this concern by pointing to differences between the short-term connections sport fans experience following an emotional win—what they term '**spontaneous *communitas***' (following the work of Turner, 1969)—and the more deeply rooted connections that are created when people make longer-term commitments to learning about others and foster relationships based around trust and obligation. The concern that many sociologists of sport hold here is that the strength and meaning of the *temporary* or *momentary* connections commonly emerging from spontaneous 'feel-good' celebrations after a major sporting victory are too often taken up as evidence that 'sport builds community'. Allison (2008) speaks to this in the following passage:

> Sport is one factor—though often a peculiarly symbolic one—in the complicated process of change in how people feel about themselves, their countries and their governments. Spain, where the national soccer team has just won the 2008 European Championship and where individual competitors like Rafael Nadal are also achieving global success surely has a 'feel-good factor' as a consequence

compared with (say) France whose sporting stardom has been on the wane in recent years. Spain must be slightly easier to govern than it might have been as a consequence. Politicians clearly believe in this effect and we cannot dismiss it . . . If China is seen to run a 'good' Olympics and also comes in the top two places in the medals table, there will surely be sound intuitive reasons for the Chinese government to feel pleased with itself. But the benefits from a 'feelgood' performance may not last longer than it takes to win the 100 meter dash.

Supporting Allison's argument that 'feel-good' performances may have only short-term impacts is a study I mentioned in chapter 1 that showed how, in the Netherlands, increases in 'national pride' and the 'stimulation of social cohesion' following athletic success are only temporary (van Hilvoorde, Elling, and Stokvis, 2010).

These attempts to clarify the meaning of community and unity should not be taken to mean that sport cannot be useful in community building. On the contrary, and following Ingham and McDonald, we can begin to consider how powerful and ongoing sport-related connections might be the basis for sustained positive relationships between groups with a history of conflict. Kidd (2007), for example, offers a more balanced and progressive view of sport's potential, arguing that while sport is commonly implicated in the exacerbation of conflict and violence, it can also be an excellent forum where 'first steps' in a longer and more complex process toward a more cohesive society can be taken.

Sport, Nationalism, and International Diplomacy

Although promoting nationalism can be useful for uniting those within a country, many sociologists of sport recognize and describe ways that sport is also used for diplomatic purposes on the world stage. James Cull (2008), in an essay on the modern Olympic Games and China's foreign policy around the Beijing 2008 Olympics, uses the term **'public diplomacy'** to describe ways that this takes place. In this context, public diplomacy refers to the engagement of and attempt to win favour from people living in other countries, and to the processes through which 'international actors have sought to engage foreign publics' (Cull, 2008, p. 118). The assumption here is that positive relationships between people in 'our' country and people in other countries will potentially reinforce or lead to positive relationships with governments of these countries. Strategies for 'doing' public diplomacy include: hosting a major sporting event—and using the event as a platform for disseminating desirable messages to international tourists and viewers/readers of international media; succeeding at international sporting competitions as a way of increasing exposure and prestige on the world stage; and participating in and publicizing sport-related cultural exchanges, where touring teams and athletes participate in exhibition matches designed for relationship-building.

One of the highest profile examples of the 'cultural exchange' form of diplomacy (i.e., 'cultural diplomacy') is what has come to be termed 'ping pong diplomacy'. Ping pong diplomacy refers to a serendipitous and friendly meeting between the captain of the US table tennis team and members of the Chinese team at the 1971 World Table Tennis Championships in Nagoya, Japan. The meeting was the first step toward what became a trip to China by the US table tennis team and delegation. This exchange contributed to somewhat warmer diplomatic relations between China and the US at the time—countries that for many years leading up the event had essentially no diplomatic contact. The event is believed by many to have inspired US president Richard Nixon's visit to China the following year (Lee, 2008).

Other lower profile exchanges have taken place with various diplomatic strategies in mind. Lee (2008) explains:

[Sport-related cultural exchanges sometimes signal] an increasing openness on the part of one or another of the countries, such as the 1989 visit to the United States of the Soviet national baseball team. Other times it is intended to maintain some level of people-to-people relationships despite the withering of official interactions, such as the visit of U.S wrestlers to Iran in January 2007. Government-initiated efforts are still robust; the United States sends American Public Diplomacy envoys Cal Ripken Jr. and Michelle Kwan around the world to speak the 'universal language of sports.' While such interactions don't necessarily open up 'new chapters of history', they do have an important impact.

Although Lee offers a useful overview of ways that sports is used in public diplomacy efforts, critical sociologists studying sport's usage in these contexts would also highlight examples of diplomatic efforts with much different consequences than the friendly or innocuous exchanges noted above. The 1936 Berlin Olympics is a classic example of a Games that was strategically used to demonstrate German dominance and promote fascist ideologies. Although these Games are sometimes remembered for the four gold medals won by African American track and field star Jesse Owens, an accomplishment that somewhat undermined the host nation's attempts to demonstrate German dominance, as Krüger (1999) notes, Germany ended up placing first in the Olympics, 'beating the United States into second and Italy into third, thus showing the world what a strong unified Germany could achieve in the world of physical culture' (p. 71).

Canada's dramatic hockey victory over the Soviet Union in the oft-celebrated 1972 Summit Series is another example of an event that would fit the definition of public diplomacy (i.e., it was a cultural exchange). However, and as with the Berlin Olympics example, many sociologists who reflect on this event emphasize how divisions between the countries (and Cold War tensions more generally) were amplified, at the same time that Canadians were brought together in this dramatic victory (Macintosh and Hawes, 1994; Scherer, Duquette, and Mason, 2007). This despite the fact that, as Scherer et al. (2007) point out, the Canadian government's key goal in setting up the series was to improve 'low level' relations with the Soviet union as a way of establishing a more unique and independent national identity (i.e., independent from the US).

Of course, what took place in the series was far from friendly, with the violence and intimidation tactics associated with Canadian players being a point of particular controversy in Canadian media at the time. As Scherer et al. (2007) describe in a reflection on Game 7 of the series:

> Like the preceding contest, game seven was replete with numerous violent acts, including a brawl that was precipitated by an altercation between Gary Bergman and Boris Mikhailov. Soviet players, who did not resort to fisticuffs, chose other methods of aggression. Mikhailov repeatedly kicked at Bergman's shins with his skate blade and after both players were banished to the penalty box, an incensed Bergman exacerbated tensions by pointing to Mikhailov while making a throat-slitting gesture. (p. 179)

Yet to this day, the Summit Series is a common reference point for those who support the view that hockey brings together a nation, as it certainly did in 1972. The point here, however, is that although these sorts of events may inspire (temporary forms of) unity, it is difficult to responsibly portray this event and form of international diplomacy as a peace-building activity.

In fact, and with events like the Summit Series in mind, Andrews and Wagg (2007) introduce their edited book *East Plays West: Sport and the Cold War* with a chapter entitled 'War Minus the Shooting?'. The title refers to a line from George Orwell's 1945 essay entitled 'The Sporting Spirit' where he famously states that 'serious sport . . . is war minus the shooting.' While most analysts are careful not to exaggerate ways that sport may contribute to serious international conflict, there are enough examples of links between sport and war that such connections cannot be ignored. Kidd (2007) reminds us of the 'soccer war' between Honduras and El Salvador that broke out during a heated soccer match, and the group of sports fans 'that became the vanguard of genocide during the Yugoslavian civil war' (p. 165). Journalist Christopher Hitchens (2010) summarized his view on these sorts of sport-related political tensions in a *Newsweek* article written in the lead-up to Vancouver 2010:

> [in Angola in] January a gang of shooters sprays the bus carrying the national soccer team of Togo...and a local terrorist group announces that as long as the Africa Cup of Nations tournament is played on Angolan soil, fresh homicides will

be committed . . . [T]he Southern African Development Community (SADC) that have the task of hosting . . . the soccer World Cup in Cape Town this summer are in disarray as a consequence of the dispute between Angola and Congo over the 'security' aspects of these allegedly prestigious sporting events . . . On my desk lies an essay by the brilliant South African academic R.W. Johnson, describing the waves of resentment and disruption that are sweeping through the lovely city of Cape Town as the start of the World Cup draws near. Cost overruns and corruption, the closing of schools to make room for a hastily constructed new stadium... constant disputes over the rigging of 'draws' for the playoffs, allegations of bribery of referees...Nothing is spared.

Recent work by sociologists like Falcous and Silk (2005), McDonald (2005), S. King (2008), Butterworth and Moskal (2009), and Scherer and Koch (2010) follow up on this sport–war theme in their descriptions of ways that sport was strategically used to garner support for the Iraq War and other post–September 11 military initiatives. Research on 'sport and terrorism' similarly speaks to ways that sport is sometimes a platform for the promotion of various political agendas (Atkinson and Young, 2003, 2008; Toohey, 2008; Wedemeyer, 1999).

In this context, it worth noting that one of the key historical reasons for promoting sport involvement after the First World War in Canada, Britain, and France was to increase the physical fitness—and thus the military preparedness—of potential recruits and volunteers for future conflicts. According to Houlihan (2000), this practice continued after the Second World War in countries like the Soviet Union and elsewhere where 'territorial security was still perceived to be under threat' (p. 215).

Public Diplomacy and Serious Diplomacy

One of the reasons that forms of public diplomacy are commonly highlighted in work around sport and politics is that there are few examples where forms of sport-related 'serious diplomacy'—referring here to 'discussions and decisions about political issues of vital national and international interest' (Coakley and Donnelly, 2009, p. 433)—have been shown to be effective. As Coakley and Donnelly (2009) point out, boycotts of sporting events are seldom seen to have major direct impacts, as the games always go on, despite the absence of nations intent on sending a political message. They also argue that while athletes may come together during international exchanges, these same athletes have little political influence and do not make major political decisions, and that connections made between leaders at international sport events have not been shown to advance relations between countries in a meaningful way.

Even common assumptions about ways that public diplomacy—referring here to the engagement with and attempt to win favour from people living in other countries, and to the processes through which international groups attempt to engage 'foreign publics' (Cull, 2008)—can be useful in changing a country's image have been subject to particular scrutiny since the 2008 Beijing Olympics. In a recent study on the topic, Manzenreiter (2010) demonstrated (drawing on global opinion polls following the Beijing Games) that the Games did little to improve China's image for international viewers, and on this basis argued that 'expectations that a sports event can improve the image of a country are overrated' (2010, p. 29). Put simply, the 'soft power' that is associated with public diplomacy is sometimes (as Manzenreiter put it) 'weak power'.

Reflections on Sport, Diplomacy, and the Nation

In this discussion of the 'old' politics of sport, I have highlighted research and thinking from various theoretical perspectives. I referred to optimistic and uncritical portrayals of sport's role in peace-promotion—portrayals that would be aligned with a functionalist perspective on sport. Questions asked by authors working from this perspective would be, for example, 'How does sport contribute to peace promotion?', and 'How does sport contribute to nation building and unity?'

Many of the key sociological articles and books I featured, however, are based around questions such as 'How is sport used by governments in their diplomatic work?', and 'What is the relationship between this diplomatic work and nation-building and/or peace-building?' In posing these questions I am assuming that sport may promote social cohesion within and among societies, and that it may also reinforce existing divisions within societies, offer forums where existing tensions may be exacerbated, and/or 'disguise' or distort the real inequalities and problems that exist outside of sport.

Of course, these are the sorts of assumptions that guide 'critical' sociologists. The hegemony concept is especially pertinent here in light of research that describes the role that sport plays in generating consent for a particular way of seeing one's home nation and other nations. Ingham and MacDonald's (2003) essay that speaks to ways of thinking about sport, community, and unity is ultimately 'critical' as the authors balance thinking about the benefits of *communitas* (i.e., short-term connections between people) for sport fans against the ways that these same fans may be exploited emotionally and financially by sport team owners concerned largely with profits (cf., Belanger, 2000). The hegemony concept is similarly useful for thinking through reasons that many governments and politicians support elite sporting competitions and commonly associate themselves with successful teams and inspirational/ evocative moments (recall the 'feeling-passion' component of hegemony). As Coakley and Donnelly (2009) note, nation leaders frequently attend major sport events and meet with championship teams as a political strategy that may increase their 'legitimacy' as leaders (p. 427).

Sport, Peace, and Cultural Studies

Sorek's (2007) suggestion that sport can also play a role in generating consent for a particular understanding of the nation—a view of the nation that deemphasizes concerns about inequality that exist outside the stadium—is especially provocative for thinking about sport, power, and peace. Not only does it highlight ways that sport may be implicated in supporting a particular hegemonic relationship, but it also points to ways that sport is, at times and ironically, perceived to be and promoted as apolitical. The point here is that the promotion of sport as apolitical is itself a political act.

However, and looking ahead to research by Sugden (2006), Keim (2003), and others that will be featured in chapter 7, we will begin to see how this perception of sport as apolitical is, in fact, crucial for those who use sport for development and peace programs in reconciliation efforts. That is to say, sport's value as a cultural forum for bringing together rivalling groups is integrally tied to this view of sport (and sport-related spaces) as apolitical.

In noting these contradictory views on sport's capacity to appear or 'be' apolitical, I am highlighting another theoretical disjuncture. This disjuncture is between an interpretive sociological view of sport and a more critical stance on sport. You may recall from chapter 2 that interpretive sociologists tend to ask questions about the meaning that people give to their sport-related experiences. With these questions about meanings and interpretation in mind, William I. Thomas (1923) famously argued that 'if men [and women] define situations as real, they are real in their consequences'—an argument and assumption that anchors much of the research conducted within the interpretive sociology tradition. For sociologists guided by this viewpoint, it does not matter if sport is, in fact, being used for political purposes at a macro level. What is important is that sport is *perceived* to be apolitical since this perception is the reality for those who share this understanding. This is relevant for thinking about micro-level interventions and programs where sport is used to support peace-building efforts (e.g., friendly soccer matches or teambuilding sport clinics for youth) because the success of these initiatives relies on this perception of sport as apolitical. That is to say, *this perception is precisely why sport spaces are sometimes ideal spaces for integration, reconciliation, and the promotion of intercultural understanding.*

Despite these benefits, those who uncritically laud sport's apolitical qualities are commonly in tension with critical sociologists who suggest that to be supportive of an apolitical view of sport is to be complicit about ways that sport may be used to reinforce and perpetuate the same inequalities and social problems that many sport programs were designed to address. The overarching concern here is that sport-related peace-building activities that are helpful in allowing people who are in conflict situations to temporarily 'feel better' and experience some intercultural connection may not be part of any real solution to the structural problems that are the underlying reasons for various forms of inequality and conflict. Having said this, and as Sugden (2006) has argued, it is important to do something to address tensions and difficulties, and positioning sport as an apolitical space is one way to do this.

Clearly, there is no 'right' answer here, although recognizing and attempting to address inequalities and social problems on multiple levels—and seeing connections between these levels—is crucial for understanding and addressing the complexities of social problems. Over the upcoming chapters I continue to explore connections and sometimes contradictions between peace-building initiatives in local communities and the diplomatic efforts of politicians. This 'multi-level' approach to peace-building is at the core of what some scholars refer to as 'multi-track diplomacy'—an approach that emphasizes the need to promote peace within and through various channels and at different levels, with the assumption that these levels interact and are integrally related.

We can begin to see here how a critical cultural studies–influenced perspective might be useful for more nuanced thinking about peace-building across these levels. That is to say, being guided by a critical cultural studies approach would help analysts think through, recognize, and respond to contradictions that exist across the various levels/contexts of social life. In doing so, analysts and practitioners will recognize that the success of any response will be necessarily imperfect (i.e., it will never be 'guaranteed'). Despite this, there is still reason to be encouraged by the idea that recognizing limitations and problems on an ongoing basis can lead to more responsible, flexible, and reflexive approaches to intervention and diplomatic relations.

Discussion Questions

1. Why might sport's potential to 'unite societies' sometimes be overstated?

2. How did the Vancouver 2010 Olympic Games, the Beijing 2008 Olympics, or another recent Olympic Games 'unite and divide'?

3. How can a contextual cultural studies approach help us see the complexities and contradictions around sport's role in diplomatic relations?

Suggested Readings

Cull, N. (2008). The public diplomacy of the modern Olympic Games and China's soft power strategy. In. M. Price & D. Dayan (Eds.), *Owning the Olympics: Narratives of the new China* (pp. 117–44). Ann Arbour, MI: University of Michigan Press. An exploration of the 'public diplomacy' concept, with particular attention the term's relevance for the Beijing 2008 Olympics.

Houlihan, B. (2000). Politics and sport. In J. Coakley & E. Dunning (Eds.), *Handbook of sports studies* (pp. 213–27). Thousand Oaks, CA: Sage Publications.

A succinct but comprehensive overview of the various 'ways of seeing' sport and politics.

Jackson, S. & Haigh, S. (2008). Between and beyond politics: Sport and foreign policy in a globalizing world. *Sport in Society*, 11(4), 349–58. An excellent summary of ways that foreign policy is articulated in a 'globalizing world', as the authors put it.

Levermore, R. & Budd, A. (2004). *Sport and international relations: An emerging relationship*. New York: Routledge. An overview of research and commentary on sport and international relations from a variety of perspectives.

Wagg, S. & Andrews, D. (Eds.). (2007). *East plays West: Essays on sport and the Cold War*. London: Routledge. A collection of essays focused around sport-related diplomacy and international relations during the Cold War.

Relevant Websites

CBC news archive
http://archives.cbc.ca/sports/hockey/topics/318
This link includes a series of CBC archived videos on the 1972 Canada–Soviet Summit Series.

CBC news archive
http://archives.cbc.ca/sports/hockey/clips/13340
This link includes an archived CBC video about the infamous Richard Riot in Montreal in 1955 in response to the suspension of Maurice 'Rocket' Richard.

The Globe and Mail Series on Sport and Society
www.theglobeandmail.com/intellectual-muscle/the-talks/article1312702
This webpage includes a series of podcasts about sport and society that were posted during the 2010 Vancouver Olympic Games. Recommended listening for this chapter is Denis Pilon's talk entitled 'The Politics of the Olympics' and the talks and panel discussion entitled 'Sport and Inclusion: Are Major Sporting Events Inclusive of First Nations and Other Groups?' that featured Waneek Horn-Miller, Valerie Jerome, Sharon Firth, Shirley Firth-Larsson, Aaron Marchant, and Sid Katz.

Key Terms

'new' or global politics of sport refers to the processes through which sport-related transnational corporations and international NGOs (e.g., the IOC) have come to play a prominent role in agenda-setting for nations and regions.

'old' politics of sport refers to ways that nations and their governments use sport as part of their efforts to promote nationalism and unity. This also refers to sport's role in foreign policy, which means considering (for example) how sport is used to attain prestige and recognition in the international community. These approaches to sport-related diplomacy are evident today, although transnational corporations and international NGOs play a heightened role in such negotiations in the current moment (see 'new/global politics of sport' entry above).

politics as it is used by sociologists, refers broadly to the 'processes through which power is gained and used in social life' (Coakley and Donnelly, 2009, p. 419).

public diplomacy refers to the engagement of and attempt to win favour from people living in other countries, and to the processes through which international groups attempt to engage 'foreign publics' (Cull, 2008).

spontaneous *communitas* refers to a transient connection and experience of togetherness—like the short-term connections sport fans experience following an emotional win for their team.

4 | Sport, Global Politics, and Peace

Questions to Consider

⊛ What is 'globalization' and how does it relate to sport, politics, and peace?
⊛ What is 'neo-liberalism' and how does it relate to sport, politics, and peace?
⊛ Why do many critical sociologists of sport think that neo-liberal policies and ideologies hinder peace and contribute to a process of de-democratization?
⊛ What is the 'Golden Arches Theory of Conflict Resolution' and how does it relate to sport and peace? What are the problems with this theory?

Introduction: Sport, Globalization, and a Vision of the Future

The year is 2018. There is no crime and there are no more wars. Corporations have replaced countries—and the violent game of Rollerball is used to control the populace by demonstrating the futility of individuality. However, one player, Jonathan E., rises to the top, and fights for his personal freedom and threatens corporate control . . . and the authorities decide he must be stopped, no matter the cost.[1]

Good science fiction films inspire viewers to consider what could happen if current social, cultural, and political trends continue into the future. William Harrison, the screenplay writer for the 1975 sci-fi classic *Rollerball*, wrote just such a film—a film that highlights ideas that have become, 35 years after *Rollerball*'s release, very familiar to those who study sport, politics, **globalization**, and peace.

For example, Harrison describes a world where nation states have disappeared in favour of corporations. Following a similar theme, sociologists like Allison (2005), Silk et al. (2005), and Scherer and Jackson (2010) describe the diminishing influence of nations in sport politics and the increasing prominence and power of transnational corporations like Nike, and NGOs like the International Olympic Committee. Harrison also depicts a world where war does not exist (i.e., a world in a state of negative peace), but where many of the freedoms and rights associated with democratic political systems—systems where positive peace is promoted—have been eliminated. For example, the resources, privileges, and decision-making power of the everyday consumer-citizen pale in comparison to those possessed by corporate owners in Harrison's vision. At the same time, and as the film's main character Jonathan E. finds out, opposition to the ideas of those in power is suppressed by corporate owners.

Following these themes, sociologists of sport commonly study how sport is used to generate consent for—and reduce resistance within—societies where high levels of inequality exist. I will take this a step further and suggest that *Rollerball*'s depiction of a society where negative peace is maintained, but positive peace is not, has particular relevance to studies of sport and peace in **neo-liberal** societies. That is to say, while there is some evidence that armed conflict is less likely when economic ties exist between nations (akin to the highly integrated corporate-economic relationships depicted in the borderless world of *Rollerball*), it is also the case, according to Cortright (2008) and others, that *when the creation of these ties is driven by neo-liberal forces, positive peace (referring, for example, to high levels of equality and equity in political and economic realms) is compromised.* As I show later in this chapter, sport is integrally tied to the promotion of these neo-liberal ideologies and policies—and in this way could be contributing to processes of '**de-democratization**' (Tilly, 2007).

Finally, Harrison's screenplay portrays fans of rollerball as disengaged from politics, but fully engaged in spectatorship. For years, sociologists concerned with sport's potential role as an 'opiate of the masses' (following Karl Marx's famous claim that 'religion is the opiate of the masses') have addressed similar concerns, although this issue seems especially pertinent at a moment when sport appears to be playing a greater and greater role as a tool for promoting the neo-liberal ideologies and policies that may inadvertently promote inequalities on a global scale.

A 'Global' Politics of Sport

Below, I build on the previous chapter's description of what Allison (2005) calls an 'old politics of sport', discussing here characteristics and debates around newer forms of sport politics, what Allison refers to as a newer or 'global politics of sport' and what Silk et al. (2005) term '**corporate nationalism**'. As I noted previously, these forms of politics—the 'old' and 'the global'—are interrelated. That is to say, sport continues to play a role in nation-building and international diplomacy, and nation states, contrary to William Harrison's vision in *Rollerball*, not only exist, but continue to be important political entities in the contemporary world. Having said this, the cautionary tale that Harrison offers remains a useful reference point for thinking about ways that transnational NGOs and corporations have increasingly come to influence various forms of international relations. While the most stark example of a powerful sport-related transnational organization is the International Olympic Committee, a group that has an astonishing influence over agenda-setting in Olympic cities around issues like urban planning and sustainability, Allison and others point to a myriad of other powerful sport-related non-governmental and corporate bodies as well—NGOs and corporations referred to throughout this and upcoming chapters.

I examine this newer politics of sport in the following sections. First, I describe the broader social and political developments that were precursors to the rise of (sport-related) transnational NGOs and corporations. I then define and discuss in some detail the term 'neo-liberalism'—a term that is central to contemporary discussions about sport-related politics. I then define and discuss the term 'globalization', another concept that is commonly used to help sociologists explain how it is that sport-related politics have become both global and corporate nationalist. In doing so, I identify concerns commonly expressed by sociologists of sport about this movement toward a global and corporate nationalist politics, focusing in particular on apprehensions about the potential impacts of these developments on democratic features of some societies. Throughout this process I will be pursuing a main argument of this chapter—that sport is integrally tied to the promotion of neo-liberal ideologies and policies, and could in this way be contributing to processes of 'de-democratization' (Tilly, 2007).

The Decline of the Nation: Setting the Stage for Neo-liberalism and Intensified Globalization

How and when did we move from a nation-centred approach to politics to a 'global politics'? How is sport implicated in this process? Although there is no firm starting point, developments associated with 'the rise of global institutions' (sport-related and otherwise) and the intensification of globalization processes more generally are commonly linked with the rise of neo-liberal policies and ideologies.

Neo-liberalism is the term used to describe an approach to governance that was increasingly adopted beginning in the 1970s in the US and UK (following an initial neo-liberal experiment in Chile in the early 1970s), an approach that is now 'hegemonic within world capitalism' (Harvey, 2005, p. 9). The neo-liberal approach was increasingly implemented at this time as a response to Keynesian economic policies (i.e., referring to the economic doctrines of British economist John Maynard Keynes) that had been adopted in Canada and many other democratic countries following the Second World War. David Harvey (2005) notes how Keynesian-influenced policies (that grew from what Rugge (1982) termed an 'embedded liberalist' philosophy) were based around the idea that the state's mandate should be to pursue 'full employment, economic growth, and the welfare of its citizens', and that 'state power should be freely deployed, alongside of or, if necessary, intervening in or even substituting for market processes to achieve these ends' (p. 10). In this system, a compromise of sorts is advocated between 'capital and labour' with the goal of ensuring 'domestic peace and tranquility' (Harvey, 2005, p. 10).

This meant that the state 'actively intervened in industrial policy and moved to set standards for the social wage by constructing a variety of welfare system (health, education and the like)', while at the same time attempting to promote corporate and industrial activity, albeit with active state intervention as well as state ownership in key sectors (p. 10–11).

In the 1970s, the economy began to stagnate, inflation was becoming a problem, and unemployment was on the rise in North America and other industrial countries around the world—trends attributed to Keynesian-related wage increases for workers, rising costs for public services, market saturation, and competition from low-wage countries (Morley and Robins, 1995, p. 27; cf., Silk et al., 2005). Although various responses to this problem were possible, Teeple (2000) points out that the stage was being set for a neo-liberal response for many years, with the slow but significant decrease in the power and role of the nation state from 1945 to the 1970s. For example, over this time overseas trade and investment (aided by advances in computer and information exchange technology) were increasing dramatically as transnational and multinational corporations 'had begun shifting profits and operations to places where the advantages in taxation, wages, and state support were greatest' (Teeple, 2000, p. 61). In doing so, according to Teeple, these corporations were assuming 'the powers of sovereign entities, ignoring and interfering in the interests of nation states', and were thus placing international pressures on nations to remove barriers to expansion, relocation, and trade (2000, p. 61). At the same time, international NGOs (like the IOC and FIFA) and intergovernmental organizations (like the United Nations) were becoming more and more influential (Hardt and Negri, 2000).

The Neo-liberal Response

With this background, we can begin to think about what neo-liberalism is, and what it means to say that neo-liberalism was a response to a Keynesian approach to governance. Neo-liberalism in this context refers to policies and ideologies that are based around the use of a market rationality and private business approach for all social, cultural, and political matters—which is to say, every action and policy is submitted to considerations of profitability (Brown, 2006). Within a neo-liberal governance model, individuals are viewed as—and encouraged to be—'rational actors' who make decisions based on the benefits of their actions for themselves. As in a private business model, the assumption here is that such responsibility will promote efficiencies in the system, since neo-liberal citizens will be motivated to be as productive as they can be—to make the best decisions they can to maximize personal benefits (e.g., maximize income, health, and status). For this reason, supporters of this system assume that a healthy open competition amongst motivated and rational entrepreneurs will produce a healthy and productive citizenry.

This system is not intended to support those who cannot support themselves, as the motivated neo-liberal citizen is expected to find a way to succeed—as a creative entrepreneur—regardless of circumstances. Only if there is a market for services to support vulnerable citizens—e.g., if there is consumer demand for facilities that cater to the needs of elderly lower-income people who may have particular health problems and challenges with mobility—would there be a need for a private sector response to this service gap. If not enough people want a service (or more accurately, if a service is not financially sustainable), then a neo-liberal system would not support it. This system, as Brown (2005) notes, 'carries responsibility for the self to new heights' as 'the rationally calculating individual bears full responsibility for the consequences of his or her action no matter how severe the constraints on this action—for example, lack of skills, education, and childcare in a period of unemployment and limited welfare benefits' (p. 42).

Proponents of this approach also argue that societal problems—problems that proponents of Keynesian economics would respond to through government intervention—can be more effectively addressed in an open market system. For example, if the environmental impacts of building a new golf course or producing golf equipment are important to consumers, then those in the golf industry will respond to consumer demand for environmentally friendly products because it is in their best (financial) interest to do so. You can begin to see here how 'moral' or 'ethical' decisions and 'economic' decisions are inseparable according to this rationality, since it is 'moral' to make 'rational' (i.e., profitable) decisions in a neo-liberal system.

You may recognize that in Canada, municipal, provincial, and federal governments have increasingly adopted variations of neo-liberal governance models (Frisby et al., 2007; McBride and McNutt, 2007), although a hybrid model of government continues to exist. That is to say, government continues to at least partially fund essential services (like healthcare and education) and offer some support systems for more vulnerable groups, even if the market might not explicitly support these. Ongoing debate exists about what priorities should drive decisions about how to strike a balance between these different models.

Finally, those adopting a neo-liberal approach encourage the ever-increasing development of global economic connections, which means removing barriers to transnational corporations moving into new, profitable contexts. I elaborate on this point later in this chapter.

Sociology of Sport and a Critique of Neo-liberalism

Many sociologists of sport and others offer a passionate and often well-supported critique of a neo-liberal approach to governance. A main concern is that more vulnerable groups (e.g., lower-income persons, children living in poverty) are often negatively impacted by these sorts of policies, since the 'competition' and 'minimal government' based approach to all things social means that those with fewer resources (e.g., lower-income women interested in access to recreational facilities) are less likely to be catered to by corporations/organizations that must be economically sustainable or profit-making (Donnelly and Coakley, 2002; Frisby et al., 2005). Those who disagree with a neo-liberal approach argue that some social problems should be the responsibility of government, and that some aspects of society should not be measured according to profitability or financial viability.

Other critics point out that an incentive system that is based purely on profit can lead to other types of problems when, for example, sport corporations catering to consumers interested in environmentally friendly business practices decide to market themselves as 'green' without substantially changing their business practices. Since altering environment-related behaviour can be expensive, this decision to 'greenwash' would be completely reasonable according to a neo-liberal sensibility (Beder, 2002). Calculating the relative risk and cost of getting caught greenwashing would necessarily inform this business decision, since moral and rational (i.e., economic) decisions are one and the same in this system. I return to this point in chapter 9's discussion of sport and environmental issues.

Additionally, and as Marglin (2008) notes in his book *The Dismal Science: How Thinking Like an Economist Undermines Community*, the principles underlying a commitment to 'community living' may be undermined by an approach to governance (i.e., neo-liberalism) designed to privilege and reward those driven only toward *personal* success and prosperity. With this critique in mind, sociologist Grant Jarvie (2006) describes the 'communitarian' perspective, which is based around the idea that the emphasis on 'individualism' that is so central to neo-liberalism overlooks the importance of cooperation and building trust in order to create and sustain peaceful societies. Jarvie (2006, cf., Coleman, 1988; Putnam, 2000) goes on to describe the communitarian view that maintaining a healthy democracy depends on encouraging the development of various networks of social groups and relationships in order to 'foster co-operative working and community' and build 'trust through taking on mutual obligations' (p. 333). The term commonly used to describe the kinds of 'networks, norms and trust' that help sustain communities is 'social capital' (cf., Bourdieu, 1984). Sport is commonly seen as a cultural form that can be used to promote the cultivation of social capital (Nicholson and Hoye, 2008—see also chapter 7).

Finally, you will remember that supporters of neo-liberal forms of governance assert that in order to continue to increase profits and support competition, corporations need access to emerging markets (i.e., the markets of 'developing' countries in the Global South) for cheap labour and to expand their consumer base. Perhaps the most well-known critique of sport's relationship to neo-liberalism is based around this kind of expansion. Those who study this issue are particularly concerned about the relatively uninhibited movement of sport-related transnational corporations (like Nike) into countries of the Global South—a movement associated with what is commonly termed 'economic globalization'. The reason for this concern is that regulations around working hours, working conditions, and child labour may not exist or be enforced in some areas—or in other cases it may be difficult for those working in factories to challenge management. In these cases, the risk of human rights violations and poor treatment of workers more generally is high.

With these concerns in mind, scholars like Sage (1999) and Knight and Greenberg (2002) have documented the activities of, and corporate responses to, various anti-sweatshop and anti-Nike activist groups (referring to the sweatshop labour practices commonly associated with major athletic apparel companies)- groups that protest against what they see as the exploitation of workers impacted by this approach to doing business. A most recent example of concerns about this form of globalization emerged in the lead up to the World Cup of Soccer in 2010, where issues were raised about working conditions for those responsible for stitching official Adidas replica soccer balls. The following excerpt from an article in the UK's *The Daily Telegraph* newspaper speaks to this:

> A report being launched . . . by the International Labor Rights Forum brings to light the plight of football stitchers who are at the very bottom of football's multi-billion pound empire. Adidas, which makes replicas of the official World Cup football, the 'Jabulani', in the world's football-making capital, Sialkot [in Pakistan], is targeting £1.2 billion sales this year. Meanwhile some of Sialkot's stitchers, who make 70 per cent of the world's hand-stitched footballs, say they do not earn enough to feed their children . . . Adidas states its stitching centre workers earn a minimum of 231 rupees (£1.85) a day. This means if they work a six-day week, they just make the monthly minimum wage of 6,000 rupees—less than £50. This is half the recognised 'living wage' of 12,000 rupees . . . for a family to be able to afford education for their children, rent, electricity, and food. (Henderson and Crilly, 2010)

Although debates are ongoing about what appropriate standards should be and what is actually taking place in factories like those mentioned, the point here is that serious concerns have been raised about the implications of inexpensive and flexible forms of producing sport-related apparel and equipment in a global age, and that the rights and experiences of people may be overlooked when the most efficient and profitable mode of production is always sought.

Globalization and the Sociology of Sport

The above concerns about the impacts of economic globalization are among many issues and critiques offered by sociologists of sport about globalization in all its forms. Although I will pursue these topics and associated critiques in more detail later on, it is important to recognize here that the term 'globalization'—as is the term 'neo-liberalism'—is complex and contested. So, and although a read of many sociology of sport articles will reveal problems with economic forms of globalization in particular, there are other interpretations of the term and phenomena that are more optimistic. Put another way, it is important to recognize that there is a vibrant debate around terms like globalization and to be aware of reasons that some scholars and others—who are also interested in the pursuit of peace and equality—see neo-liberalism and globalization differently than do many critical sociologists.

So What Is Globalization?

Before exploring these various perspectives on sport's role in globalization, I discuss what it means to study globalization in the sociology of sport and to offer a working definition—since 'globalization and sport' is one of the more widely studied and wide-ranging areas in the field. In broad terms then, globalization refers to the 'compression of the world and intensification of consciousness of the world as a whole' (Jarvie, 2006, p. 95; Robertson, 1992; Thibault, 2009). Although globalization is sometimes described as a relatively new (i.e., late twentieth century) phenomenon, scholars like Maguire (1999), Bairner (2001), and Miller et al. (2001) are quick to point out that processes of globalization have been in operation for centuries through world exploration, empire-building/colonization, and trade. What distinguishes the contemporary era is the magnitude and speed of globalization.

Arjun Appadurai (1996) summarized some key processes (what he terms 'scapes') through which globalization takes place. He does so using the following set of interrelated terms:

- ideoscapes (referring to ways that ideas are transmitted across border);
- financescapes (referring to the transfer of capital across borders);
- mediascapes (referring to the global reach of mass media);
- technoscapes (referring to the global movement of technologies); and
- ethnoscapes (referring to the movement of people across borders).

Jarvie (2006) offers an excellent summary of ways that sport is taken up through these various scapes:

Sporting ethnoscapes might involve the migration of professional or non-professional personnel through player, manager or coach transfers; sporting technoscapes could include sports goods, equipment . . . and transporting of sports technology [more generally]; sporting financescapes refer to the global flow of finance brought about through the international trade of players, prize-money, endorsements, and sporting goods; sporting mediascapes refer to the sport-media complex that transports sport across the globe . . . [and] sporting ideoscapes are bound up with the ideologies and philosophies expressed by, in and through sport. (p. 100)

With these processes in mind, sociologists of sport have conducted studies on topics like the impacts of the internationalization of sporting competitions and sport tourism on cities (Gold and Gold, 2007; Maguire, 1999); the influences of globally disseminated forms of sport media on local cultures/identities and the related impacts of transnational entities like Nike or the NBA on local cultures/identities (Carrington et al., 2001; Jackson and Andrews, 1999); relationships between transnational organizations like the International Olympic Committee and the World Anti-Doping Association and national sport governance structures (Houlihan, 2006; Lenskyj, 2006); and, as above, the labour practices of transnational athletic apparel companies (Sage, 1999).

Concerns and Debates about Sport-related Globalization

Although sociologists explore a variety of issues around sport-related globalization, one of the key debates is about the impacts of global forces (summarized in Appadurai's five scapes) on the distinctiveness of local cultures/identities, and on the meaning and importance of nation states in a global age. Bairner (2005) notes that this concern is manifested in various ways. Many commentators are fearful that a neo-liberal approach will become 'the' form of governance on a global stage—a concern that is at the core of anti-globalization protests that commonly take place during meetings of groups like the World Trade Organization (WTO). Others focus more broadly on what they see as the looming demise of nations and local identities—and the possible global spread of a homogenous, Americanized form of culture.

Although there are ongoing debates about what happens when global forces and local cultures converge and interact—and about what the future holds for the 'the local' as these convergences and interactions continue and accelerate—one of the more convincing arguments is made by sociologist of sport and globalization theorist, Joseph Maguire. Maguire (1999), a professor at the University of Loughborough, argues that interactions between 'the local' (which commonly refers to civic or ethnic cultures and identities) and 'the global' has led to a situation where there are 'diminishing contrasts' between nations as the various forces of globalization continue to circulate, but also 'increasing varieties' of local/national forms of culture and politics as these always-circulating forms of culture (e.g., images of celebrity icons like Yao Ming; Nike basketball sneakers; Manchester United soccer jerseys; the sport of hockey) are understood and utilized in various and distinctive ways. Bairner (2005) nicely summarizes this process, indicating that 'the nation as we have known it may well be about to disappear but it will do so not because of the triumph of a single unidirectional tendency—e.g., Americanization—but rather because all national cultures borrow and continue to borrow from each other' (p. 88).

With these processes in mind, researchers like Jackson and Andrews (1999; cf., Silk and Andrews, 2001) describe how transnational corporations intentionally cater their products to local audiences, and how local audiences will sometimes use products in unintended ways. What is created in these situations are '**glocalized**' forms of culture (i.e., combinations of local and global cultural forms). Although Jackson and Andrews's, Bairner's, and Maguire's portrayals of global–local interactions depart from the view of a homogenized monoculture portrayed in William Harrison's *Rollerball* and by some sociologists, there should be no mistake here that nation states are not the only all-powerful characters on the world stage in this era of accelerated globalization. As Bairner (2005) notes, even if nations resist or reinterpret global influences, a glocalized national identity is still not an authentic, distinctive, or stable identity as processes of globalization will continue to impinge on, influence, and change what is meant by 'the nation'.

For example, ice hockey is commonly celebrated for being an authentically Canadian sport, yet with the ongoing integration of players from other countries into the National Hockey League (and Canada's exposure to other playing styles and sport cultures through international competitions), the sport of hockey in Canada is in some ways glocalized in its look and meaning. With this in mind, MacNeill (1996) points out in her study of Olympic hockey at the 1988 Calgary Olympics that Canadian sport announcers commonly explained how countries that had experienced hockey success had often been influenced by Canadian hockey (e.g., through coaches or players that had been part of non-Canadian hockey systems). Following MacNeill's findings, we can begin to consider not only how hockey in Canada and in other countries is glocalized, but also how in Canada there may be a perceived threat to an identity as 'the dominant and authentic hockey nation' when other countries are successful (noting that Canada performed poorly at the 1988 Games). That is to say, and as MacNeill notes, in order to legitimize popular and mythologized links between hockey and national identity in Canada, there may be a perceived need to highlight how even the success of other countries is attributable to the Canadian hockey tradition. This response is well aligned with studies that focus on ways that globalizing influences are resisted because of fears about the threat of external/globalizing influences on valued forms of national identity and culture (Jackson and Andrews, 1999).

Glocalization and Corporate Nationalism

While some celebrate the power of people in local/national contexts to resist homogenization (Rowe, 2003), authors like Andrews and Ritzer (2007) argue that *all* local cultures are in some way 'glocal' (also known as 'hybridized' or 'creolized'), since it is essentially impossible for nations to completely avoid the ever-present and ongoing influences of globalization in an increasingly interconnected world. With this argument in mind, Silk et al. (2005) edited a book entitled *Sport and Corporate Nationalisms* which includes a set of essays focused around the idea that the 'context and processes through which national cultures are produced and reproduced are being transformed' with the increasing influence of transnational corporations (p. 7). While Silk et al. acknowledge in their introduction to the book that the 'internal political forces previously responsible for harnessing and contouring national identity' have not been 'rendered obsolete', they are unambiguous in their suggestion that we have entered an era where the influence of the nation 'is being eroded by external, commercially driven, forces' (p. 7). As they explain:

> As human civilization becomes increasingly corporatized, the nation and national culture have become the principal (albeit perhaps unwilling) accomplices within this process, as global capitalism seeks to, quite literally, capitalize upon the nation as a source of collective identification and differentiation. (Silk et al., 2005, p. 7)

Of course, there are various forces that have led to the glocalization of national cultures around the world (e.g., international travel, global media). What Silk et al. are arguing, however, is that the contemporary transnational corporation is a preeminent glocalizing force because of its scope of influence, its ongoing need to make inroads into new markets, and the often-subtle, tactical, and insidious ways that they make these inroads. That is to say, these ways in are made through the use of marketing strategies that allow corporations to gain widespread exposure for their brand, and at the same time link this brand—and the products associated with it—with nationalist symbols. The idea is that when brands become linked with non-corporate symbols like flags or an Olympic victory, the emotional attachments and loyalties that are commonly associated with the symbol become linked with the brand as well. While this is certainly an effective technique for promoting products and brands, critics like Silk et al. raise questions about the social implications of merging corporate brands and nationalist symbols, noting that the companies that benefit from such loyalties and attachments are ultimately (and by mandate) concerned first and foremost with profit. In Box

4.1, I describe how the corporate nationalism identified by Silk et al. is associated with a global politics of sport. I do this by highlighting interconnections between corporations (Adidas and Li Ning), an international sport organization (the IOC), and a nation (China) at a global sporting mega-event, the Beijing Olympics.

These issues are also explored by Jackson and Hokowhitu (2005) in their study of ways that the traditional indigenous *haka* dance of the Māori in New Zealand/Aotearoa—a dance now well known as a pre-match ritual for the New Zealand All Blacks rugby team—came to be appropriated in a global advertising campaign by Adidas. The advertisements in question feature the All Blacks rendition of the *haka*. The authors point to the complex ways that the Adidas–*haka* relationship could be seen to impact a society where the indigenous *haka* dance is itself contested, since the dance was part of a unifying national team ritual in a society where race-related inequalities, divisions,

---

BOX 4.1 ❋ LI NING: EMBODYING CORPORATE NATIONALISM AND A GLOBAL POLITICS OF SPORT

. . . as I sat in Ditan Park last Friday evening with hundreds of other Chinese and foreigners watching the opening ceremony [for the Beijing 2008 Olympic Games] on two big TV screens, I couldn't help wonder what Olympic sponsor Adidas was thinking as former six-time Olympic medalist Li Ning, who began a rival athletic apparel company under his own brand, lit the Olympic flame while suspended by wires 75 feet in the air.

> From Chi-Chu Tschang's *Businessweek* article 'Olympic ambush heats up Li Ning-Adidas rivalry' (Tschang, 2008)

Li Ning was a dominant gymnast, renowned for his six medal performance (3 gold) at the 1984 Olympic Games in Los Angeles. While this Olympic success made Li a national icon in China, Li Ning is best known in recent years for his success as founder of *Li Ning*, the athletic apparel company that bears his name.

With this in mind, reflect on the above quotation from *Businessweek* and consider the various meanings of Li Ning in his appearance at the Beijing Games. He is a national icon for China, a symbol of the international Olympic community and committee (as torchbearer for the Games), and a representative for two transnational athletic apparel corporations (Li Ning, and temporarily at least, Adidas)—and thus a symbol of China's long-awaited engagement with the global marketplace. Li Ning thus connects an international NGO, transnational corporations, and national politics. In these ways Li Ning embodies the 'corporate nationalist' and 'global political' sensibilities that are characteristic of twenty-first century sport.

and disagreements around land claims persist. Jackson and Hokowhitu raise important questions about what is lost and who might be exploited when a company like Adidas uses a local-national ritual like this for profit-making purposes. They ask whether the selective use of warrior images by Adidas to represent a complex indigenous culture might reinforce stereotypical views of the Māori as primitive, naïve, and violent, as noble savages, as exotic others, as humorous archetypes, and/or as hypersexual predators. For example, the expressions of *haka* dancers (e.g., wide-open eyes and protruding tongue) are meaningful within a culture that considers the eyes to be windows of the soul and the tongue 'an avenue whereby thoughts of the mind is [sic] conveyed to the audience' (Karetu, 1993; quoted in Jackson and Hokowhitu, 2005, p. 76). Consider how such expressions, taken out of context, could fuel some of the stereotypes noted earlier.

A broader issue is that the Māori have in many respects lost control over how their culture is represented in an era where images are quickly and easily disseminated across a global mediascape. Noting that Adidas did consult with Māori cultural leaders when constructing the initial advertisements in question, Jackson and Hokowhitu emphasize now the global dissemination of these images means that the *haka* has come to be reinterpreted and appropriated in other contexts.

Globalization, Peace, and Democracy: Contemplating the Golden Arches Theory of Conflict Prevention

Although sociologists of sport are commonly critical of these sorts of impacts of globalization, other commentators describe how processes underlying globalization have been associated with the promotion of peace. One of the more captivating but controversial propositions was put forth by Pulitzer Prize–winning author/journalist Thomas Friedman who offered the '**Golden Arches Theory of Conflict Prevention**' in his 2000 book *Lexus and the Olive Tree: Understanding Globalization*. The Golden Arches Theory refers to Friedman's observation that no two countries that possessed a McDonald's restaurant have ever fought against each other in a war. Friedman uses the theory as a metaphor to highlight the idea that in today's increasingly interconnected world, there are important disincentives for any country thinking about declaring war on another country when there are economic links between these countries and shared perspectives on the importance of international trade and commerce. As he explains:

> Today's version of globalization—with its intensifying economic integration, digital integration, its ever-widening connectivity of individuals and nations, its spreading of capitalist values and networks to the remotest corners of the world. . . makes for a much stronger web of constraints on the foreign policy

behavior of those nations which are plugged into the system. It both increases the incentives for not making war and it increases the costs of going to war in more ways than in any previous era in modern history. (Friedman, 1999, p. 250)

At the same time, Friedman argues, corrupt and oppressive governments are not 'good for business', so there is pressure on these governments to be more democratic and peaceful in their operations—or at least to stabilize themselves enough to accommodate international trade.

This argument is intriguing in that it inspires thinking about links between economic growth and global interconnections (processes that sport is a part of, as noted earlier in this chapter), and peace. In fact, and along the same lines as Friedman, Cortright (2008) points out in his book *Peace: A History of Movements and Ideas* that 'there is widespread agreement that promoting equitable and sustainable economic development is an effective strategy for peace' and that 'raising economic growth may be the single most important step that can be taken to reduce the incidence of global conflict' (p. 275).

While interesting and provocative, the Golden Arches Theory is not without major flaws—and I am not referring here to the exception to the rule that has arisen since the first edition of Friedman's book was published (when Russia invaded Georgia—both nations with McDonald's restaurants!). For example, and unlike Friedman, Cortright (2008) argues in no uncertain terms that *the way that development and growth is achieved is a crucial consideration for those interested in a broader view of peace promotion.* That is to say, although economic relationships between countries and widespread economic growth more generally may be associated with (a certain version of) peace, evidence showing that market liberalization is a useful strategy for fostering peaceful societies is questionable. For example, Nobel Prize–winning economist Joseph Stiglitz in his 2002 book *Globalization and its Discontents* describes the lack of evidence that economic globalization generally and trade liberalization specifically (as forms of neo-liberalism) are helpful for those who are not associated with major corporations and their investors. As Cortright (2008) suggests, 'privatization, reduced public services, and the loosening of market regulation [i.e., neo-liberalism] . . . had many side effects on the supposed beneficiaries in the developing world—fostering corruption, undermining local economies, exacerbating inequalities, and exposing weak economies to destabilizing financial shocks' (p. 276).

A broader problem with the idea that economic globalization promotes peace is that the term 'peace' is narrowly defined in this context. Even if Friedman is correct in his argument that there are fewer wars when countries are tied to one another through trade and other forms of economic integration, this does not mean that these countries are more peaceful. Remember here the definition of positive peace, which links peace with equality and an engaged citizenship, not a citizenship at the mercy of transnational

corporations and organizations that have a major influence over governmental decision-making.

Consider in this context Tilly's (2007) definition of a 'democratic' regime:

> . . . a regime is democratic to the degree that political relations between the state
> and its citizens feature broad, equal, protected and mutually binding consulta-
> tion. Democratization means net movement toward broader, more equal, more
> protected, and more binding consultation. De-democratization, obviously, then
> means net movement towards narrower, more unequal, less protected and less
> binding consultation. (p. 14)

With this definition in mind, it does not seem a stretch to consider how
forms of economic globalization (associated with neo-liberal forms of government) might be implicated in the *de-democratization* of many countries.
I say this because when transnational corporations and international non-
governmental organizations have enormous influence over decision-making
by governments, then, in turn, citizens have less direct say about issues of
concern to them (i.e., they do not vote for corporate leaders or NGO leaders).
This would seem to align with Tilly's description of de-democratization as the
movement toward a situation where government consultation with citizens is
less protected and less binding. At the same time, if various forms of inequality are exacerbated by these economic and social trends, then it is likely that
consultation around decision-making would be 'more unequal' (to use Tilly's
words). Again, democracy suffers in this situation.

Of course, and as noted earlier, since sport plays an integral role in the types
of globalization and neo-liberalization noted above, sport cannot be separated
from this de-democratization process. This is a point I pursue and follow-up
on in other parts of this book, where I discuss the impact of sport-related economic developments on the environment (chapter 8), the role mass-mediated
sport sometimes plays in the promotion neo-liberal ideologies (chapter 9),
and the role of sport in international development (chapter 7).

Reflections on Theory

Although there are ongoing debates about the value and impacts of economic
globalization and neo-liberalism, most would agree that it is a dominant approach to governance and international relations in the current historical moment. This raises questions that will return us to the theories that underscore
all chapters of this book. These questions include: 'How is it that neo-liberal
ideologies and forms of governance have become and continue to be privileged?', and 'What role has sport played in these processes?'

Theorists who draw on the work of Michel Foucault might point out that
the language of and assumptions underlying neo-liberalism—language and

assumptions that speak to (for example) the importance of competition, in-dividualism, privatization, and minimal government intervention—become taken-for-granted, interwoven into the public speech of politicians and busi-ness leaders, and most importantly, into the everyday behaviours and beliefs of the 'citizen-entrepreneurs' in a neo-liberal system (Brown, 2006). In fact, theorists Michael Hardt and Antonio Negri (2000), in their book *Empire*, draw on Foucault's term 'biopower' as a way of describing how social con-trol is exercised through the diffusion of messages within and around soci-etal institutions like schools, religious organizations, and mass media, as well as through the work of international NGOs like Amnesty International and Oxfam. Equally important for thinking about a global politics of sport is Hardt and Negri's acknowledgement (again, drawing on Foucault) that the channels of power and communication that are used to oppress and gener-ate consent can also be used productively by those who want to resist the seemingly irresistible global political and corporate-related bodies. I return to this point in my discussion of social movements and sport in the next chapter.

Through a different (but still critical) lens, we could also consider how groups that benefit from the promotion of neo-liberal forms of governance (e.g., those who run transnational corporations and those who benefit from their successes) strategically and intentionally generate consent for an ap-proach that may not be favourable for less powerful or marginalized groups. For example, some theorists who discuss the reasons behind the US-led invasion of Iraq in 2003 point to ways that the war directly benefited pri-vate industries in Western countries. Cortright (2008) describes how social movements that emerged in response to the invasion did so because consent had (initially) been sought by some politicians for a war for reasons related to 'freedom' and 'safety', whereas in fact the invasion was very much about economic expansion (i.e., about controlling oil in Iraq, and subsequently employing preferred corporations in the post-invasion reconstruction and development).

What Cortright is describing here is a hegemonic relationship between those who promoted the war, those who initially consented to the war, and those who organized counter-hegemonic movements in an attempt to undermine the hegemony of those making decisions about the invasion. It is of course pertinent here that attempts to secure consent for the war often included the use of imagery and language at major sporting events, and the explicit promo-tion of the troops in and around sport. As Mary McDonald (2005) notes in her discussion of sport and war in the aftermath of the September 11 attacks, it was not uncommon to hear the argument that attendance at sporting events or the viewing of televised sport were expressions of support for the American way of life—as declarations of (consumer) freedoms that need to be protected (see chapter 9).

In fact, and although MacDonald's point was that sport's role in relation to the 2003 Iraq war and other military efforts is problematic, we can also see here how sport could be seen to *serve a function* during times of war. That is to say, spectator sport may be used to garner support for war efforts, and perhaps even recruit participants. In this sense, from a functionalist perspective, generating support for an international war effort (itself a form of globalization) would be a positive contribution of spectator sport. As you might expect though, this function is troubling for many who feel that more open and transparent strategies for recruiting support for (and participants in) war efforts is more democratic and genuine.

Other Understandings of Globalization: Looking Ahead

Although sociologists of sport often focus on links between sport and economic globalization, there are various others forms of globalization that have inspired research and debate. For example, sport scholars are increasingly taking note of the international sport for development and peace work of NGOs like Right To Play—groups known to promote peace-related values and information through sport on a global scale (Giulianotti, 2006). Similarly, by declaring 2005 the International Year of Sport and Physical Education (IYSPE), and by linking sport with the promotion of the Millennium Development Goals, the United Nations explicitly linked sport with its international development system. Also, when sport scholars like Donnelly and Kidd (2000) and the authors in Giulianotti and McCardle's collection (2006) invoke human rights–related legislation in discussing the rights of children who are involved in high performance sport or of workers producing sport equipment, or the rights of citizens around the world to 'play' (i.e., to have access to forms of sport and recreation), these scholars are commonly referring to legislation agreed upon and signed by multiple countries in an international system of governance and justice (Donnelly and Kidd, 2000).

As a segue to the next chapter, it is also worth noting that the 'social movements' that Cortright refers to above—the groups of everyday people who collectively respond to what they see as injustices and global problems—also operate in many cases on a global level (Wilson, 2007a). To the extent that global movements are sport-related—and as we will see in the next chapter, they sometimes are—we can begin to see how 'globalization from below' (referring to worldwide connections created throughout grassroots organizations, instead of those imposed by multinational corporations) can take place. If we look at globalization though this lens, we can begin to see how the activities of people on a micro level are influenced not only by the activities of powerful groups and the structural conditions they exist within, but also by the proactive work of those who connect with one another, with the goal of creating global communities and/or motivating large-scale social change.

Note

1. Adapted from summaries by Jeff Hanson and David Landers, found at: www. imdb.com/title/tt0073631/plotsummary.

Discussion Questions

1. Can you think of examples of glocalization and sport?

2. What are the implications of powerful corporations having a major presence in our lives?

3. Do you think we are moving towards William Harrison's vision of a few corporations 'outlasting' nations? What other trends do you see in the globalization of sport? What are the intended and unintended consequences of these developments?

Suggested Readings

Allison, L. (Ed.) (2005). *The global politics of sport: The role of global institutions in sport.* New York: Routledge. An edited collection that offers an excellent overview of issues around sport, international relations, and global politics.

Andrews, D. & Ritzer, G. (2007). The grobal in the sporting glocal. In R. Giulianotti & R. Robinson (Eds.), *Globalization and sport* (pp. 28–45). Malden, MA: Blackwell. An intriguing essay that summarizes and assesses arguments around glocalization and sport.

Brown, W. (2006). *Edgework: Critical essays on knowledge and politics.* Princeton, NJ: Princeton University Press. This book includes a thorough and insightful examination of the neo-liberalism concept.

Maguire, J. (1999). *Global sport: Identities, societies, civilizations.* Cambridge: Polity Press. This classic text in the sociology of sport field includes an overview of issues around sport and globalization and reflections on key studies by the author.

Miller, T., Lawrence, G., McKay, J. & Rowe, D. (2001). *Globalization and sport.* Thousand Oaks, CA: Sage. Another outstanding text examining globalization and sport with particular sensitivity to issues around neo-liberalization.

Silk, M., Andrews, D., & Cole, C. (Eds.). *Sport and corporate nationalisms.* Oxford: Berg. This collection includes several excellent essays that describe and assess ways that corporations and nations have become interrelated within and around the world of sport.

Relevant Websites

The Globe and Mail **Series on sport and society**
www.theglobeandmail.com/intellectual-muscle/the-talks/article1312702
This webpage includes a series of podcasts about sport and society that were
posted during the 2010 Vancouver Olympic Games. Recommended listening for
this chapter is Kevin Wamsley's 'Vancouver—the 6th North American Winter
Games: What Does History Tell Us about Hosting the Olympic Games?', Bruce
Kidd's 'What do the Olympic Games Contribute to Society?', and Stephen
Wenn's 'The Olympic Movement and the Road Ahead: Status Quo or Will the
IOC Tackle the Big Issues?'

**Royal Society for the Encouragement of Arts, Manufactures and Commerce
(RSA)—'Crises of Capitalism'**
http://comment.rsablogs.org.uk/2010/06/28/rsa-animate-crisis-capitalism
The above website includes a link to a lecture by renowned social geographer
David Harvey, and to a intriguing animated video that is narrated by Harvey,
called 'Crises of Capitalism'.

Key Terms

corporate nationalism refers to interconnections between nations and
corporations, and especially when corporations use images of and (positive)
feelings associated with nations and nationalism to promote private goods.

democratization refers to the movement towards 'broader, more equal, more
protected, and more binding consultation' (Tilly, 2007, p. 14).

de-democratization refers to the movement towards 'narrower, more unequal,
less protected and less binding consultation' (Tilly, 2007, p. 14).

globalization refers to a set of processes that have led to an increasingly integrated
and interconnected world. These processes include: the movement of people and
ideas/ideologies around the world; the development of technologies and media
forms/outlets that promote, enhance, and allow global connections; and the
promotion of economic ties throughout the world—a process that has accelerated
with the adoption of neo-liberal policies and ideologies since the 1970s.

glocalization a process whereby local forms of culture are integrated into and
combined with forms of culture from elsewhere. The term is commonly used
to describe processes through which corporations integrate characteristics of
targeted local markets into their products and product campaigns (e.g., the use
of the indigenous *haka* dance from Māori groups of New Zealand in Adidas
advertising campaigns).

Golden Arches Theory of Conflict Prevention refers to an observation
by journalist and international affairs specialist Thomas Friedman, who
noted (at the time of his observation) that no two countries that possessed a
McDonald's restaurant had ever fought against each other in a war. Friedman
uses the theory that emerged from this observation to highlight the idea that
in today's increasingly interconnected world, there are important disincentives

for any country thinking about declaring war on another country when there are economic links between these countries, and shared perspectives on the importance of international trade and commerce.

neo-liberalism refers to policies and ideologies that are based around the use of a market rationality and private business approach for all social, cultural and political matters—which is to say, every action and policy is submitted to considerations of profitability. Within a neo-liberal governance model, individuals are viewed as and encouraged to be 'rational actors' who make decisions based on the benefits of their actions for themselves. The assumption here is that such responsibility will promote 'efficiencies' in the system, since neo-liberal citizens will be motivated to be as productive as they can be—to make the best decisions they can to maximize personal benefits (e.g., maximize income, health, and status).

PART III

Peace Activism, Peace Education, and a Sporting Praxis

5

Pursuing Peace from Below: Sport, Social Movements, and (Ironic) Activism

Questions to Consider

⊛ What role can and do sport-related social movements and certain forms of sport-related activism play in peace-promotion?

⊛ How do processes known as 'detraditionalization' and 'individualization' impact the types of political action in which people are engaging?

⊛ How might we assess the success of sport-related movements using resource mobilization and political opportunity perspectives?

⊛ What is 'ironic activism', and is it possible that certain 'sport for peace' groups actually perpetuate the very problems they are meant to solve?

Introduction: A History of and Opportunities for Sport-Related Activism

Globalization . . . is also the creation of new circuits of cooperation and collaboration that stretch across nations and continents and allow an unlimited number of encounters. (Hardt and Negri, 2004, p. xiii)

. . . networked global power enables and prompts global opposition, allowing the opposition to flourish, taking advantage of new formations and offering new configurations for resistance. (Wall, 2007, p. 260)

A main argument underlying the previous two chapters is that although sport can act as a tool in facilitating successful international diplomatic efforts and fostering (global) communities, it is often used in ways that do quite the opposite. Especially alarming for some commentators is sport's role in the promotion of certain policies and ideologies that may be associated with the perpetuation of structural and cultural violence—and with de-democratization processes more generally.

Although many sociologists are justifiably pessimistic about these developments, others focus on the processes through which inequalities and injustices can be, and have been, challenged on a local and global level. In fact, and with the opening quotations from Hardt and Negri (2004) and Wall (2007) in mind, we can begin to think about why in the current historical moment—a moment where communication across and within global networks is both possible and relatively accessible—there are unprecedented opportunities for people to disseminate information about and collectively organize around social concerns in unique and powerful ways.

Many sociologists of sport engage these issues and others related to social change and social resistance by attending to the various ways that athletes and others respond to sport-related social problems and oppressive structures. In this chapter, I discuss this body of work, focusing in particular on the range of ways that sport-related social change and social resistance have been promoted, and how these changes and forms of resistance have been understood by sociologists. In doing so, I will define the terms '**activist**' and '**social movement**', discuss their relevance to the sociology of sport, and offer examples of studies on sport-related resistance and collective action.

The argument underlying this chapter is that activists respond in various ways to sport-related injustices and social problems—with some responses being more effective than others, and some responses (ironically and unintentionally) perpetuating the status quo. I also note that in the current historical moment, there is immense potential for positive global and local changes and social resistance efforts because of advances in communication technology. I conclude the chapter by pointing out how oppositional movements and protest groups—while often portrayed as social problems in themselves—are fundamental to maintaining democratic and peaceful societies. In this context, I suggest that in order to see how important these movements are—i.e., to see how these movements have led to important social changes—a sociological imagination is needed.

Sport and Social Movements: Background

There is a long history of sport-related activism. The 'worker's sport movement', which can be traced back to the mid and late 1800s is perhaps the earliest example of sport-driven collective action (Riordan, 1999), and early iterations of the women's movement are associated with challenges to social practices around sport that excluded and denigrated women (Hall, 1996, 2007; Hargreaves, 1994; Harvey et al., 2009). While the broad issues and concerns dealt with by these two movements remain relevant today (i.e., issues around working class exclusion/alienation and women's rights), many point to the 1960s as a time when activism within and around sport was at a peak.

In fact, perhaps the most well-known and well-publicized act of social resistance in a sporting forum took place at the 1968 Mexico Olympics, when African-American sprinters Tommie Smith and John Carlos stood on the podium following their gold- and bronze-medal performances in the men's 200 metre final—each with shoes off, wearing black socks, eyes facing down, and holding a Black Power salute (i.e., a black-gloved fist held above their heads). The event remains a key reference point for those interested in showing how sport has been and could be used as a forum for protest and awareness-raising around social issues. In this case, and as authors like Edwards (1973) and Hartmann (1996, 2003) note, Smith and Carlos were raising awareness and inspiring further protests around the fight for civil rights in the US. Of course, the civil rights movements of the 1960s inspired various forms of activism, including attempts to promote equity and equality in and around women's and girls' sport (Cahn, 1994; Hall, 1996, 2007; Hargreaves, 1994). One of the key successes of that movement was the groundbreaking implementation of Title IX in the US, which required federally funded institutions to follow regulations around equitable support for male and female sport programs (Wushanley, 2004).

Since the 1960s, sociologists of sport have studied a variety of movements and forms of activism. These include studies on:

- movements to ban team mascots that appropriate Native American culture or imagery (Davis-Delano and Crosset, 2008)
- the 'anti-golf' and 'surfers against sewage' environmental movements (Stolle-McAllister, 2004; Wheaton, 2007, 2008)
- the disability sport movement (Depauw and Gavron, 2005; Thomas and Smith, 2009)
- the Gay Games movement (Symons, 2010)
- the 'anti-jock'/anti-bullying movement (Wilson, 2002)
- anti-Olympics movements (Lenskyj, 2002, 2008)
- movements against exploitation of workers in the production of sport-related goods by transnational corporations (Sage, 1999)
- movements to block funding of sport stadiums (Davis-Delano and Crosset, 2008)
- movements to save community-based sport stadiums from demolition and development efforts (Wilson and White, 2002)

Although the various forms of activism examined in these studies share a focus on some aspect of sport (i.e., they are often about an *athlete-driven* response to a social problem, and/or they are a response to *sport-related* problem by athletes and others), they also differ from one another in important ways. For example, some of these groups are well organized, have a large and official membership, have concrete goals and a developed strategy for creating change, and often work closely with government in their attempts to reform policy and alter the culture in and around sport. The non-governmental organization the Canadian Association for the Advancement of Women and Sport and Physical Activity (CAAWS)—which is mandated to foster 'equitable support, diverse opportunities and positive experiences for girls and women in sport and physical activity'[1]—is an excellent example of this kind of organization.

Other groups are less well organized and do not have an 'official' mandate or membership, and are instead (loosely) linked by a shared sense of dissatisfaction with the status quo, and a common set of symbolic gestures and cultural practices that are used to express this dissatisfaction. I discuss this sort of group formation in more detail below, but will point here to one of the most well-known examples of this type of resistance/expression, which was portrayed in C.L.R. James's 1963 book *Beyond a Boundary*. In James's classic reflection on his experiences with and the meaning of cricket, he described how many men in the West Indies saw their success in cricket—a sport introduced initially to the Caribbean by the colonial British powers—as an anti-colonial expression. That is to say, and although cricket playing may not have changed the existing set of power relationships (i.e., it was not 'counter-hegemonic'), it held important symbolic value for these men who had few other means by which to (at least temporarily) resolve frustrations associated with living in a disempowering context.

We can see from this example how the symbolic response to the social problem described by James differs from the more formalized actions of groups that work more directly with representatives of government and business in an attempt to alter policy or change corporate behaviour through negotiation. Still other groups—also more organized and strategically 'activist' than the men described by James, but less structured than CAAWS—operate outside the system in their attempts to raise public awareness of their concerns through protest. Around recent Olympic Games, for example, these groups consistently organize public demonstrations (sanctioned and unsanctioned) intended to bring attention to environmental and social problems related to hosting sporting mega-events (Lenskyj, 2000, 2008).

With some of these differences and variations in mind, Harvey et al. (2009) note—following the classic work of Raymond Williams (1977)—how particular forms and goals of collective activism (sport-related or otherwise) are dominant at particular moments in history. For example, they note how the dominant social movements from the 1960s to the late 1990s focused around changing societal views on topics like gender, race, and environmental issues—with 'anti-racist', 'feminist', and environmental movements being some of the leaders of the period. These **new social movements**, as they were termed, were somewhat distinct from the worker's movements of previous eras (i.e., 'older' social movements), which were focused around the economic concerns of the working classes and disenfranchised and, at least in early/classic writing on these movements, saw a proletariat/working-class revolution as a main strategy for social change.

Alongside these dominant forms of social movements are 'residual' forms (meaning they were previously dominant, but now are more peripheral) and 'emergent' forms (meaning they are groups that have come into existence—although they may or may not become dominant). As we discuss later on, these historically based distinctions are especially relevant for thinking about the sorts of movements that are dominant in the contemporary era, where interconnected **anti-globalization** and **alter-globalization movements** are responding to problems that exist within increasingly neo-liberal and globalized societies.

But What Is Activism, and What Are Social Movements?

The term 'activism' refers to acting on issues of social, political, and environmental significance; to attempts by people to move beyond theory (while hopefully using theory as guide) in order to 'make a difference', to 'do something about oppression' (Watts et al., 2003, p. 186). Watts et al. (2003) elaborate on this basic definition in their outline of what an activist does:

> . . . an activist is a person who acts strategically with others, on the basis of shared values, to create a more just society. The strategies include changing how society or its institutions operate (reform, evolution) and creating new institutions or a new society on the basis of alternative principles (revolution, transformation). Methods and tactics include political participation, pressure tactics aimed at gaining concessions, armed struggle, or operating an organization with a mission of social change or liberation. These methods require knowledge, skills, and capacity; so activism also includes methods aimed at building capacity through community organizing, training, educating, and mobilizing. (p. 186)

Although this is just one definition of activism, it is one that best describes the activist work outlined in this book—i.e., the work of those intent on promoting equity and equality and striving towards positive peace. Other forms of activism also exist that are not based around these kinds of social justice issues. It is possible, for example, using a broader definition of activist (meaning any sort of collective action intended to bring about social change) to consider the work of lobby groups or interest groups who operate on behalf of the tobacco industry, or those who promote racist ideologies, to be activist. Though that definition is technically accurate, by and large the term now carries a connotation of left-leaning ideology, and that is how I use it in this book.

The term 'social movement' is also a frequently referred to and well-developed concept that is commonly utilized in sociological research on various forms of collective action. The term has a variety of meanings which are nicely encapsulated in Suzanne Staggenborg's (2008) book *Social Movements*. I list key definitions below:

collective challenges, based on common purposes and social solidarities, in sustained interaction with elites, opponents, and authorities (Tarrow, 1998, p. 4; quoted in Staggenborg, 2008, p. 5)

a set of opinions and beliefs in a population which represent preferences for changing some elements of the social structure and/or reward distribution of society (McCarthy and Zald, 1977, 1217–18; quoted in Staggenborg, 2008, p. 6)

loose and changing coalitions of groups and individuals (Staggenborg, 2008, p. 34)

political entities aiming to create social change (Staggenborg, 2008, p. 34)

Authors like Harvey et al. (2009) and Harvey and Houle (1994) also distinguish between the 'old(er) social movements' (like the worker's movements noted above) and 'new social movements', which Harvey and Houle (1994) define as follows:

new social movements [e.g., the feminist, anti-racist movements noted above] differ from older ones since they [the new social movements]: (a) are not linked to specific economic interests, (b) work toward change in society's values, and (c) work for the collective good. They are fluid, their membership diverse, they take different organizational forms, and they vary in size, composition, and forms of actions. They are often active at local, national and transnational levels in the form of loose networks of groups and organizations (p. 347).

More recently, authors like Sage (1999) have identified sport-related anti-globalization movements (like the anti-sweatshop/anti-Nike movements) that protest against forms of corporate-driven economic globalization, while Harvey et al. (2010) studied sport-related alter-globalization movements that attempt to change *how* globalization takes place. As they put it, alter-globalization movements 'support new forms of globalization based on values of democracy, justice, environmental protection, and human rights rather than economic concerns' (p. 384). Harvey et al. (2009) note how alter-globalization is a 'multifaceted form of resistance to neo-liberal globalization', which includes 'global social movements and a myriad of nongovernmental organizations [that] have been active at the local and global level in advocating for more humane globalization' (p. 385). We can begin to see here how the types of social movements that emerge at any historical moment are integrally tied to broader social issues and developments of that moment—with the global social movements linked to the emergence and heightened significance of various global political forms, including the ongoing implementation of neo-liberal policies and practices.

As with the term 'activist', the social movement concept usually refers to oppositional groups, groups that are outsiders to the established power structure—unlike interest groups and political parties that are more integrally tied to government or other established institutions (Staggenborg, 2008). Of course, as social movements become more organized and institutionalized they evolve into what are sometimes termed 'social movement organizations'—organizations that may be part of a 'social movement industry', like the sport for development and peace industry/movement (see chapter 7). These organizations, in structure and in practice, commonly work more closely with established groups in their attempts to negotiate change.

Different Perspectives on Sport and Social Movements

Just as there are diverse social movement formations (ranging from 'diffuse and informal' to 'hierarchical and well-organized'), there are various ways that scholars have understood activist-oriented groups and their social and cultural practices. Below, I provide an overview of these perspectives and describe studies conducted in the sociology of sport field to help illustrate key features of these perspectives.

'Pre-Political' Resistance and Symbolic Resistance: Social Movements and Sport-Related Subcultures

There are many intriguing sociological studies focused on what are commonly termed sporting **subcultures**—with the term 'subcultures' referring to social and cultural groups that are 'focused around certain activities, values, certain uses of material artifacts, territorial spaces etc. which significantly differentiate them from the wider culture' (Hall and Jefferson, 1976, p. 22). Those who study subcultures commonly describe the symbolic ways that subculture members express their dissatisfaction with and/or undermine aspects of mainstream culture. In the case of sport subcultures, this means that the styles of clothing, the use of equipment, the approach to sporting competitions, and the practice of sport more generally by subculture members would be 'oppositional' when compared to more accepted and commonly practised approaches to sport.

A commonly cited study of an oppositional sporting subculture was conducted by Becky Beal, a professor at California State University, who focused research on a skateboarding subculture in the southwestern US. In her study, Beal (1995) describes how participants in skateboarding competitions were less focused on winning or maintaining a disciplined approach to their sport, and more focused (at least compared to those who participate in more mainstream sport competitions) on supporting their peers who were attempting impressive skateboard tricks, and on maintaining a relaxed communal atmosphere. In a similar way, Rebecca Heino (2000) explains how in the early days of the snowboarding subculture, participants commonly used the snowboard itself as a site of resistance—covering boards with stickers and personalized designs, and purchasing boards with pre-existing imagery that would range from 'impressionistic snowflakes to animation bordering on obscene' (p. 180). Heino suggests that the snowboard became 'a highly expressive piece of equipment, representing the individual's personality and resistance to the uniformity and sterility of skiing' (p. 180).

Although these might seem like trivial forms of resistance—symbolic gestures and practices easily associated with stereotypical expressions of teen angst and rebellion—many scholars argue that it is important to keep an open mind about the potential meanings and implications of these gestures and practices. For example, authors like Willis (1990) suggest that there is something to admire in the ways that many young subculturalists find creative ways to use the limited resources they have at their disposal to make a statement about their dissatisfaction with, for example, the ways that mainstream sporting items are marketed to them, or the culture of mainstream competitive sports more generally. Duncombe (1997) calls this 'the personalization of politics', arguing that when subculture members (who are often young people, who often lack the same voice in society as adults) collectively participate in counter-mainstream activities (like alternative sports), they are finding ways to 'confront the distance between themselves and a mainstream political world in which they effectively have no say' (Duncombe, 1997, p. 30).

Even more pertinently, the activities of these subculture members might be considered '**pre-political**'. That is to say, many young people use subcultural activities as a way to find a language to express themselves and their concerns, to prepare themselves for active engagement with politics through the micro-political and personal identity work that takes place in subcultural contexts (Duncombe, 1997, p. 176; cf., Hobsbawm, 1959). This perspective aligns well with arguments made by Morris and Herring (1987, cf., Staggenborg, 2008, p. 14), who suggest that socially connected people (i.e., not isolated people) are most likely to be (eventually) politically active people. This final observation would seem to bode well for those who are active participants in (youth) subcultural communities, and for democratic societies more generally—since active citizen engagement is a fundamental feature of healthy democracies.

Although these are reasonable arguments for viewing sport subcultures as important entities in the realm of sport politics, there are also reasons to avoid overstating the oppositional potential of these groups (Wheaton, 2007; Wilson, 2006b). For example, and as authors like Bennett (1999, 2000) point out, it appears that many young people are often more likely to be transient and temporary affiliates of any particular subcultural group (instead of committed members), preferring to move between groups and to have a variety of diverse associations. This observation has led some commentators to describe the activities of young people as 'neotribal' and individualistic (Bennett, 1999), instead of subcultural and oppositional. Those who work in this research area are also quick to note that subcultural groups are commonly (and often quickly) incorporated into mainstream culture, meaning that the alternative status of groups like snowboarders and skateboarders is diminished when it becomes 'fashionable and common' to participate in these groups (Hebdige, 1979; Wilson, 2006b).

New Social Movements, Subcultures, and Sport

While these critiques are well-supported and deserve attention, some of the most recent research and writing on (sport) subcultures has highlighted instances where subcultural groups are *more political* and *more influential* than ever before (Meikle, 2002; Wheaton, 2007; Wilson, 2006b). These scholars note that in the current historical moment—with the availability of communication technologies that enable new and global opportunities for political engagement—there are unprecedented possibilities for political engagement by less powerful groups (e.g., young sport subculture members).

With these possibilities for resistance in mind, sociologists of sport have begun to highlight the political—and increasingly global—character of various oppositional sporting groups. In fact, some scholars are beginning to see how what have historically been coined 'sport subcultures' might also be called 'new social movements'—a term that may better reflect the form of political engagement and group structure of some subcultures. That is to say, some groups are 'not linked to specific economic interests', and are 'working towards changing society's values and toward the collective good' (all characteristics of new social movements, according to Harvey and Houle's definition, provided earlier). These same groups are also commonly fluid in their membership, vary in size, and are 'active at local, national and transnational levels in the form of loose networks of groups and organizations' (Harvey and Houle, 1994, p. 347).

In a study I conducted on an online sport-related community that called themselves the 'anti-jocks' (Wilson, 2002, 2008), I considered the relevance of the new social movements concept for a group of youth that, before the Internet, would have found it nearly impossible to collectively mobilize (e.g., it would have been logistically and financially difficult to share resources and strategies among group members). The anti-jocks are a collection of adolescent (i.e., high school–aged) males who had in many cases been bullied by athletes who play 'hypermasculine' sports (e.g., gridiron football, hockey, basketball). The anti-jocks—who appeared to be located, for the most part, in the US—felt that in their schools and in society more generally, hyper-masculine sport athletes often receive special and undeserved privileges, while those who participate in other activities (like the school band) are treated like second-class citizens.

Some anti-jocks extend their critique to the use of public funds to support sport teams and stadium building—funds they felt could be better spent on activities that did not perpetuate what anti-jocks called a 'jockocracy' and the injustices they associate with it. On their 'anti-jock webpages', some anti-jocks included references to studies by sociologists of sport that uncover certain myths about the value of sport (e.g., like Miracle and Rees's [1994] renowned critique of the idea that sport builds character) and research on the problems associated with hypermasculine sport cultures more generally (Sabo and Runfola, 1980; Wilson, 2002). I argued in the article that the anti-jocks could be considered a new social movement (n.s.m.) because of their disconnect from economic interests, their goal of changing society's values and working toward a collective good (e.g., high schools with less bullying and more attention to non-sport successes), as well as their fluid and diverse membership that was connected (at least theoretically, because of their Internet presence) across local, national, and transnational levels (recall here Harvey and Houle's definition of n.s.m.).

Other sociologists similarly highlight the overtly political sensibilities of—and thus the 'movement-like' characteristics of—some sport-related subcultures. Michael Atkinson (Atkinson, 2009; Atkinson and Young, 2008), for example, did this in his work on the *parkour* subculture. *Parkour* refers to a subculture of (usually male) youth who run over, under, around, and through human-made and natural obstacles in urban environments (e.g., climbing fences, scaling buildings)—in all cases attempting to keep a constant and uninterrupted flow of movement. According to Atkinson, *parkour* participants (known as '*traceurs*', 'free runners', or 'urban freeflowers') see their activity as a form of resistance against hypercompetitive sport and the overdevelopment of city spaces. As Atkinson and Young (2008) put it:

> Traceurs expressed disdain for highly organized, scripted, contained, competitive and consumer-based sport experiences . . . When discussing their playing field, the traceurs described a need to 'take back' local city space for their own purposes, and use their 'natural environment' to meet their own physical, emotional and psychological needs. (p. 59)

Atkinson explicitly links this transnational movement (noting *parkour*'s existence in many major cities around the world, and its presence on various websites) to the new social movements concept, arguing that *parkour* can be linked with other diffuse and global movements that critique cultures oriented around hyper-consumption, as well as environmental movements.

In a similar way, Wheaton (2007; 2008) and Heywood and Montgomery (2008) describe the activities of surfers who have banded together to protest pollution and environmental damage. Wheaton notes that, in keeping with a definition of new social movements put forth by Alberto Melucci (1996), the Surfers Against Sewage (SAS) group she studied was 'not aligned with traditional class or party politics' and often used diverse and often non-traditional approaches for bringing attention to their issue of concern—which includes staged media campaign events with 'highly morally charged symbolic messages' (Wheaton, 2008, p. 122; cf., Anderson, 1997, p. 207). As she describes:

> The success of SAS as a pressure group stems from its ability to gain media attention by adopting dramatic and evocative symbols of environmental damage such as gas masks and a large dark brown inflatable 'turd', signifying untreated raw sewage in the sea. These 'media hits' have involved a small group of protesters, usually wearing wetsuits and gas masks, carrying surfing or water-sport equipment, and transported in the 'SAS Tour bus'. (p. 123)

One of the other striking observations in Wheaton's article was that SAS was just one of a 'groundswell of "interventions" by youth who had previously been characterized as dispossessed individuals'—interventions that took the form of 'non-violent protests' on an unprecedented and transnational scale (p. 113). According to Wheaton (2008), these groups, which ranged from 'local environmental organizations to those concerned with fair trade, [and] labour rights' were commonly linked 'under the banner of anti-capitalism' and anti-globalization (p. 113).

Alter-Globalization and Sport

As you can see, the most contemporary research on sport and social movements in the sociology of sport has engaged questions about how sport-related groups are responding to some of the problems associated with globalization and neo-liberalism noted in chapter 4. Wheaton's recognition that these different sport-related movements are part of a 'movement of movements' is especially pertinent as we begin to think about ways that various social groups committed to social change work together in response to an overarching set of issues, and the different strategies they use to respond to concerns about inequality, workplace exploitation, environmental damage, and so on.

Of course, and as Harvey et al. (2009) note, the movement of movements includes various sport-related groups that are often quite different from one another, using often-distinct approaches to dealing with the problems they see with globalization, and focusing on different topics of concern. Despite these differences, these groups tend to share some key ideological viewpoints— including the fundamental belief that 'another globalization is possible', and that:

every one of us is part of a single world, a world that has been fragmented by a neo-liberalism that exacerbates individualism and, as a result, is in need of a reart-iculation of the social, the political, and the economical through new, more legit-imate and democratic forms of global governance. (Harvey et al., 2009, p. 388)

You will note here that there is a difference between alter-globalization movements and what are commonly termed anti-globalization move-ments—movements that, by a strict definition, would be seen to 'reject' glo-balization (Harvey et al., 2009, p. 387). Harvey et al.'s goal in emphasizing the 'alter' instead of the 'anti' is to point out that many groups commonly considered to be against globalization are, to the contrary, in support of a 'different form' of globalization. As importantly, however, Harvey et al. show that the alter groups attempt to achieve an alternative form of global-ization in various and diverse ways (following Scholte, 2005 and Held and McGrew, 2007).

Harvey et al. identify, on one hand, groups interested in *transforming* glo-balization through 'grassroots and broader social movements' that resist and replace the current power structure with a more decentralized and citizen-driven governance model. The authors also, on the other hand, point to groups focused on *reforming* the current system of governance, by promoting more democratic and accountable forms of global capitalism (pp. 389–90).

Harvey et al. go on to identify various types of reformist and transform-ist organizations. They refer to the Surfers Against Sewage (SAS) group de-scribed earlier as a 'sport organization concerned with social change *outside of sport*' (i.e., with environmental problems related to pollution). Harvey et al. refer also to the Play Fair campaign (associated with the British NGO Oxfam) as a 'non-sport organization that is focused around challenging a global *sport-related problem*'—that is, the 'injustices in the global labor sup-ply chains that underpin sporting events' (p. 394). Both SAS and Play Fair are considered reformist organizations because of their interest in inspiring changes within existing institutions. They are both 'alter-global' in the sense that they both recognize that the environmental problems and labour-related injustices that are their *raison d'être* are inherently and unavoidably global—and for this reason require a response from people around the world. In this way, these groups are interested in altering particular processes that underlie globalization.

According to Harvey et al., an example of a transformist, non-sport group is Reporters Without Borders (RWB). Members of RWB are interested in trans-forming practices and norms around press coverage in places where report-ing is controlled or limited by government or others. The group focused, for example, on media coverage during the Beijing Olympics because of concerns about what they saw as undemocratic approaches to the press by government (Harvey et al., 2009). The group is transformist in the sense that the goal is to undermine a system of state-controlled media, in hopes of inspiring a more independent and democratic approach to reporting. Another example of a transformist group is the `organic' golf movement, a movement by some golf course superintendents (and others who support the idea that golf is a worthwhile leisure activity) to completely discontinue the use of pesticides on golf courses—a practice that would undermine what has become a well-established relationship between the golf industry and chemical industry, and interrupt a key strand of the supply chain for golf industry members (Wilson and Millington, 2011).

Of course there are various other groups that fit in the categories offered within Harvey et al.'s typology. The main point here, however, is that many sport-related social movement groups may share concerns about global issues, but they differ in their approaches to dealing with these problems.

Life Politics, Lifestyle Politics, and Sport

Life politics is a politics, not of *life chances*, but of *life style*. It concerns disputes and struggles about how . . . we should live in a world where what used to be fixed either by nature or tradition is now subject to human decisions. (Giddens, 1994, p. 14–15)

In the previous sections we focused on the characteristics, activities, and goals of social movement *groups*, and their responses to societal challenges and changes associated with globalization. In this section we consider the idea that (seemingly) fragmented, individual-political acts are, in some respects, still collective actions—and that these acts are a distinct feature of the contemporary moment.

A leading proponent of this view is renowned British sociologist Anthony Giddens, who suggested that forces associated with globalization and modernization have led to a situation where people are increasingly being political through the choices they make in their everyday activities and consumer purchases. Giddens uses the term 'life politics' to describe this more nuanced version of the personalized politics referred to earlier in this chapter. He suggests that life politics has overtaken **'emancipatory politics'** as the dominant political form—with emancipatory politics referring to collective actions intended to promote political and personal freedoms, such as the civil rights movement. Giddens explains this shift from emancipatory to **life(style) politics** through two key processes. The first process, known as **detraditionalization**, refers to the loosening of the usual bonds that have historically held groups of people together and offered particular securities (e.g., family-related, location-related, or social class–related bonds and securities). The second and related process is **individualization**, which refers to the increase in the number and type of choices people have about where they can live, the jobs they can pursue, and the lifestyles they can construct— freedoms that have emerged because of the loosening of ties associated with detraditionalization.

While the freedoms associated with detraditionalization and individualization are enabling in the sense that people have more choice about the life trajectories they follow, people are also required to make more decisions on their own (Giddens, 1994). Furlong and Cartmel (1997), in their study of contemporary youth in reflexive modernity, describe how feeling 'on one's own' has led some to experience a heightened sense of uncertainty and anxiety about one's place in the world, what the authors refer to as an 'ontological insecurity'. These feelings are exacerbated in the current historical moment because, as German sociologist Ulrich Beck (1992) notes in his writing on 'risk' societies, individuals are now exposed to sometimes frightening global concerns in unprecedented ways (e.g., through pervasive and real time media), and must deal with problems that are direct results of modernization (e.g., technological innovations), like the threat of nuclear weapons and widespread environmental destruction.

According to Giddens, this is where life politics comes in. Giddens notes how people are beginning to respond to these new insecurities by creating a sense of order in their lives through the construction of coherent lifestyles. These lifestyles are assembled through the sets of choices people make about the leisure activities they participate in, the clothing they buy, the food they purchase, and so on. Giddens's point is that these personalized lifestyle choices are often strategic, and underlie people's attempts to become 'self-actualized' (Giddens, 1991, p. 214). These lifestyle decisions are political to the extent that our day-to-day choices can often be linked to key social issues and global processes—which is not difficult to do in a consumer society where the purchases we make and activities we choose can often be traced back to transnational corporations (who produce our shoes) and/or global-environmental issues (how they produce our shoes).

In this way, the decisions people make about what athletic apparel brand to buy, whether to purchase tickets to a mega–sporting event, about the donations one chooses to make (or not make), about whether to buy local food, or whether to limit consumption altogether, are political decisions. The idea is that if more and more people make similar lifestyle decisions, then structural changes will take place as a response to these choices, as businesses (sometimes transnational corporations) respond to these consumer preferences/demands.

We can begin to see in Giddens's comments how life politics and the politics of alter-globalization movements—such as anti-sweatshop movements that target Nike and other apparel and clothing producers—are linked. They are linked not only in ways that the lifestyle decisions of individuals may ultimately influence or alter decision-making by corporate leaders aiming to appease consumers, but also in the sense that they both bypass conventional political streams. That is to say, alter-globalization activists directly confront transnational corporations and global political entities through various forms of protest, while those practising life politics make everyday (personal) decisions that speak to their personal and consumer values.

As you might expect, there are ongoing debates about the extent to which forms of life politics that are not associated with some kind of organized consumer movement will, in fact, make a difference on a global level. At the very least, and if we believe Giddens's portrayal of reflexive modernity, life politics can be seen as a personal response—as a coping strategy—in contemporary societies.

Reinterpreting Subcultures: Lifestyle Sports and the Post-political Moment

These debates are front and centre when it comes to the expression of life politics through participation in what Belinda Wheaton, a research fellow at the University of Brighton, commonly refers to as 'lifestyle sports'. While the term 'lifestyle sports' is often used interchangeably with terms like 'alternative sports' and 'extreme sports'; Wheaton (2004, 2005) argues that lifestyle sports are particular kinds of alternative sports. She explains:

> While each lifestyle sport has its own history, identities and development patterns, there are nonetheless commonalities in their ethos, ideologies and increasingly the national and transnational consumer industries that produce the commodities that underpin their cultures . . . With their roots in the counter-cultural social movements of the 1960s and 1970s many have characteristics that are different to the traditional 'dominant' institutionalized, Western 'achievement' sport cultures. Unlike some alternative and extreme sports, lifestyle sports are fundamentally about participation, not spectating . . . Participants show high commitment in time and/or money and a style of life that develops around the activity. They have a hedonistic, individualistic ideology that promotes commitment, but denounces regulations and institutionalization, and are often critical of, or ambivalent towards, commercialism and formal 'man-on-man' style competition. . . . (2005, p. 141)

Wheaton links the development of lifestyle sports—like surfing, skateboarding, and emergent sports like kite surfing—with the same processes that Giddens points to in his writing about the context for the emergence of life politics. Specifically, she refers to the ways that individualization is reflected in the more personal and reflexive approach to day-to-day decision-making that is typical of lifestyle sport participants. She also points to the strategic importance of consumption for those attempting to carve out meaning and a coherent identity in late modern times—noting that the emergence and evolution of lifestyle sports was based around the selling of 'a complete style of life' to participants, not merely a sport or leisure activity.

The Surfer's Against Sewage group mentioned earlier is an excellent example of a subculture with a lifestyle and orientation that transcends sport. For example, the values and activities of group members are based around a pro-environment and 'selective consumption' ethic. Selective consumption refers here to the group's preference for surf clothing and apparel brands that are aligned with environmental values. In Wheaton's study of this group she offers the example of an SAS member's condemnation of the brand (and multinational corporation) Quicksilver for sponsoring a surfing competition in an area of Indonesia where coral reefs could easily be damaged (Wheaton, 2005).

Wheaton (2005) notes, however, that surfers and other groups have demonstrated a selective consumption ethic that is, at times, contradictory. For windsurfers, equipment and associated brands are commonly viewed as a necessarily evil for a group that sees themselves to be anti-style. Conversely, Wheaton and Beal (2003) note in their study of skateboarders that knowledge of brands is a marker of subcultural membership and being 'in the know'—with skaters preferring brands that 'had authentic status, primarily through demonstrating their long-standing commitment to the culture's "core" attitudes', despite the fact that many of these brands are now the faces of international or transnational corporations.

By highlighting these contradictions, Wheaton is pointing to some of the limitations of life politics as a strategy for challenging a system that commonly favours the interests of transnational corporations and neo-liberal forms of governance. The idea is that these challenges are always based around the choices of *consumer*-citizens, and in this way privilege a consumer-driven form of politics (which favours those with greater purchasing power) over a politics driven by the lobbying and decision-making of voting citizens.

The Success of Movements:
Political Opportunity and Resource Mobilization

While sociologists of sport like Wheaton have outlined how the sport-related lifestyle choices of people may have political ramifications, and Harvey et al. have done well to begin to document various types and goals of contemporary (global) social movements, Davis-Delano and Crosset (2008) point out that few researchers have systematically examined the characteristics of successful sport-related movements (global or otherwise). Of course, evaluating success is challenging and complex, especially if we consider the diverse goals that guide social movements—goals which could include (among other possibilities):

- raising awareness around a set of social concerns;
- creating a cohesive 'social movement community' and sense of belonging for community members;
- becoming a recognized representative for an issue;
- inspiring a sense of empowerment for movement members who feel marginalized and/or oppressed;
- inspiring a change in government policy or a change in cultural norms and practices;
- interrupting activities of powerful groups whose goals and actions are unacceptable to the activist group;
- bringing attention to an alternative approach to, for example, the practice of sport (e.g., to a non-competitive and anti-corporate sport, like *parkour*)

Acknowledging the diverse goals of these groups and the challenges associated with evaluating particular outcomes, it is still difficult to argue with Davis-Delano and Crosset's (2008) view that it is helpful to better understand what tactics and strategies seem to be most effective for creating change in particular contexts—and which social movement theories help us explain why some social movements are successful and others are not. Responding to the lack of research on these topics, Davis-Delano and Crosset decided to examine two sport-related social movements—one that challenged sporting teams that currently have a Native American mascot like 'Redskin' or 'Indian' (which are commonly considered to be derogatory representations of Native Americans) to change their mascots; and another that protested and attempted to prevent the use of public monies to fund sport facilities that house privately run teams. In these cases, 'success' meant that a 'mascot was changed' (for the first movement mentioned above), or the 'stadium/facility was not funded' (for the second).

Although Davis-Delano and Crosset offer many insights into the factors that impact the effectiveness of social movements, they argue that the success of the particular movements they studied was best explained by resource mobilization theory, political process theory, and framing theory—theories commonly referred to by social movement researchers. Although not exhaustive descriptions, I outline below some of the principles associated with these theories. Each point I outline is based around an assumption about the circumstances under which social movements are most likely to be successful. According to these theories then, movements are successful when:

- ***resources can be mobilized***—movements are most likely to be successful when, for example, a critical mass of people can be recruited into the movement, when the support of members of media or other influential people (e.g., politicians) can be attained, and when financial and technical support can be secured (e.g., to help set up a website, or develop promotional materials)

- *political opportunities are available and utilized*—movements are most likely to be successful when the political climate is most favourable for social change and when dominant groups are most responsive to challenges from social movement groups (e.g., around election times; when other movement groups have already 'opened the gates' for political changes that may benefit the group; when the government was elected on a mandate that is aligned with some of the values of the social movement group) (Amenda, 2005)

- *social movement entrepreneurs* (i.e., leaders/visionaries of social movements—see Box 5.1) are effective in creating *collective action frames* (i.e., key messages that rally and inspire movement members and others). Effective framing commonly includes strategically identifying an injustice, attributing blame, and proposing a solution that requires the support and action of movement members.

BOX 5.1 ⁙ ELITE KENYAN RUNNERS AS 'SOCIAL MOVEMENT ENTREPRENEURS'

In response to a wave of violence in parts of Kenya following a disputed election in December 2007, many of the country's elite distance runners took the lead in promoting 'run-for-peace' reconciliation events. Organizers of these events were intent on creating forums (i.e., running races and associated pro-peace ceremonies) where members of the Kikuyu and Kalenjin tribes, which were at the centre of the conflict and disputed election, could come together peacefully. The success of these events hinged on the idea that providing safe and positive spaces for friendly inter-tribal interactions is an important first step towards a more peaceful and united Kenya.

The best publicized of these events took place on 15 March 2008 in the town of Iten, in Kenya's Rift Valley region, where many of the country's top runners train and live. The event featured 560 girls from local schools running through the streets in a four-kilometre race. Several current and former elite runners oversaw the competition, including former world marathon champions Douglas Wakiihuri (a member of the Kikuyu tribe) and Luke Kibet (a member of the Kalenjin tribe). The event received coverage in international publications like *Runner's World*, which lauded race organizers for their successful contributions to the reconciliation effort.

These run-for-peace events can be understood in a variety of ways. They are relevant to thinking about ways that national sporting successes may help 'unite' those in divided societies by promoting feelings of connection among citizens (see chapter 3)—noting that the previous athletic successes of figures like Wakiihuri and Kibet were celebrated by Kenyans of various affiliations. The events are similarly relevant to research that explores the role that sport can play, and does play, in micro-level conflict transformation efforts (see chapter 7). They also pertain to the study of international development and sport (also chapter 7), given that international aid for some of these events was mobilized, in part, through the international NGO Shoe4Africa—an organization with international celebrity representatives such as actors Natalie Portman and Anthony Edwards (although Shoe4Africa remains Iten-based, and is run locally).

For me and a team of researchers—including Professor Mike Boit of Nairobi's Kenyatta University, an Olympic medallist himself who has been a participant-organizer in run-for-peace events— who travelled to the Rift Valley in May 2011, the focus was on the particular role that elite Kenyan runners played in organizing and promoting these events, and the importance of these athletes to the success of these events. Put simply, we were interested in understanding whether and how these athletes might be considered 'social movement entrepreneurs'.

Guided by Suzanne Staggenborg's (1988) definition of a social movement entrepreneur as a leader 'who initiate[s] movements, organizations, and tactics' (p. 587), we studied the role that elite runners played in the response to the post-election violence. Our research was based on in-depth interviews with a sample of former and current Kenyan runners and other high-profile members of the elite Kenyan running community who led the organization of sport-for-peace events, including former Boston marathon champion Moses Tanui, former New York marathon champion Lorna Kiplagat, and Kenyan athletics coach Joseph Ngure, who works out of the renowned Eldoret High Performance Training Centre (based in the Rift Valley region, and founded by Kenyan running legend Kip Keino).

Our findings showed that these high-status figures shared the assumption that run-for-peace events help demonstrate, at least symbolically, that inter-tribal rifts can be overcome, even after a violent conflict. According to interviewees, the decision to hold running events (instead of another kind of cultural event) was strategic, since: (a) the feelings of prestige and pride associated with Kenya's success at elite distance running are thought to transcend tribal boundaries; and (b) it is known that elite runners often model inter-tribal collaboration—noting here that athletes with various tribal affiliations are known to work together as teammates at international competitions, where they represent 'one Kenya'.

In this way, our findings offer some evidence that elite Kenyan runners who chose to be involved in these events played a key role in the success of these events. While the mere presence of celebrity runners at the events was thought to be important for attracting participants and spectators, our findings suggest that those athletes who were *actively* involved in organizing the event (i.e., as movement entrepreneurs) had an immense capacity to mobilize resources because of their prominence and high status in communities affected by the conflict. For example, some athletes (especially those who grew up in the Rift Valley and/or trained there) had well-developed and positive relationships with local media, who would publicize the run-for-peace events. These 'runner-entrepreneurs' were also able to attract volunteers for the events through their highly developed sets of contacts. They were also in a better position to influence those who have the power to fast-track the sort of community-based work that is needed for events like this to happen, such as road closures for races. It is also noteworthy that many of these athletes have high-profile friendships with teammates from rival tribes, giving them credibility in their attempts to organize reconciliation activities.

From this case study, we can begin to see how in Kenya—where running is highly valued for cultural, political, and economic reasons—opportunities exist for elite athletes to emerge as trusted leaders in a movement for peace, especially during times when confidence in formal political leadership is low (as was the case following Kenya's 2007 election). Interviewees in our study also noted that the 'runner/movement entrepreneur' may have been especially influential at the time the conflict took place because the 2008 Beijing Olympic Games were on the horizon, and the ability of athletes to train in the Rift Valley was compromised during the conflict. To the extent that many Kenyans are concerned about the performance of these athletes on the world stage, it is possible that the pre-Olympic moment was a politically opportune time for elite athletes to take on leadership roles, to remind people of the pride that Kenyans of various tribes feel when the country's elite runners perform well, and that internal conflicts can stand in the way of the successes that a unified Kenya can achieve. In these ways, this recent research on the run-for-peace work of Kenyan runners in 2008 and beyond illuminates a particular context in which social movement entrepreneurs led the way in pursuing political opportunities, and mobilizing resources in a sport for peace movement.

It is important to note here how these theories (especially resource mobilization and framing theories) imply, on one hand, that there are features of social movements that are in some respects 'transhistorical'—meaning that, regardless of context, social movement organizations will be more effective when they are able to mobilize in particular ways and with the guidance of tactically astute social movement entrepreneurs and leaders. On the other hand, though, there is clear recognition that context matters here—that 'different sorts of strategies are likely to be necessary to win collective benefits in different political circumstances' (Amenta, 2005, p. 34). This latter point is important if we begin to think about how, for example, anti-Olympics activists might be more or less likely to influence the work of government or Olympic organizing committees at different stages in the process (e.g., the moment before a city has decided to bid for a Games, compared to moments when a city has been awarded the Games, compared to the moment when the Games are on), and how different types of protest and collective action might be necessary to raise awareness and inspire change at these different moments (Amenta, 2005).

It is also worth noting here how different types of social movements—e.g., more established organizations like Greenpeace as compared to less formal organizations like the environmental group Earthfirst! (renowned for blocking logging roads and other acts of civil disobedience)—specialize in different types of activism and social engagement (Staggenborg, 2008). More established groups are better positioned to create sustained relationships with government, and to lobby for policy changes on an ongoing basis. More informal groups are better able to innovate and raise awareness immediately—although they are limited in their ability to develop the relationships that may lead to policy changes in the long term.

With the exception of Davis-Delano and Crosset (2008), little attention has been paid to these kinds of nuances around sport-related activism, or to the theories that help explain the success of social movements in particular contexts. In light of the attention that is consistently paid to protests around hosting the Olympics in particular—and the role that critical sociologists might play in raising important and questions and concerns about globalization, neo-liberalization, and sport—it would seem that this area deserves more attention.

Do Movements Matter?
Hegemony, Ironic Activism, and Reflections on Theory

As you may recall from chapter 2, sociologists who use the hegemony concept are attentive not only to ways that power is maintained by some groups over other groups, but also to ways that hegemony is interrupted and overturned by resistant groups (i.e., counter-hegemony), and how social changes that do take place may or may not threaten the existing power structure. With this in mind, we can begin to think about ways that a concept like hegemony can help sociologists ask more nuanced questions about the success of movements and about changing (and sustaining) power relationships—questions such as: 'When does social resistance make a difference?', and 'When do social movements matter?'

In her essay on the history of cultural struggle and resistance around women's sport in Canada, sociologist Ann Hall (2007) speaks to these questions when she describes how increased opportunities for women's involvement in sport over time were 'granted' by the powerful men that (conventionally) controlled sport 'providing traditional gender roles went undisturbed and the gender order of society was left intact' (p. 69). Others who have studied progressions around women's sport have made similar arguments about the implementation of Title IX in the US, which led to more opportunities for female involvement in sport, but an accompanying movement by men into coaching and administrative positions that were previously held by women.

The irony here, as authors like Hargreaves (1994) note, is that while women and girls were able to participate more often in sport than in years past because of a policy change, the ability to make decisions about how these sports were run was diminished. My point here is that progressive social changes are not always what they seem, since any kind of social change is commonly accompanied by unintended consequences, unanticipated complexities, and new problems. In some cases, the structural reasons why certain inequalities or problems exist may not be have been addressed by the change, or may, ironically and inadvertently, be perpetuated by the change!

For example, in a recent study I conducted with Lyndsay Hayhurst on sport for development and peace organizations (Wilson and Hayhurst, 2009), we found that while these organizations were proactively responding to concerns associated with neo-liberal governments (e.g., decreases in government-supported recreation opportunities for marginalized populations), to be successful in this system still meant perpetuating a competitive neo-liberal system that is itself responsible for some of the inequalities that these organizations are attempting to deal with. That is to say, to survive in the current NGO climate, these organizations need to be successful in funding competitions, and to effectively manage their image for donors. Being effective at these activities does not necessarily mean that these groups will be effective at collaborating with those in local communities, or qualitatively impacting the lives of those targeted by their programs. For example, rigorous self-monitoring and self-evaluation by SDP groups might not serve the competitive (as opposed to altruistic) interests of these groups—because identifying internal weaknesses and problems might not be helpful when attempting to appeal to the corporate and government donors that contribute to and sustain these organizations. In fact, it may serve the competitive interests of these groups to only self-evaluate in areas that are strengths (for example, some groups may serve many young people, so counting the number served would be a good measure), while avoiding evaluations that may reveal shortcomings around the quality or long-term impacts of programming (Coalter, 2008). With these problems in mind, Lyndsay Hayhurst and I labelled this SDP work in a neo-liberal system '**ironic activism**'—meaning that many SDP NGOs are both responding to and perpetuating problems with neo-liberalism *at the same time* (Wilson and Hayhurst, 2009).

The Importance of Context

The idea that certain activist tactics tend to be more effective under certain circumstances (and less effective under others) has particular relevance for those guided by a cultural studies approach. That is to say, those working with a cultural studies sensibility recognize the contingent and context-specific features of any attempt to make sense of power relationships and, at the same time, are interested in using critical theory and research to inform practice.

If we consider the types of social movements outlined throughout this chapter, we can see how at least some movements are informed by an understanding of how forms of oppression are perpetuated. At the same time, however, and as Davis-Delano and Crosset (2008) note, sociologists of sport (and many sport-related activists) are only beginning to learn about the ways in which, and contexts wherein, certain tactics for change are most effective. With this in mind, we can begin to think about the shared characteristics of successful (sport-related) movements, the different definitions of success for various movements, and the circumstances under which certain approaches to activism are more or less likely to make a difference (Wilson, 2007a). We can also begin to think about how sociologists who are interested in promoting social change can contribute to interventions and initiatives that support inclusion and social justice. If we remember back to the first chapter of this book, it is in this linking of theory, research, and practical action that praxis emerges—a point I develop further in the next chapter.

Thinking more broadly about ways sociologists can contribute is especially important in a moment when debates about what are 'acceptable' forms of activism have come to the fore around events like the Vancouver 2010 Olympics. There is a body of research that speaks to ways that activists are commonly portrayed as 'extremists'—or ways that the more radical and violent forms of protest become the *only* face of activism (Hackett and Gruneau, 2000). Often lost in discussions about 'the problems with activists' is that protest and activism are ways that citizens can actively participate in the democratic process, as well as an understanding that various strategies for awareness raising and inciting social change (whether these be reformist or transformational) have all been shown to be useful in promoting progressive forms of democratic change (Kennelly, 2008).

The reason that looking at historical examples of activism and their impacts is useful—which is to say, the reason that examining activism and social change using a sociological imagination is useful—is that we can see how certain forms of protest actually made a difference, even though the inevitable disruption and tension that occurred at the time was not appreciated by everybody. The Black Power salute that took place on the podium at the 1968 Olympics, mentioned earlier, is an oft-cited example of this. It is sometimes forgotten that the two athletes that made this important symbolic gesture were initially vilified for disrespecting the Olympics, for bringing politics to the 'politics free' zone of sport (Hartmann, 2003). There were threats to have the athletes' medals revoked and to have the athletes themselves banned from the Olympic village. Of course, in hindsight, these athletes have come to symbolize the importance of taking a stand, raising awareness, and rallying support around key social issues. Such grassroots activism is considered crucial for healthy democratic societies, and as I have argued throughout this chapter, sport can and does often play a key role here.

Looking Ahead

There are ongoing debates about the role that sociologists of sport can and should play in promoting the types of social change often sought by activist groups (e.g., around social justice/equality and inclusion). Even among those who work in a cultural studies tradition—who tend to be united around a concern with linking theory, research, and social action—there is ongoing debate about what counts as appropriate and progressive intervention. For example, in his article 'One-Dimensional Sport', Ian McDonald (2009) of the University of Brighton challenges sociologists of sport to think seriously about the extent to which and ways in which their work makes a difference, and argues that not all forms of sociological critique are easily translated into intervention.

McDonald's point is an important one that inspires the next chapter's discussion of peace education and sport, since for many sociologists it is through forms of (critical) pedagogy that peace promoting social change is commonly sought.

Note

1. Taken from www.caaws.ca/e/about/mission_vision.cfm.

Discussion Questions

1. What are the differences between a new social movement and older social movements?

2. Are there distinguishing features of sport-related social movements?

3. What makes a social movement successful? Under what conditions does it seem most likely that a social movement will be successful?

4. How is a subculture similar to and different from a social movement?

5. How can a social movement be ironic?

Suggested Readings ··

Davis-Delano, L. & Crosset, T. (2008). Using social movement theory to study outcomes in sports-related social movements. *International Review for the Sociology of Sport,* 43(2), 115–34. In this impressive examination of two sport-related social movements, the authors assess the explanatory power of five social movement theories.

Harvey, J., Horne, J. & Safai, P. (2009). Alter-globalization, global social movements and the possibility of political transformation through sport. *Sociology of Sport Journal,* 26(3), 383–403. An innovative exploration of the alter-globalization concept as it relates to sport-related social movements.

Sage, G. (1999). Justice do it! The Nike transnational advocacy network: Organization, collective action and outcomes. *Sociology of Sport Journal,* 16(3), 206-235. A foundational study of the anti-sweatshop movements that underlie many critiques of transnational sport-related corporations.

Wheaton, B. (2005). Selling out? The commercialization and globalization of lifestyle sport. In L. Allison (Ed.), *The global politics of sport: The role of global institutions in sport* (pp. 140–61). New York: Routledge. A discussion of the emergence and meaning of lifestyle sports, and issues around the seeing participation in lifestyle sports as a form of politics.

Wilson, B. (2002). The 'Anti-Jock' Movement: Reconsidering Youth Resistance, Masculinity and Sport Culture in the Age of the Internet. *Sociology of Sport Journal,* 19(2), 207–34. A case study of an Internet-based youth movement that arose in response to concerns about bullying by athletes, and other social problems associated with hypermasculine sporting cultures.

Wilson, B. (2007). New Media, Social Movements, and Global Sport Studies: A Revolutionary Moment and the Sociology of Sport. *Sociology of Sport Journal,* 24(4), 457–77. A discussion the influence of the Internet on the potential for impact of various sport-related social movements.

Wilson, B. & Hayhurst, L. (2009). Digital activism: Neo-liberalism, the internet, and 'sport for development'. *Sociology of Sport Journal,* 26(1), 155–81. A study of 'sport for youth development' groups and ways that these groups are in some cases participating in a form of ironic activism.

Wilson, B. & White, Phil. (2002). 'Revive the Pride': Social Process, Political Economy and a Fan-Based Grassroots Movement. *Sociology of Sport Journal,* 19(2), 119–48. A case study of a social movement to save the Ottawa Rough Riders CFL team and stadium.

Relevant Websites ··

Surfers Against Sewage
www.sas.org.uk
   This is the home page for the Surfers Against Sewage (SAS) environmental group.

National Coalition on Racism in Sport and in Media
www.aimovement.org/ncrsm
> According to the website, 'the National Coalition on Racism in Sports and Media exists to fight the powerful influence of major media who choose to promulgate messages of oppression.' Issues around the use of native mascots is a key issue taken up by this group.

Media Watch (Canada)
www.mediawatch.ca
> Mediawatch is a national, not-for-profit feminist organization which includes information about media literacy, research on portrayals of females and others in mainstream media, and information for those interested expressing concerns to media regulatory agencies.

Key Terms

activist refers to someone who 'acts' on issues of social, political, and environmental significance, and to someone 'who acts strategically with others, on the basis of shared values, to create a more just society' (Watts et al., 2003, p. 186).

alter-globalization movement A movement—sometimes thought of as a 'movement of movements', because of the various groups involved—with the broad and shared goal of changing *how* globalization takes place, with an emphasis on promoting human rights.

anti-globalization movement A social movement that consists of various social movements (sometimes known as a 'movement of movements') that are resistant to different aspects of globalization. Although these movements differ from one another in their concerns, the anti-globalization movements commonly referred to the sociology of sport are 'anti-sweatshop' and 'anti-Nike' movements that are concerned with the treatment of workers and human rights violations by companies that outsource the production of athletic apparel to countries of the Global South (commonly in Southeast Asia).

detraditionalization refers to the loosening of the usual bonds that have historically held groups of people together and offered particular securities (e.g., family-related, location-related, or social class–related bonds and securities).

emancipatory politics refers to collective actions intended to promote political and personal freedom, such as the civil rights movement.

individualization refers to the increase in the number and type of individualized choices people have about where they can live, the jobs they can pursue, and the personalized lifestyles they can construct—freedoms that have emerged because of the loosening of ties associated with detraditionalization. Sociologists argue that the freedoms associated with individualization and detraditionalization have led to a situation where people are more likely to feel 'on their own' in society.

ironic activism When the collective actions intended to resolve and deal with a particular issue or concern lead to outcomes that actually *perpetuate* the issue or concern.

life(style) politics refers to a more personalized form of politics, where one expresses a political stance through the choices that are made about consumer purchases, everyday activities, and other personalized lifestyle choices.

new social movement A term used to describe groups that operate on local, national, and transnational levels, vary in size and organizational forms, are concerned with social change, and are not specifically concerned with economic issues (unlike 'older' social movements—acknowledging that debates have persisted on the issue of whether 'new' movements are distinct from older' movements). Examples of these movements are feminist movements, environmental movements, and anti-racist movements.

pre-political (subcultural activities) refers to subcultural activities that (perhaps inadvertently) help young people find a language to express themselves and their concerns, and to prepare themselves for active engagement with politics through the micro-political and personal identity work that takes place in subcultural contexts.

social movement a concept used to describe various forms of collective action and 'political entities aiming to create social change' (Staggenborg, 2008, p. 34).

subcultures refers to social and cultural groups that are 'focused around certain activities, values, certain uses of material artifacts, territorial spaces etc. which significantly differentiate them from the wider culture' (Hall and Jefferson, 1976, p. 22).

6

Pursuing Praxis: Peace Education, Critical Pedagogy, and the Sociology of Sport

Questions to Consider

⊕ What are the meanings of the terms 'praxis' and 'conscientization', and what do they have to do with sport and peace?

⊕ What do the terms 'peace education' and 'critical pedagogy' mean, and how can these forms of education be used to raise awareness about and address sport-related social problems?

⊕ In what ways can sport-based prevention and education programs be peace-promoting?

⊕ In what practical ways can scholar-educator-activists raise awareness about sport-related social problems, and how are theory and practice linked in these efforts?

Introduction: 'Educated Hope' and the Influence of Paulo Freire

Praxis: reflection and action upon the world in order to transform it
(Paulo Freire, from *Pedagogy of the Oppressed*, 1970, p. 36)

The influence of Brazilian philosopher and educator Paulo Freire—renowned for his efforts to promote literacy among impoverished workers in Brazil in the early 1960s (before he was jailed and exiled for these 'subversive' activities)—remains strong through his classic 1970 book *Pedagogy of the Oppressed*. The book encapsulates Freire's approach to teaching and his belief that oppressed people are generally not encouraged or equipped to know and to respond to the concrete realities of their world. As Shaull (2000) notes in his Foreword to a recent edition of the book, Freire felt that many oppressed people are 'submerged' in a 'culture of silence' where 'critical awareness and response [are] practically impossible' (Shaull, 2000, p. 12).[1]

Many of those interested in ways to promote peace through progressive forms of education still use the Freirian notion of '**conscientization**', which is a pedagogical approach intended to promote awareness about how current systems of domination and oppression operate. For Freire, conscientization is a strategy that can be adopted in the pursuit of **praxis**—the translation of critical awareness into action. Influenced by Freire, activist-educators like Henry Giroux (2007) argue that there is a need to explore the possible responses to power regimes that perpetuate the forms of oppression that Freire and many others have identified. Giroux suggests that a goal of such awareness-raising should be to inspire an 'educated hope' for those interested in social change, and contribute to the development of a 'language of possibility' that will support the work of those interested in social changes intended to enhance democracy and promote social justice (Giroux, 2007, p. 33).

Conscientization, Praxis, and the Sociology of Sport

Inspired by the work of Freire and others, I have argued throughout this book that in order to responsibly incite and carry-out 'peace promoting' social and cultural changes in and around sport, it is crucial to first understand why certain forms of change are necessary—and how the oppression of some groups and privileging of others may be taking place. That is to say, without recognizing how power operates, and the contexts that allow for the perpetuation of inequalities, the kinds of change sought by those interested in more peaceful, inclusive, and democratic sporting worlds may fall flat for the reasons outlined in the previous chapter.

Of course, it is one thing to recognize the need for this sort of awareness about why and how to link theory with sport-related forms of transformational practice; it is quite another to support the development of this awareness—and of skilled critical sociological thinking more generally. With this in mind, I spend this chapter outlining ways that educators, scholars, and activists guided by a cultural studies sensibility—and in many cases influenced and motivated by Freire—have responded to this need to raise awareness about sport-related social problems, and processes through which power operates. Initially, I discuss the many ways that peace might be promoted through education, and identify tensions and controversies that exist around the 'doing' of **peace education**. Featured here is a discussion of **critical pedagogy** as an approach to education that Freire was referring to, an approach that is commonly adopted by educators who teach sociology of sport classes and do other kinds of pedagogical work within and around sport. I then consider how the 'reflection' that Freire refers to in his definition of praxis is translated into a form of action in a series of sport-related educational contexts. Featured here, among other critical pedagogical and action-oriented approaches to social change is a case study of the widely-used Mentors in Violence Prevention (MVP) program—a program designed to promote theoretically informed interventions into gendered violence in and around sport.

What will also become evident throughout this chapter is that peace education as a concept and area is complex and not without its problems. In fact, forms of peace education are at times implicated in the perpetuation of certain social problems, a point I demonstrate below and into the next chapter's discussion of international development and sport.

So What Is Peace Education?

The term 'peace education' is commonly used to describe the range of peace-related pedagogical practices, although, like many broad concepts, it is ambiguous and contested. Harris's (2004) encompassing definition offers a starting point:

> [Peace education] refers to teachers teaching about peace: what it is, why it does not exist and how to achieve it. This includes teaching about the challenges of achieving peace, developing non-violent skills and promoting peaceful attitudes. (p. 6)

Examples of peace education include, but are not limited to, the following:

- Conflict Resolution (or Conflict Transformation) Education—which includes using pedagogical approaches to promote better relationships between countries and cultures, or to deal with micro-level, interpersonal conflicts (like bullying in schools)
- International Education—which includes learning about different cultures as a way of developing empathy and breaking down cultural barriers
- Environmental Education—which includes promoting holistic thinking about relationships between nature and humans
- Media Literacy Education—which includes learning about how portrayals of race, ethnicity, class, gender, and disability may reflect and reinforce unequal social relations
- Human Rights Education—which includes learning about how certain strategies for peace-building are grounded in (or could be grounded in) human rights legislations, and how legal systems more generally can be useful for promoting peace
- Global Education—which includes inspiring contemplation about the positive and negative impacts of globalization
- Development Education or Critical Pedagogy—which includes examining reasons for and the circumstances surrounding the perpetuation of structural and cultural forms of violence, and inciting action-oriented responses to social problems (cf., Harris, 2004)

As a read of other chapters in this book will reveal, many sport scholars draw on sociological research pertaining to most or all of these issues in their work with students, although such work may not always be framed as peace education per se. For example, those who teach about international development and sport will consider ways that sport can be used to support conflict transformation efforts. Those who study media portrayals of race and gender will be interested in issues pertaining to cultural violence that are associated with the dissemination of negative and demeaning stereotypes. Efforts to inspire thinking about how these images or texts are problematic—and the importance of thinking about the contexts these images/texts exist within—are forms of media literacy education, and perhaps global education (when, for example, these images are produced by transnational corporations).

However, and although many of the key topics outlined above are dealt with by sociologists of sport, sport practitioners, activists, and others, the actual strategies used to raise awareness about these topics differ significantly. There are good reasons for this, including:

• that pedagogical strategies used to explore issues around peace and conflict would be different for groups that are actively involved in conflict with another (e.g., in efforts to resolve/transform conflict among Israeli and Palestinian youth at a soccer camp), compared to those who are not directly involved in active conflict (e.g., bystanders to incidents of bullying by high-status male athletes);
• that education efforts for marginalized groups (e.g., those living in poverty) compared to more privileged groups (who may be inspired to contribute to solving problems like 'widespread poverty') may be different; and
• there are various ways that peace can be defined, so educational efforts will vary depending on the peace-related goals and preference of the educator (Coté, Day, and de Peuter, 2007; Harris, 2004).

It is also known that approaches to sport-related peace education—whether they focus on using sport as a tool for peace, or on the need to promote peace within sport—may at times be in tension with one another. The most obvious difference would be based around the ways that educators connect theory with practice, since teaching about the power of sport to promote peace from a functionalist perspective as compared to a critical perspective is different, for reasons outlined in chapter 2. For example, a theoretically driven tension would arise between those who uncritically endorse the use of sport as an educational tool for promoting character building and conflict resolution for youth in developing countries, and those who see these attempts to educate/intervene in developing countries/contexts as forms of colonization (e.g., when the pedagogical practices used by volunteers representing international NGOs are insensitive to indigenous approaches to learning and local cultural traditions).

With such debates about *how* to educate for peace and democracy in mind, Coté, Day, and de Peuter (2007) suggest that education is too often equated with simply delivering information—information that is based around and perpetuates an uncritical acceptance of the status quo. In making this argument, they draw on the work of Ivan Illich (1971) who famously wrote *Deschooling Society* as a call for more critical, collaborative, deinstitutionalized, and politically inspired thinking that is not 'top-down'. Following Illich, Coté et al. (2007) acknowledge that, in many cases, traditional schooling may, in fact, '*alienate* us from our learning, and force us down pathways that serve to perpetuate the existing order instead of allowing us to pursue avenues that call out to us as particular subjects' (p. 8). In fact, students and instructors working in (or with a background in) kinesiology and physical education–related departments at universities may recognize a particular need for a more reflective approach to education in these contexts (see Box 6.1).

BOX 6.1 ❋ QUESTIONING ASSUMPTIONS IN PHYSICAL EDUCATION

The instructor . . . pulled the cover from a partially dissected cadaver. . . lifted the abdominal muscles. . . and revealed the intestines,,,This was my first visit to the gross anatomy lab. . . 'The only way you really learn anatomy,' [the instructor] said, 'is to get your hands inside and manipulate the parts of the body.' While I was keen to learn about the body, I was reluctant to make such a dramatic entry. But I did it anyway and learned what I needed to know about the structure of the peritoneum. And I felt a tremendous sense of power . . .Here was the confirmation of what science had always told me about the body, but which from my own experience had always rung false: The body is an object . . . As a student of physical education, I realized that the power of my profession lay in its ability to manipulate the body, to make it an efficient resource. (Pronger, 1995, p. 427)

By introducing his article *Rendering the Body: the Implicit Lessons of Gross Anatomy* with this evocative—and what we learn later in his piece to be ironic—description of his initiation into the rituals of gross anatomy, Brian Pronger provokes thinking about how many students in kinesiology, human kinetics, and other physical education–related programs commonly learn about the body and, in turn, about physical activity and sport. Most notably, he highlights how (physical) education is a socializing agent, and therefore, the viewpoints and taken for granted assumptions of students in physical education are shaped by the dominant messages that are promoted in PE contexts. Although this may seem commonsensical, if we remind ourselves of this—and of the powerful ideological consequences of promoting certain ways of thinking and seeing, and the deemphasizing of others—we can begin to understand how certain ways of seeing the world (e.g., through the eyes of an objective scientist) come to be taken-for-granted and unquestioned.

Pronger (1995) takes this a step further—as do many sociologists of sport—to explicitly argue that there are negative social (and often physical) implications associated with viewing of the body exclusively as an object. For example, seeing the body as an object is commonly associated with seeing the body as a 'high performance machine'. Research by scholars like Rob Beamish (2008) and John Hoberman (1992) shows how such a view of the body might lead high performance athletes and those working with them to more easily and unreflexively alter, tweak, and tune the body using whatever methods are available to them—without regard for the negative health consequences. They further argue that although steroid-using athletes are commonly stigmatized, we should, in fact, be completely *unsurprised* (and far less judgmental) when we find out that many athletes have used illegal performance enhancers. That is to say, with our culture's emphasis on high performance and success in major sporting events, along with the accepted view of the body as an object to be manipulated and improved with this performance in mind, it should not surprise us when some athletes to 'do what it takes' to succeed. In a not unconnected way, sociologist Michael Messner (1990) has famously argued how the high rates of violence and injury in many sports are attributable to the dominant view of the body as a 'weapon'—an 'object' of destruction for athletes in high contact sports where the long-term negative effects of the physical abuse of self and others are still coming to light.

Seeing the body as an object that can be 'made stronger' and 'kept young and beautiful' is also associated with the view that we have a *moral* responsibility to control what the body looks like (White, Young, and Gillett, 1995). According to Pronger and others who study sport and health, this (dominant) view of the body is a reason that many social and health problems have emerged for people who make unhealthy attempts to conform to unrealistic and gendered body ideals—ideals only achieved though cosmetic surgery or risky and problematic eating and exercise-related practices by men and women (i.e., who are attempting to 'get huge/strong' or 'get skinny'). The view of the body as object is also associated with a belief that the natural changes that take place in the body as one ages are to be avoided through cosmetic surgeries and obsessive/unhealthy eating and exercise habits—points made starkly in Gullette's (1997) book *Declining to Decline* and in sociological studies by Hurd Clarke (Hurd Clarke, 2010; Hurd Clarke, Repta, and Griffin, 2007).

All this to say, sociologists commonly and understandably raise important concerns when the body is unreflectively treated as an object in formal education contexts, and elsewhere.

Sport, Cultural Studies, and Critical Pedagogy

With these sorts of concerns in mind, many sport scholars have recognized the need for alternative and critically oriented approaches to education—approaches that inspire people to reflect on their taken-for-granted assumptions about sport, to consider their positioning in a broader system of power relations, and to use this knowledge to intervene when they become aware of inequalities and social problems (Giardina, 2005). For example, in their essay 'Cultural Studies: An Interventionist Practice', Howell et al. (2002) highlight the need to link theory with efforts for social change, and suggest that by using a 'contextual cultural studies' approach—an approach that allows students to see 'how particular sporting practices are positioned into specific contexts', and 'how sporting contexts get their meaning and identity through the power structures and relationships to which they are connected'—scholar-educators can help 'destabilize connections that appear natural and extremely stable in any given historical context' (p. 155). The point is that by showing how various forms of oppression are perpetuated—and demonstrating that widespread inequalities in society are neither natural nor necessary—people will be better positioned to envision possibilities for change.

Underlying these arguments is a set of assumptions about the role sport can and should play in critical pedagogical work. These include:

1. That sport and other forms of popular culture are impactful and significant cultural forms precisely because of the often-unnoticed ways they perpetuate and reflect existing systems of power relations and structures of inequality. That is to say, because sport is not always taken seriously, it is a venue where imagery and messages that may perpetuate unequal power relations may be accepted uncritically, and thus consented to by audiences.

2. That sport oftentimes *reflects* extant power relations and inequalities, and for this reason, it makes sense to use representations of sport as teaching devices for thinking about broader social issues. Put another way, the sociological study of sport and other forms of popular culture in a given society can help us teach and learn about the social and cultural features of that society—and demonstrate how an awareness of history and context can help us see why inequalities and social problems exist, how they are perpetuated, and how they might be dealt with.

3. Recognizing the role that sport plays in the lived experiences of many, it makes sense, following Giroux (1981), to use pedagogical practices that draw on 'the lived experiences of the students themselves as a starting point for developing classroom experiences' (p. 29). In this way, student reflections on their own sporting experiences are an excellent starting point for critical pedagogical work.

Questions about *how* the critical awareness-raising that Howell et al. (2002) and others are talking about has, and should, take place is a little less clear—at least in the sociology of sport literature. Ian McDonald (2009) makes this point in his article 'One-Dimensional Sport', where he lauds cultural studies scholars like Howell et al. (2002) for their well-theorized attempts to create change, but is apprehensive about their claims to actually connect their cultural critiques with any sort of intervention (McDonald, 2009, p. 41). McDonald goes on to suggest that although radical interventionist opportunities might be limited in the realm of sport, sociologists of sport have an excellent opportunity to raise awareness about and make progress on important social issues through their position as educators in universities:

> . . . it seems that all we can and must do [as critical sociologists of sport] is engage in rearguard and defense strategies: such as exposing relations of power, engaging in campaigns for equality, formulating critiques. Sport does not have equivalents of avant-garde artistic movements or revolutionary cinematic and literature movements. However, unlike its more radical counterparts, it does have a public profile and presence that suggest political possibilities, particularly for those of us involved in teaching critical sport sociology in universities. (McDonald, 2009, p. 44)

McDonald's argument is important for its emphasis on the need to focus on educational contexts as 'spaces of intervention' where the promotion of more peaceful sporting cultures can take place.

Some Sport-Related Critical Pedagogical Practices

With McDonald's critique in mind, I spend this section discussing some examples of sport-related pedagogical practices that are aligned with a cultural studies sensibility—where '(critical) theory meets practice'. It is worth noting here, by way of introduction, that the examples I provide below are part of a long history of critical pedagogy by those working in and around the cultural studies field. As Coté et al. (2007) note, 'the history of cultural studies is rife with examples of scholars and activists developing relays between critically oriented education, bottom-up pedagogy, and oppositional social movements' (p. 4). This includes work by forerunners in the field of cultural studies like Raymond Williams and E.P. Thompson, who were concerned with adult education for workers, as well as greater access to education for working-class students. Of course, Paulo Freire's influence is powerful and central to the work of peace educators working with a cultural studies sensibility. Henry Giroux's (2007) attempts to instigate awareness-raising—with the goal of inspiring the development of a 'language of possibility' for pro-democratic social changes—is an example of this (Giroux, 2007, p. 33). It is with these aims in mind that the following sport-related pedagogical practices emerged.

Performance and Critical (Sporting) Pedagogies

At a special ceremony during the opening of the 1999 Pan Am Games in Winnipeg, Manitoba, seven First Nations men in their fifties entered the stadium in war canoes. One of them held the Games torch. In 1967 when Winnipeg first hosted the Pan American Games, ten outstanding athletic teenage boys were chosen to run 800 kilometers over an ancient message route with the Games torch. When the runners arrived at the stadium, they were not allowed to enter with the torch. Instead, a non-Aboriginal runner was given the honour. Thirty-two-years later, the province of Manitoba issued an official apology.

Nine of the ten young men chosen for the 1967 Pan Am Games torch run were from residential schools. [The film] *Niigaanibatowaad* is about the segregation of the Aboriginal athletes and the despair and abuse suffered in the school system. *Niigaanibatowaad: FrontRunners* is a story of survival, hope, reconciliation and a dream for a new beginning that transcends hatred and racism.

Synopsis of National Film Board production *Niigaanibatowaad: FrontRunners*
© Laura Robinson, the screenwriter and a coproducer of *Niigaanibatowaad*

In 2007, the National Film Board of Canada released *Niigaanibatowaad: FrontRunners*, a one-hour dramatic film that is based on a set of stories recalled by the runners mentioned above. The stories are about running, and about the horrors suffered by many aboriginal children in the residential school system. The film has particular pertinence to thinking about ways that sport reflects and can perpetuate existing inequalities and practices of oppression. This point is clarified in an essay by Laura Robinson, one of the film's producers, and the writer of the original play (entitled *FrontRunners*) on which the film is based. Robinson writes:

> . . . in 1967 there were unwritten rules about who could and couldn't be in celebrations and stadiums. This was also Canada's centennial year, and though there was an increasing political understanding of racism in Indigenous communities, sport officials lagged sadly behind. The runners [from the torch relay] either went home or back to residential school. Nine out of ten of the runners were what we now call residential school survivors. (Robinson, 2002a)

Robinson, a journalist and well-known author of books on gender, violence, and sport, presented *FrontRunners* at the North American Society for the Sociology of Sport (NASSS) Conference and at the CanWest Global Theatre in Winnipeg as part of the North American Indigenous Games (among other venues). Robinson is certainly not alone in her efforts—although her credentials as a regular contributor to the sociology of sport community are unique here—as she was joined by athletes from the 1967 relay in public discussions about the issues raised in the play/film. She was also joined by the film's director and producer, Lori Lewis, an indigenous educator and member of the Kwaguilth indigenous nation of the Northeastern Coast of Vancouver Island.

The use of dramatic and evocative theatre performances and film to inspire critical thinking about and action on issues such as the treatment of aboriginal peoples is increasingly recognized as an important pedagogical approach. This type of learning has been called 'performance pedagogy' or 'spectacle pedagogy' (Denzin, 2003, 2009). Norman Denzin (2009) explains how such an approach links critical theory to practice (i.e., how it is a form of praxis):

> This performance paradigm travels from theories of critical pedagogy to views of performance as intervention, interruption and resistance. It understands performance as a form of inquiry; it views performance as a form of activism, as critique and as critical citizenship. (p. 257)

Influenced by Denzin, sport scholars like Giardina (2005, Giardina and Hess, 2007; Giardina and Weems, 2004), Silk (2008), Markula (2006), Rinehart (2010), McDonald (2008), and others have begun to explore ways that film, poetry, theatre, dance, experimental/evocative writing, and other forms of **critical performance pedagogy** can 'promote a radically progressive democratic consciousness' (Giardina, 2005, p. 159). A key argument underlying this approach is that there is a crucial emotional and corporeal component to praxis—and that connecting to ideas on multiple levels (i.e., across the intellectual, emotional, and corporeal levels) is important to generate the understanding and commitment that is required to inspire theoretically informed transformative practice.

With this idea in mind, sociologists of sport Brett Smith and Andrew Sparkes (2005) discuss ways that emotion-evoking forms of scholarly writing are instructive and essential for those working in disability studies. These authors, who study athletes who have experienced spinal cord injuries, conducted in-depth interviews with these athletes and assembled their stories/narratives, presenting them in articles such as 'Men, Sport, Spinal Cord Injury and Narratives of Hope,' published in the journal *Social Science & Medicine* (Smith and Sparkes, 2005). Smith's and Sparkes's articles include reflections on the athletes' hopes, successes, disappointments, and depression—reflections that, according to the authors, 'encourage connection, empathy and solidarity,' and/ or 'inform, awaken and disturb readers by illustrating their involvement in social processes' that underlie society's expectations and treatment of badly injured and disabled people (Smith and Sparkes, 2008, p. 25). In the same way, according to Smith and Sparkes, athletes, researchers, or others who offer written reflections on their own experiences with any number of issues (as Smith [1999] does with depression)—in what are commonly termed 'autoethnographies'—have a great deal to offer readers of such narratives. For example:

[readers may] find the consequences of their involvement (or lack of it) unacceptable and seek to change the situation [they are presented with in the narrative]. In such circumstances the potential for individual and collective change is enhanced. Accordingly, a valuable use of autoethnography is to inspire in someone critical reflection. Here readers may recontextualise what they knew already in the light of their encounter with someone else's life . . . [In fact], well-crafted autoethnographies can be a call to witness and open up possibilities to get research across in a thought-provoking and accessible manner to a variety of diverse audiences and not just to 'expert' readers of academic journals. This further enhances the potential of the research to initiate individual and institutional change and make a difference in the 'everyday' world. (Smith and Sparkes, 2008, p. 25; cf., Denzin, 2003, 2009)

We can begin to see from such examples how connecting theory with practice—and engaging students around issues to do with social justice, democracy, and inequality—can take place in various ways.

Low Income Women, Recreation, and Feminist Participatory Action Research (FPAR)

With a similar concern for awareness-raising and inciting social changes that are beneficial for marginalized groups, University of British Columbia professor Wendy Frisby and her colleagues (cf., Frisby, Reid, and Ponic, 2007) undertook an innovative research and intervention project that was intended to create opportunities for more inclusive recreation-related experiences for a diverse group of low-income women in British Columbia (including single mothers, women with a disability, older women, and recent immigrants), who were experiencing various difficulties associated with poverty (e.g., social isolation). The researchers—along with the women they worked with—collectively sought out opportunities to discuss, question, and challenge the (neo-liberal) policies that were seen to be responsible for many of the broader problems experienced by these women.

Frisby et al.'s project is commonly described as a 'feminist' **participatory action research** (FPAR) project—which means, among other things, that the project is a *collaboration* between the researchers and the participants. A goal of these sorts of projects is to avoid conducting research in a top-down, hierarchal manner—a manner that often privileges the researchers' pre-determined definition of the study problem over the needs, interests, and viewpoints of the participant-collaborators (Frisby, Maguire, and Reid, 2009).

The feminist part of the project refers to conducting the research with a shared understanding that women are much more likely in Canada and globally to live in poverty and to be the victims of various forms of violence, and that feminist participatory work is intended to help deal with some aspect of these issues and disparities. Feminist work, in this context, is intended to recognize not just the issues women commonly face, but also the processes through which the marginalizing experiences of certain groups come to be ingrained and taken for granted. Conducting research in a non-hierarchical fashion is an attempt to break away from forms of research that may reflect cycles of oppression, recognizing that research-driven relationships can be unequal and exploitative (cf., Frisby, Maguire, and Reid, 2009).

In a similar way, the assumption underlying a non-hierarchical approach to the study of widespread social inequalities is that *all* members of the collaboration are learning about power, poverty, and oppression through the research, and although the researcher-academics came to the relationship with training in the theories of power, the organic knowledge of non-academics is equally important. In this context, Freire's 'conscientization' is relevant in the sense that all members of the collaboration are learning more about their positioning in relation to dominant power structures, with the shared goal of using this enhanced understanding as a platform to act.

Functionalism, Prevention, and a Sociological Imagination? Exploring Sport Programs Designed to Support Underserved Youth

Unlike action research projects like Frisby et al.'s that are developed and enacted with critical sociological perspectives in mind, sport-related prevention programs intended to support underserved youth are often designed with functionalist principles in mind. Sociologists of sport are commonly skeptical of these sorts of programs, especially those designed to 'get youth off the streets' and 'control deviance and violence'. There are many reasons for this skepticism. The first reason will be fairly obvious by now for readers of this book—playing sport, in itself, does not solve social problems. As Jay Coakley (2002) notes in his article 'Using Sport to Control Deviance: Let's Be Critical and Cautious', research focused around sport participation and the behaviours of young people demonstrates that 'those who play sports are less likely than comparable others to engage in deviant or violent behavior *only when* participation is accompanied by an emphasis on a philosophy of nonviolence, respect for self and others, the importance of fitness and control, confidence in physical skills, and a sense of responsibility, (p. 24). In situations where sport programs promote winning over participation and fair play, where hostility and aggression towards opponents is fostered, and where 'referees and coaches make calls that young people should learn to make for themselves', then sport may inhibit the development of nonviolent and empathetic young people (Coakley, 2002, p. 24; Martinek and Hellison, 1997).

Another concern is that that over-emphasizing the benefits of sport programs—even programs shown to be effective in supporting the holistic development of young people—may distract from the root causes of various forms of deviance and violence. The idea here is that perpetual poverty and deprivation are key indicators of various social problems for young people, and that these structural level issues are in no way addressed by these programs. Put simply, if sport programs remain the primary solution for dealing with youth-related social problems, then the underlying problems (poverty, deprivation) are never actually dealt with.

While these criticisms are powerful and important, they should not be taken to mean that well-designed and context-sensitive sport-related programs for youth (and underserved youth especially) do not serve an important purpose. To the contrary, it is well known, for example, that young people of all backgrounds face difficult challenges, and that programs offering social support and opportunities to develop strategies for dealing with day-to-day issues can be helpful.

Don Hellison's 'Responsibility Model': Steps Toward Peace-Promotion

Don Hellison, a professor at the University of Illinois at Chicago and a long-time leader and mentor in programs for underserved youth, is recognized for developing a set of pedagogical principles intended to help teachers lead sport-related activities that support the holistic development of young people. Although it is largely functionalist in its orientation, as you will see, aspects of Hellison's work are guided by a sociological imagination and a goal of linking theory with (peace-promoting) practices.

Hellison organized his principles and approach into what he calls the 'Teaching Personal and Social Responsibility' (TPSR) model, commonly referred to as the Responsibility Model. The model has been adopted by leaders of sport and physical education programs throughout the US, Canada, New Zealand, England, and elsewhere. His model and influential work are featured in a curriculum guide for physical educators in the Canadian province of Saskatchewan, and appear alongside other related work in a recent document prepared for the United Nations Development program entitled *Harnessing the Power of Sport for Development and Peace: Recommendations to Governments* (Sport for Development and Peace International Working Group, 2008). A TPSR Alliance has been created to connect the community of scholars and practitioners who study, refine, and use the approach, or as the Alliance's mission statement indicates: '[The Alliance] seeks to apply sport and physical activity to youth development in schools and after-school and summer programs through workshops, clinics, publications, and other means—which has led to the development of a TPSR annual conference and website.'[2]

Hellison's (2003) model is based around the idea that through sport-related programming, young people begin to learn about the following principles:

1. respect for the rights and feelings of others
2. participation and effort
3. self-direction
4. caring about and helping others
5. using these values outside of physical education classes

Hellison conceptualizes these five principles as interrelated 'levels of development', and suggests that teachers support young people in their attempts to develop skills relevant to each level.

These principles are fundamentally related to peace in a variety of ways. For example, the first level—respect for the rights and feelings of others—reflects Hellison's concern with young people learning about peaceful forms of conflict resolution, and why nonviolent solutions to problems should be a right. This same level is intended to promote behaviour that is inclusive, and develop an understanding of why being included should also be a right. Level 3—self-direction—includes an emphasis on resisting peer pressure, which is crucial for young people who may (for example) take leadership in anti-bullying interventions, where bystanders are expected to stand-up for others.

Level 4's theme of helping others is based around the development of compassion and empathy for others. This emphasis is also relevant for young people learning to deal with conflict since nonviolent forms of resolution require sensitivity to the feelings and perspectives of others. The theme is also meant to underscore the idea that there is a benefit to supporting others without any expectation of reward, since strong communities are founded on selfless acts of support. At the same time, by encouraging young people to be compassionate and empathic—and seeing results of this encouragement in and outside sport—role models are being developed. With this last point in mind, Level 5 invites program participants to reflect on ways that they can enact—and are enacting—principles 1–4 outside of the sport program or physical education environment. In this way, direct links are made between personal responsibility and awareness of ways to contribute to the community.

While TPSR may be carried out in various ways, there is a consistent set of principles that underlies its implementation. For example, a TPSR-driven program is focused on the young person, not the sport-related activities they are learning. Leaders are encouraged to be sensitive to the social, educational, and economic needs of the young person, as well as the 'cultural differences, developmental needs, and behavioral fluctuations due to the intense pressures' that many young people encounter in their day to day lives (Martinek and Hellison, 1997, p. 42). In this way, a more holistic and context-sensitive approach is encouraged, as young people are treated as resources to be developed, not problems to be solved.

Thinking Critically and Sociologically about the TPSR Model

Many critical sociologists, like Coakley (2002), recognize the value of the functionalist-oriented work of Hellison and his TPSR-inspired colleagues (cf., Hellison et al., 1996; Hellison and Walsh, 2002; Martinek and Hellison, 1997; Martinek et al. 2006), despite the reservations noted earlier. The reason for this recognition is that programs founded on Hellison's TPSR principles are meant to be implemented with a healthy understanding of the strengths and (especially) the limitations of individually-focused programs intended to 'develop' young people. For example, Martinek and Hellison (1997) acknowledge that it is a mistake to see character development and sport involvement as inherently linked—an acknowledgement that has led to the development of well-thought-out strategies for using sport as a tool to promote learning about respectful relationships and conflict resolution. In a similar way, programs inspired by TPSR principles are meant to discourage the blaming of young people for the circumstances in which they find themselves. Blaming is not only unjustified—as many problems encountered by young people can be traced to broader social and political factors, such as 'ineffective schools and social services' and 'meager economic opportunities and unresponsive government'—but youth are, quite simply, not interested in programs that 'blame the victim', 'fix deficiencies', 'or control deviant behavior' (Martinek and Hellison, 1997, p. 42).

For this reason, Hellison and his colleagues urge practitioners to see youth as people who are 'at promise', not 'at risk'. This positive orientation is thought to be more effective in the sense that young people are more likely to develop a sense of autonomy and, in turn, an independent voice when the focus is on their strengths and potential for development. Following this argument, Coakley (2002) suggests that sport programs that inspire autonomy and confidence might be seen as 'sites for enabling young people to become critically informed about their connection to the world and the social, economic and political forces that are at work in the world around them' (p. 27).

Of course, Coakley remains pragmatic about the potential of even the best initiatives, noting that programs that support this level of awareness are quite rare. Still, if we consider that the development of a sense of control over immediate sport settings and personal lives is necessary before one can begin to influence and engage issues in the community at large, then there are good reasons to be supportive of such sport programs.

An Extended Case Study of Theory Meeting Practice: The Mentors in Violence Prevention (MVP) Program

Few violence prevention programs of any kind foreground discussions of mascu-linity. This is unfortunate, because whether the victim is female or male, males commit more than 90 per cent of violent crimes . . . When many of these crimes are examined, we can see that attitudes about manhood are often among the critical variables leading to assault. This is especially obvious in extreme cases of men's violence against women (e.g., rape, battering). Considering this reality, discussing issues of gender, as we do in MVP, should be regarded as a basic com-ponent of any violence prevention program. (Katz, 2005, p. 398)

Jackson Katz is a scholar, activist, educator, and former college football player who has been taking on the issue of male violence in the US since the early 1990s. The Mentors in Violence Prevention (MVP) program he created and leads was 'designed to train student athletes and other student leaders to use their status to speak out against rape, battering, sexual harassment, gay-bash-ing, and all forms of sexist abuse and violence' (Katz, 2006, p. 209). Although in this section I focus on male athletes as both trainers and as the target audience, the overall program includes male and female leaders and audi-ences—all of whom are invited to reflect in various ways on: (a) how norms of masculinity play into the perpetuation of a cycle of violence by men; (b) ways to respond to scenarios where male violence commonly takes place; and (c) how the culture of silence and passivity around these forms of violence can be broken.

Since its inception in the early 1990s, MVP has been 'the most widely uti-lized gender violence prevention model in college athletics—for both men and women' (Katz, 2006, p. 209). The program has been adopted for the training of players, front office staff, and coaches for the New England Patriots and New York Jets NFL teams, the Boston Red Sox Major League Baseball team, as well as Major League Lacrosse. This is in addition to the numerous ses-sions MVP holds for the US Marine Corps, and especially for high school and middle school students around the US.

The program is based around a series of training sessions that are led by an MVP facilitator. The sessions feature a visualization exercise, where those in the audience are asked to close their eyes and visualize a situation where a female who is close to them (e.g., a family member) is in a potentially abusive situation, and where bystanders choose not to intervene. Those in the audi-ence are then asked to comment on their feelings about the bystander, and what they should have done to intervene.

The exercise is intended to highlight the need for men, and in this case high-status male athletes, to be leaders on these issues—and the specific role that bystanders can/must play if incidents of violence against women are to be reduced. The exercise is also intended to trigger a discussion about what those in the audience would do if *they* were a bystander (the facilitators offer a number of common scenarios), and what sorts of interventions are desirable and possible in different contexts. According to Katz, discussions tend to focus on the reasons it is difficult in hypermasculine cultures to intervene in such situations. It is commonly acknowledged in these sessions that certain cultural norms and values protect those who are perpetuators of violence. Such values and norms include: the deeply rooted sexist attitudes that are revealed in disrespectful/misogynist comments about females as sexual objects not deserving of respect or safety; and/or victim-blaming remarks about females who are thought to 'ask for' problems with the way they dress or act.

Katz (2006) notes that answers to questions about 'why many males do not intervene' reveal much about 'the dynamics of male-peer cultures and the pressures on young men to conform' (p. 215). He elaborates:

> For example, many guys admit that they would not be happy to see a guy treat his girlfriend this way [abusively], but they would not say anything. The guy who is abusing his girlfriend might be older than him, or bigger. He might be more popular. People might not think he is 'cool' if he tries to get involved. It is much easier to intervene in theory than it is when the pressure is on, your palms are sweaty and your heart is pounding. (2006, p. 215)

Questions arising from such discussions include:

> 'Why do men hit women? Why do men sexually assault women? How do cultural definitions of manhood contribute to sexual and domestic violence and other sexist behaviors?' Why do some men make it clear that they won't accept this sort of behavior from their peers, while others remain silent? How is the silence of peers understood by abusers? What message is conveyed to victims when abuser's friends don't confront him? Why do some heterosexually identified men harass and beat up gay men? Does the accompanying silence on the part of some of their heterosexual peers legitimize abuse? Why or why not? (Katz, 2006, p. 214)

Theory and Practice in MVP

We can begin to see how, in the MVP program, solutions to the problem of bystander passivity—a form of consent to violence—are built on a set of theoretical foundations and sociological explorations of tolerated violence in all-male peer cultures. For example, the micro-sociological theories described in chapter 2 inform thinking about the ways that young males learn 'appropriate' ways to act in order to be an accepted member of a group (e.g., how they are socialized into cultural groups such as all-male sport teams).

In fact, and as sociologists of sport like Coakley and Donnelly (1999) and Donnelly and Young (1988) reasonably suggest, young athletes are in many cases extremely motivated to learn the ropes and appropriately manage impressions in order to be accepted into sport-related subcultures. Understanding how this takes place—and noting the strong cultural barriers that prevent members from breaking accepted codes of behaviour within these groups (e.g., not undermining high-status members)—is crucial if we are to begin to understand what it means to speak out and act, which must happen if certain forms of physical and cultural violence are to be challenged. This point is even more powerful if we consider McKay's (2002) argument that members of hypermasculine subcultures who commit acts of violence against women and other men should *not* be considered 'psychopathic individuals'. Instead, using sociological theory as a guide, they should be viewed as exhibiting behaviour that is normalized within a context where misogynistic, homophobic, and physically violent acts are common and at times encouraged.

Such an understanding of the dynamics of status hierarchies informed Katz's decision to invite higher-status athletes to be leaders of MVP sessions—since challenges to long-standing and ingrained cultural norms are more likely to be effective when these sorts of individuals are the instigators of change. The rationale around this is encapsulated on Katz's website:

> Why the initial focus on working with student-athletes? Ever since battered women's programs and rape crisis centers established their first educational or 'youth outreach' initiatives in the schools in the 1970s, one of the key challenges they have faced is the apathy, defensiveness—and sometimes outright hostility— of male athletic directors, coaches, and student-athletes. While men and young men in the school-based athletic subculture have hardly been unique in their reluctance to embrace gender violence prevention education, they typically occupy a privileged position in school culture, and particularly in male peer culture. As such, male student-athletes—especially in popular team sports such as football, basketball, hockey, baseball, wrestling, and soccer—tend to have enormous clout when it comes to establishing or maintaining traditional masculine norms. Their support or lack of support for prevention efforts can make or break them.[3]

Existing research around masculinity and identity demonstrates that the sorts of cultural behaviours that support violence are not only learned, but also 'performed' and 'context-dependent'. That is to say, understanding that men act in different ways depending on the context in which they find themselves makes it easier to see that there is nothing natural or unchangeable about violent behaviours (Connell and Messerschmidt, 2005; Millington and Wilson, 2010a). Katz referred to the hypermasculine performances expected of many men as the 'tough guise'—akin to the 'cool pose' that Majors and

Billson (1992) have written about in their work on Black masculinity—as a way of illuminating the fact that such behaviours are not innate, but are a front that is used to impress and fit into cultures where such behaviours are the norm (Jhally, 1999).

Using Theory to Link MVP with Other Strategies for Change: Sport Media and Anti-violence Education

At the same time that a micro-sociological lens can be helpful for considering how to design interventions like MVP, these sorts of programs will only have limited impact if the broader, systemic ways that violence is promoted are not understood and responded to. A most obvious example of a powerful socializing agent that highlights violence-promoting masculinities is mass media. Those who study gender, violence, and media (especially sport media) often describe how these 'violent masculinities' are commonly featured as the most desirable forms of masculinity (Darnell and Wilson, 2006; Messner et al., 2000; McKay et al., 2005; Wilson, 2007b). With this context, consider the potential impacts of messages offered through media productions of professional wrestling, or mixed-martial arts (MMA), like the reality TV show *Bully Beatdown* (on MTV). *Bully Beatdown* features a cage fight between an MMA professional and a 'bully'—who has been identified by one of the bully's victims (who has contacted the show). Although the show includes short segments where the reasons for the bully's behaviour are outlined, the show is ultimately based around the idea that the (usually male) bully 'gets what he deserves' (i.e., he is 'beat down'). An implicit message here, of course, is that the bullying victim (who is also usually male) is not 'man enough' to take care of the problem himself. At least two violence-promoting ideas are featured here. First, it is presumed that physically confronting a bully is a preferred response to the problem. The second message is that victims of bullying (and others) might look to MMA fighters or other models of desirable (hyper)masculinity to bring justice in situations of conflict.

The main point here is that these popular and mass-mediated television sport and entertainment productions feature messages about the 'best' way— or certainly the most 'honourable' or 'manly' way—to resolve conflict: through displays of physical dominance. With this in mind, it should be no mystery as to how such messages may contribute to the problems that MVP and other violence prevention programs are intent on addressing. That is to say, without understanding the mechanisms through which these sorts of messages help generate consent for a dominant understanding of what it means to 'be a man', it is unlikely that interventions like MVP will lead to a tipping point in North American culture, a point where violent masculinities are no longer desirable and dominant.

A Pro-feminist Media Education Program

Sociologist Jim McKay, a leader in the study of masculinity, sport, and media, offers educators a guide for responding to these problems by focusing, in his case, on media and its relationship to broader forces that socialize males and females into accepting the status quo around violence (McKay, 2002). McKay does this in his article 'Teaching Against the Grain: A Learner-Centered, Media-Based, and Profeminist Approach to Gender and Nonviolence in Sport,' where he describes a series of media literacy/education strategies he uses in the classroom to connect theory with practice. One of McKay's pedagogical goals is to inspire students to ask questions about how homophobia, violence, and sexual harassment in sport are framed in media, and how a critical sociologist would frame/interpret the same media. With this background, students can begin to think critically about the sorts of problematic sport-related images that help legitimatize certain forms of violence. McKay (2002)—like Messner and Stevens (2007)—emphasizes in classroom discussions that although most male athletes are not violent towards women and others, we *all* still live together in a culture that is tolerant of and perpetuates various forms of violence, and that sport media is a central part of this culture (see Box 6.2). McKay concludes his session using a clip of a media campaign that features a number of high-profile athletes speaking out against violence against women to trigger a discussion about ways that privileged groups have used (and can use) their position to assist oppressed groups. McKay (2002) offers an insightful reflection on his pedagogical work that speaks to the need to link theories of gender with his own media literacy intervention:

> I have found these strategies useful in stressing that . . . masculinity per se is not the problem, but rather that *a* very restrictive way of being a man is idealized as *the* way that *all* men should act . . . [They similarly stress] that there is nothing inherent in sport that makes men rape women [or denigrate gay men]. Rather, the way in which sports are organized [in part, through the way they are portrayed in media] to glorify violence and devalue and objectify women produces the male 'groupthink' that so often rewards male athletes for their abusive and violent behavior. (p. 111)

McKay's work is pro-feminist in the sense that: (a) it is critical—it is intended to provoke questions about and raise awareness about how unequal power relations are perpetuated, and go unquestioned; and (b) the questions that drive McKay's intervention are informed by an understanding of the sociological research that has uncovered some of the nuances of gender-based inequalities in various contexts. That is to say, and as with other critical pedagogical work, McKay's assumption is that people must understand how cultural norms around masculinity are perpetuated (e.g., in sport media, and in

Box 6.2 ❖ Why Focus on Male *Athlete* Violence?

In their compelling and instructive article 'Scoring Without Consent', Messner and Stevens (2007) note that in recent years incidents of sexual violence by male athletes against women have begun to receive a great deal of attention in mass media and increasingly through programs like MVP. This raises the question, why male athletes?

While acknowledging that ongoing research is needed—and that male athletes are certainly not the only men who commit or are complicity involved in violence, and that 'the vast majority of male athletes *do not engage* in violence against women'—Messner and Stevens (2007) argue that this is not a reason to ignore the idea that peer group dynamics of male sport teams contribute to a culture where certain forms of 'misogyny, homophobia and violence' are deemed acceptable (p. 110). They go on to argue that 'it is important to confront male athletes' violence against women because the world of sport is a key institutional site for the construction of hegemonic masculinity, and thus a key potential site for its contestation' (p. 10).

With this in mind, Messner and Stevens (2007) summarize themes drawn from social science literature that help explain how it is that certain all-male sport team environments are places where sexual violence may be enabled—where a 'rape culture' exists. They refer, for example, to:

- The role of competitive, homophobic, and misogynist talk and joking in the form of 'dominance bonding' in the athletic peer group
- The 'culture of silence' among peers, in families, and in the community that enables men's sexual violence against women (Messner and Stevens, 2007, p. 111; cf., Kirby, Greaves, and Hankivsky, 2000)

Benford (2007) and Engle Folchert (2008) also note that the sport-related rape culture exists because it is enabled by a 'lack of appropriate institutional response to incidences of sexual assault' (Engle Folchert, 2008, p. 20). An example of this, according to Benford (2007), was the apparent cover-ups and attempts to downplay by officials at the University of Nebraska at Lincoln in the early and mid-1990s, who were apparently protecting members of the university's highly successful football team who were involved in physical and sexual assaults on women. The idea here is that a culture of privilege and invincibility is (re)produced when male athletes are shielded from the usual consequences for such behaviours, which, in turn, perpetuates this rape culture (Rozee and Koss, 2001).

many hypermasculine sport contexts) if they are to devise strategies for undermining these norms, and thus interrupting cycles of gender-based violence of all kinds. The term 'pro-feminist' is sometimes used instead of 'feminist' by McKay and others who work on gender-based violence and similar issues in an attempt to acknowledge the important role that men can play in the movement toward reducing gender-based violence and related problems, while at the same time noting that the feminist movement is in many respects grounded in and based around the experiences of women—and thus should not be taken over by men. These distinctions remain subject to debates about the use of such biologically deterministic understandings of 'women' and 'men' (debates related to, for example, the positioning of transgender and transsexual people in these movements), and about the role men can and should play in the feminist movement more generally.

Jackson Katz similarly recognizes the importance of media in his work, and takes on problems around masculinity and media in an educational video called *Tough Guise: Violence, Media & the Crisis in Masculinity* (Jhally, 1999) which features Katz as narrator. The video and accompanying instructor's manual are designed to support media literacy training for those intent on exploring the role and impact of violent masculinities in mass media, and how (through understanding the prominence and prevalence of these images) men and women can begin to address problems associated with them. Again, a theoretical understanding of how violence comes to be associated with manhood—and how this linkage becomes taken for granted and thus consented to—is the basis for a (video-based) intervention intended to counter this hegemonic understanding. At the same time, and crucially, *Tough Guise* explores the possibilities for alternative models of masculinity that are based around non-violence and a respect for others. Katz refers to male role models in sport and music who freely undermine the 'tough guise' persona, including former Major League Baseball power-hitters Sammy Sosa and Mark Maguire who had an unconventionally supportive relationship with one another in their joint pursuit of the home-run record in 1998. He refers also to soul music legend Marvin Gaye, who was known to combine a respectful and sensitive form of masculinity with his powerful anti-war messages.

Evaluating Change

There are many ways that critically oriented research, education, and activism are integrated in the MVP program and others like it. Having said this, and although there is some evidence that the MVP program in particular has been effective in altering attitudes to and understandings of violence—and apparently changing behaviours[4]—continued evaluation of the long-term and institutional impacts of programs like MVP are needed. This is particularly important, because if sport teams or schools implement a program like

MVP—and the program has little or no impact on the underlying factors that perpetuate violence—then the publicized implementation of MVP could lead to the perception that the problem is being addressed, *when in fact the root causes and contextual factors have not been deal with*. Messner and Stevens (2007) encapsulate this crucial point as follows:

> We suspect that interventions that are not organically linked to longer term institutional attempts to address men's violence at its psychological, peer group, and organizational roots will have little if any effect. At their best, such programs may provide a context in which some individuals will be empowered to remove themselves from the role of passively complicit (but not fully comfortable) participants in the daily practices that feed rape culture . . . In fact], intervention programs that do not address these contextual factors are unlikely to radically alter the annual reproduction of sport as a pedagogical site for boys and men's learning of violence against women [and I will add, other men]. (p. 119)

Educator and/or Public Intellectual? Reflecting on the Roles and Responsibilities of the Sociologist of Sport

This final comment from Michael Messner, a sociologist at the University of Southern California, and his co-author Mark Stevens, a clinical psychologist specializing in men's violence prevention—both of whom have been involved in violence prevention interventions with men's athletic teams—invites thinking about the role and (perhaps) responsibility of researchers to make a difference through various forms of peace-related educational and activist work. Authors like Sugden (2007) argue that it is important for sociologists to do something about pressing concerns around violence and other issues, and that sport-related interventions can be helpful. In a similar way, Michael Atkinson and Kevin Young (2008), leaders in the study of sport, violence, and social problems, similarly assert that sociologists of sport should matter in the public sphere, in public education venues—that they should be taking on issues like player violence, and the abuse and exploitation of athletes and animals, through policy intervention, within public debate, and other contexts for awareness-raising (cf., Carrington, 2007). These sorts of arguments for a critical sociology that matters underlie a cultural studies imperative—to link theory with various forms of practice (Andrews and Giardina, 2008).

On the other hand, and as Bairner (2009b) powerfully argues, there are real constraints for many academic-educators when it comes to doing critical educational work that may adversely impact their career advancement. Community-action research like that conducted by Frisby et al. requires the development of trust and long-term relationships with collaborators— collaborators who are not invested in the same academic outcomes that are demanded of scholars (e.g., peer-reviewed publications). Such engagement may be discouraged for university research-educators, those who are often evaluated according to how many articles they produce, with less emphasis on other (often less easily measured) contributions.

Moreover, the kinds of critical pedagogy promoted by Freire and others demands a form of education that is not top-down, not dictated by power relationships between instructors and students. This is challenging work, since people always come to relationships (educational or otherwise) with social positions that already impact how they engage with others. As Frisby et al. (2007) note, it is easy to fall into traditional top-down relationships between privileged and oppressed, where the 'teaching' is one-way, where one group has the knowledge and the other does not.

All this to say, there is need to remain reflective about how peace education is implemented in different contexts, and the enabling and potentially problematic consequences of these challenging—but crucially important—interventions. With such challenges in mind, the next chapter's discussion of international development and sport begins to examine the role of peace education and other development efforts in countries of the Global South.

Notes

1. We can begin to see here how Freire's arguments are akin to those made by Michel Foucault and Antonio Gramsci, as both authors spoke (albeit in distinct ways) about how oppressive conditions come to be taken for granted, unquestioned, and perhaps 'consented to'.

2. Quoted from www.tpsr-alliance.org.

3. Taken from: www.jacksonkatz.com/aboutmvp.html.

4. Ongoing evaluations of the MVP program can be found at: www.sportinsociety. org/vpd/mvp.php.

Discussion Questions

1. What forms of peace education are you aware of that take place outside of traditional school contexts? What advantages are there to pedagogy in alternative contexts?

2. How could forms of critical pedagogy be built into physical education?

3. What obligations (if any) should sociologists of sport have to make a difference, beyond doing basic forms of sociological research?

Suggested Readings ···

Frisby, W., Reid, C. & Ponic, P. (2007). Levelling the playing field: Promoting the health of poor women through a community development approach to recreation. In P. White & K. Young (Eds.), *Sport and gender in Canada* (pp. 121–36). Don Mills, ON: Oxford University Press. A thought-provoking and informative overview of a feminist participatory action research project intended to address the problem of access to recreation, social isolation, and other social and health issues for a diverse group of low-income women, including single mothers, women with a disability, older women, and recent immigrants.

Howell, J., Andrews, D. & Jackson, S. (2002). Cultural studies and sport studies: An interventionist practice. In J. Maguire & K. Young (Eds.), *Theory, sport & society* (pp. 151–77). New York, NY: JAI. A reflection on ways to make a difference and intervene when injustices are recognized through critical sociological work.

Katz, J. (2005) Reconstructing masculinity in the locker room: the mentors in violence prevention project. In P. Leistyna (Ed.), *Cultural studies: From theory to action.* (pp. 397–407). Malden, MA: Blackwell. A reflection on issues around men's violence more generally, and an anti-violence education program.

McKay, J. (2002). Teaching against the grain: A learner-centered, media-based, and profeminist approach to gender and nonviolence in sport. In M. Gatz, M. Messner, & S. Ball-Rokeach (Eds.), *Paradoxes of youth and sport* (pp. 103–18). Albany, NY: SUNY Press. A reflection on a media education strategy intended to raise awareness about how sport media is implicated in the perpetuation of violence.

Messner, M. & Stevens, M. (2007). Scoring without consent: Confronting male athletes' violence against women. In M. Messner (Author), *Out of play: Critical essays on gender and sport* (pp. 107–19). Albany, NY: SUNY. A reflection on issues around male athletes' violence against women, and an anti-violence education program.

Wright, J. (2004). Analysing sportsmedia texts: Developing resistant reading positions. In J. Wright, D. Macdonald & L. Burrows (Eds.), *Critical inquiry and problem-solving in physical education* (pp. 183–96). London: Routledge. An excellent guide to teaching and thinking about media literacy and sport media.

Relevant Websites ···

Mentors in Violence Prevention Website and Jackson's Katz's homepage.
www.jacksonkatz.com/mvp.html
> This website includes a wealth of resources related to Gender Violence Prevention Education & Training and background on prominent anti-violence educator Jackson Katz.

Media Education Foundation—'Tough Guise'
http://mediaed.org/videos/MediaGenderAndDiversity/ToughGuise
> This foundation produces and distributes video documentaries to encourage
> critical thinking and debate about social issues, including those related to sport,
> gender, and media. The specific link is for the video *Tough Guise: Violence, Media*
> *and the Crisis in Masculinity.*

Canadian Writers in Person (feature on *FrontRunners*)
http://cwip.artmob.ca/contributors/front_runners
> This webpage features a write-up on and video featuring the play and film
> *FrontRunners* (written by sport journalist Laura Robinson), described in the
> chapter. According to the website, '*FrontRunners* deals with a true story of ten
> aboriginal boys who were chosen to carry the torch to the 1967 Pan Am Games
> in Winnipeg. Nine of the ten young men chosen for the 1967 Pan Am Games
> torch run were from residential schools.'

Teaching Responsibility Through Physical Activity (TPSR) website
www.tpsr-alliance.org
> This is the home website for an alliance of physical educators who apply Don
> Hellison's TPSR approach to teaching respect, nonviolence through physical
> education.

Key Terms

conscientization refers to promoting awareness about how current systems of
domination and oppression operate, and awareness of ways that one is implicated
in and impacted by these systems and operations.

critical pedagogy refers to the educational approach that is used to promote
awareness about how current systems of domination and oppression operate (i.e.,
to promote conscientization) and inspire thinking about ways that this awareness
can inform strategies of action. These strategies of action are conceptualized
as constructive responses to and challenges of these systems, guided by pro-
democratic principles.

critical performance pedagogy (a.k.a., spectacle pedagogy) the use
of dramatic and evocative theatre performances, film, poetry, dance, and
experimental/evocative writing to inspire critical thinking about and action on
issues, with the broader goal of promoting 'a radically progressive democratic
consciousness' (Giardina, 2005, p. 159).

participatory action research (PAR) refers to a type of research project that
is, among other things, a collaboration between the researchers and those
being researched—such that all of those being studied in the project become
researchers and leaders in the project's design. The assumption underlying a
non-hierarchical approach to the study of widespread social inequalities is that all
members of the collaboration are learning about power, poverty, and oppression
through the research. A social action and transformative component is central to
such pro-democracy projects.

peace education refers to teaching about peace, which includes teaching about
what peace is, reasons for the absence of peace in particular situations, and

ways to achieve forms of peace. Harris (2004, p. 6) notes that peace education refers also to 'challenges of achieving peace, developing non-violent skills and promoting peaceful attitudes' (Harris, 2004, p. 6). Types of peace education include: conflict resolution education; international education; environmental education; human rights education; global education; development education; and critical pedagogy (Harrison, 2004).

praxis refers to the process of attempting to understand and explain social problems and the workings of the social world (and becoming aware of how current systems of domination and oppression operate)—and using this information to act on and ultimately transform the social world.

PART IV

Key Topics and Pressing Concerns in Sport and Peace: International Development, the Environment, and Media

7

Reflections on Intervention and Imperialism in the Sport for (International) Development and Peace Industry

Questions to Consider

- What is the meaning of the terms 'development' and 'international development' and how do they relate to sport and peace?
- What types of sport for development and peace initiatives are there, and what are their various goals?
- What does the term 'social capital' mean and how can it be used to explain the effectiveness of (and problems with) programs like the Mathare Youth Sports Association in Nairobi?
- In what ways can a sociological imagination guide the work of those leading a conflict transformation intervention?
- What are the relationships between neo-liberalization, post-colonialism, and sport-related international work?
- Are there reasons to be cautious about sport for development and peace interventions?

Introduction: Exploring Tensions around Sport and International Development

For many observers, the sport–peace relationship is embodied in the work of the humanitarian organization Right To Play (RTP)—an organization that uses sport as a means to facilitate conflict resolution in war-torn environments, to support children and prevent disease in areas of immense poverty, and to promote community development more generally. With 50 employees in its headquarters in Toronto and 450 staff that support programs in regions of Africa, Asia, the Middle East, and South America (Jermyn, 2010), Right To Play stands out in the **sport for** (international) **development and peace** (SDP) field for its success in making a difference in the lives of underserved groups. It also stands out for its ability to be economically sustainable in a sector where many organizations are engaged in an ongoing battle for survival.

This success is due in no small part to the passionate and savvy entrepreneurial work of RTP's founder, President, and CEO Johann Olav Koss, himself an Olympic speed skating legend. With Koss's skill in marketing RTP as both a humanitarian organization as well as a brand—with name recognition, a desirable image, well-publicized support from celebrity athlete-ambassadors, and endorsements from respected political figures like Canadian diplomat Stephen Lewis—it is no wonder that RTP has secured sponsorships from powerful corporations like Mitsubishi and Microsoft.

However, and at the same time that RTP is respected for its leadership and achievements in the sport for development and peace field, the organization—along with a range of other successful SDP NGOs that have emerged in recent years—has become a target and reference point for those who see many disconcerting, yet under-reported, problems with this style of international development. Sociologists like Darnell (2007, 2010a, 2010b), Giulianotti (2006), Levermore (2009), Coalter (2010), and Black (2010), for example, have written thought-provoking articles on ways that the sport-related international development work of RTP and others might not be as progressive as their promotional campaigns would suggest—and that these organizations continue to face many barriers as the SDP 'industry' develops through its infancy (Hayhurst and Frisby, 2010; Kidd, 2010).

In this chapter I explore these tensions. I do this, first, by outlining and considering the myriad ways that sport for development and peace work is carried out. In doing so, I examine approaches to conflict resolution and community-building that inform the work of some groups, and discuss two case studies of SDP programs. I then outline the range of concerns and critiques that are commonly expressed about international SDP work. This includes a look at assumptions about the 'power of sport' that drive some SDP work, the potential post-colonial features of SDP work, and issues around the evaluation of SDP programs. I also reflect on ways that some SDP work might be considered an accomplice to neo-liberal developments thought by many critics to perpetuate some of the same problems SDP is designed to address.

Sport in International Development: What It Looks Like and What It Is

In the first chapter of this book, I referred to the rise of not only the number international SDPs that have come into existence over the past several years (cf., Levermore, 2009), but also the range of organizations and people that have come to associate themselves with the SDP movement. This includes: corporations like Puma, Adidas, and Nike; governmental development agencies (like Canada's CIDA—the Canadian International Development Association); multilateral organizations like the United Nations and the Commonwealth; sport leagues and federations like the NBA, FIFA, FIBA, and the IOC; as well as the many athletes, students, and interested youth who are now pursuing research and volunteer work in international SDP contexts (cf., Akindes and Kirwin, 2009; Black, 2010).

There are also various types of these programs, including what Levermore and Beacom (2009) term 'sport plus' and 'plus sport' development programs. **'Sport plus' programs** are driven by the idea that promoting skill development and excellence in sport is linked with positive social and economic outcomes outside the sporting realm (Coalter, 2009; Levermore, 2008; Levermore and Beacom, 2009, p. 9). FIFA's Goal Program, which is intended to support 'national football programs and athletes that are presently unable to support themselves', is an example of this type (Akindes and Kirwin, 2009, p. 228).

'Plus sport' programs, on the other hand, are mandated to directly promote various forms of social development, with sport simply being a tool to assist in the achievement of these outcomes (e.g., disease prevention or reconciliation). Right To Play is this type of program, as is Kicking Aids Out, a program that uses to soccer as a forum for peer education about HIV/AIDS and its prevention (Nicholls, 2009).

In Bruce Kidd's (2007, pp. 178–80) overview of the best practices among sport and peace–related initiatives, he offers a more specific outline of the various and often interrelated goals of organizations attempting to promote peace. These include:

- **To promote relationship building and reconciliation**—For example, the Run for Peace event held in Iten, Kenya in 2008, described in chapter 5, was organized by celebrity athletes/runners, local community members, and the NGO Shoe4Africa following the inter-tribal violence that took place during the elections in late 2007. The event was intended to help young people and others in the community affected by the violence to move forward and build cross-tribe relationships. The Football 4 Peace intervention (described later in this chapter) is similarly intended to build relationships between Arab and Jewish youth in Israel.
- **To promote a truce or the cessation of hostilities**—The Olympic Truce, initially designed to allow athletes safe passage to the Games, is a celebrated example of this. The Truce has at times been successful, as the IOC and United Nations have worked together to, for example, negotiate a temporary ceasefire in Bosnia during the 1994 Olympic Games in Lillehammer. As Kidd (2007) notes, that particular ceasefire 'allowed for the vaccination of an estimated 10,000 children' (p. 178).
- **To protect children**—Programs that raise awareness about child safety in and around sport are examples of this. The RespectED violence and abuse prevention program offered by the Canadian Red Cross does pedagogical work in sport contexts (e.g., minor hockey associations). Armstrong (2004) and Kidd (2007) refer to a football league in Liberia (run by Don Bosco missionaries) that promotes awareness around domestic and physical abuse of young people more generally.
- **To provide peace education of all kinds** (see chapter 6)

- **To rehabilitate victims of war, including refugees and child soldiers**. Right To Play in particular is known for their work using sport to promote psycho-social health for these groups.
- **To offer remembrance of and reflection on tragic events**. Kidd (2007) refers to an invitational basketball tournament that takes place in the Great Lakes region of Rwanda as an example of an event intended to remember a star basketball player—Gisembe Ntarugera Emmanual—who was killed during the 1994 genocide. The event is also intended to bring together inter-ethnic teams in friendly competition. The event is accompanied by community theatre performances and public speeches that inspire reflections on and lessons learned from the event.

Defining International Development

One of the central debates within development studies revolves around a basic and underlying question —'What is meant by international development?' Seemingly straightforward responses to this question include, 'processes by which there is an attempt to improve life chances throughout the world but particularly in countries considered to be low income' (Levermore and Beacom, 2009, p. 7), or 'the organized intervention in collective affairs according to a standard of improvement' (Pieterse, 2001, p. 3; cf., Black, 2010). In a report prepared for the Sport for Development and Peace International Working Group (SDPIWG), Kidd (2007) draws heavily on literature provided by the United Nations Development Programme (UNDP) to define the term—pointing to the use of 'development' to describe attempts to improve the 'well-being' of populations. Kidd notes how a Human Development Index (HDI) has been devised by the UNDP as a measurement tool that gives analysts a gauge as to how well a population is developing; to 'measure improvements in the quality of life of humans' (p. 163). The measure is focused around: life expectancy; knowledge (based on literacy and education scales); and standard of living (based on per capita purchasing power scales) (Kidd, 2007, p. 163; cf., Human Development Report, 2006, p. 394). Kidd (2007) also indicates how, more recently, measures that emphasize differences between the standards of living for the 'most well-off' and 'least well-off' within countries are being taken into account, noting that these disparities are relevant for understanding health, well-being, and social relations in these contexts.

Still others, like political scientist David Black of Dalhousie University in Halifax, Nova Scotia, describe development as a process that could be considered large scale and top-down and/or small scale and bottom-up. Large-scale and top-down interventionist work is commonly initiated by Western-based agencies *for* countries believed to be in need of development, what Darnell (2010a) and others refer to as the Global South and Low and Middle Income

Countries (LMICs). While such work is associated with the interventions of groups like Right To Play that initiate and carry out programs in LMICs, it is most obviously related to the awarding of sport mega-events like the FIFA World Cup or the Olympics to such countries. That is to say, the awarding of a major sporting event to China, South Africa, or Argentina is framed as a development project to the extent that the work that is needed to host such an event requires countries to make progress in areas like housing, transportation, human rights, and the environment. There is also, of course, an oft-debated assumption that that the economic boost associated with hosting the event will help a country move forward on issues around poverty and inequality (Cornelisen, 2008, 2009). Although 'development' used in this way commonly refers to benefits accrued by LMICs, the same sorts of arguments are made around bids to host events in places like Vancouver or London, since the economic, social, and environmental benefits that are linked with such events also apply in these contexts.

Small-scale and bottom-up development projects, on the other hand, are grassroots projects that are initiated in underserved areas *by* those in a local community to address any number of issues. Projects intended to, for example, support the health of young people or build a sense of community following conflict would be examples of this. As Black (2010) notes, however, the line between bottom-up and top-down is commonly blurred when it comes to this sort of development work:

> [M]uch of the work of organizations such as the Mathare Youth Sports Association (MYSA), Right To Play, and Athletes for Africa/Gulu Walk consists of small-scale, community-level interventions in rural and marginalized urban communities or refugee/Internally Displaced Persons (IDP) camps. Yet much of it also depends on the support of large official development agencies and/or the profile and resources generated by transnational linkages and celebrity 'athlete ambassadors'. (p. 123)

In this observation Black recognizes the various connections that exist between those working in grassroots movements for change, and the broader/ structural factors that frame the activities of movement-members—a point I return to later.

Issues and Ambiguities around Development

There are many controversial features of the development concept. For example, and as Kidd (2007) notes, there is no straightforward way of determining what forms of development are appropriate for a given country or what the appropriate roles are for foreigners in the development of another country. Black's (2010) and Cornellisen's (2008, 2009) examinations of sporting mega-events as development projects are interesting here because if *all* countries (i.e., even wealthier countries like Canada, that sometimes host events like the Olympics) can derive economic, social, and environmental benefits from hosting such games, then *all countries are 'still developing'*, although some are considered more developed than others (using measures like the Human Development Index).

The salient point here is that the framing of international development work—as 'developed' countries helping 'underdeveloped' ones—presumes that developed countries do not have major social problems and inequalities of their own and, moreover, that they are more 'advanced' (a word with a much more loaded connotation) than developing countries. Darnell (2010a), following Hardt and Negri (2000, p. 282), suggests that it is more accurate to think of developed countries and developing ones (i.e., LMICs) as being in 'distinct situations' that are circumscribed by the radically different social and cultural contexts within which they exist, instead of thinking about international relations in terms of a competition measured according to linear economic and social developments, with the finish line being a country's 'arrival' into the developed world.

Another problem with a developed versus developing understanding of the world's countries is that it presumes that there is little that underdeveloped countries have to offer developed ones (i.e., that only the Global North/First World has access to the resources and knowledge helpful for addressing social problems and building community)—an assumption that negates the important experiences and local knowledge that exist within all cultures and contexts. Others raise concerns about the often taken-for-granted assumptions that: (a) development work is equated with progress, and especially with success in enhancing health, community-building, and so on in targeted countries and contexts; and (b) that the most desirable and effective strategy for achieving development goals more broadly is within a neo-liberal system of governance.

Regarding the first point, Black (2010) and others have documented instances where development-focused interventions were not only ineffective, but also extremely harmful:

Perhaps the most disturbing contemporary example is Rwanda which . . . was widely portrayed as a developmental 'success story' virtually right up to the genocide of 1994, and in which development policies and projects both failed to anticipate the possibility for genocidal violence, and contributed to the conditions from which it emerged. However, scholars in rich and 'highly developed' countries such as Canada need think no further than the tragic legacies of interventive development in our own First Nations communities to appreciate its risks and dangers. (Black, 2010, p. 123)

Regarding the second point, development scholars have noted in recent years how a 'development through neo-liberalization' approach has become dominant, which in this case means that international institutions like the World Bank have been guided by the view that LMICs should receive financial aid only on the condition that they adopt particular policies that will encourage their participation in a global economy. Critics—including former chief economist for the World Bank and Nobel Prize winner Joseph Stiglitz (2002)—demonstrate how such policies have had devastating effects on the economies of many LMICs. Stiglitz explains how a study of the particular contexts and economies where these problems occurred should have tipped off decision makers, who should have understood that opening markets under certain conditions is risky and dangerous. Put simply, a neo-liberal approach, according to critically oriented economists, should not be considered a one size fits all strategy for development. Han-Joon Chang (2008), an economist at the University of Cambridge, follows this point in his description of how South Korea made immense strides in their economic development from the early 1960s to present by *not* participating in the world market, by protecting local industries from global forces that might undermine development.

Of course, serious concerns remain about the implications of what many might consider to be successful neo-liberalization, as I discussed in chapters 4 and 5. This is pertinent for thinking about international sport for development and peace efforts because NGOs like Right To Play are, in fact, participants in a neo-liberal response to problems related to conflict and AIDS that exist in some LMICs (Wilson and Hayhurst, 2009). I reiterate here the description of ways that the work of some SDP NGOs could be considered forms of ironic activism—or perhaps, in this context, ironic development.

'On the Ground' with Sport for Development and Peace NGOs: Connecting Theory and Practice

Remembering back to chapter 2, we considered how the Susan G. Komen Race for the Cure was shown to be an important and empowering event for many participants and a success in raising funds for and awareness about an important social and health issue. At the same time, we used a cultural studies sensibility and a sociological imagination to help us see how this event—on one level effective in achieving particular goals—was, on another level, problematic because of its reliance on a corporatized approach to solving social problems that is, according to many critics, less democratic than other approaches. In the following sections, I work through and across these different levels in order to explore how sociologists have evaluated and understood on the ground interventions in the SDP industry. As you will see, the sorts of contradictions that emerged in King's analysis are also evident here.

The Power of Sport? Guiding Principles in the Sport of Development and Peace Movement

Sport, with its joys and triumphs, its pains and defeats, its emotions and challenges, is an unrivalled medium for the promotion of education, health, development and peace. Sport helps us demonstrate, in pursuit of the betterment of humanity, that there is more that unites us than divides us.

> Adolph Ogi, former UN Special Adviser on Sport for
> Development and Peace (United Nations, n.d., p.2)

Quotations like this one embody a particular optimism about the power of sport that underlies the activities of many who work in and around sport-driven international development work. That Adolph Ogi, former United Nations Special Advisor, made this statement is especially pertinent as it represents how SDP work has come to be aligned with human rights related initiatives, and the pursuit of the Millennium Development Goals that were set out by world leaders at the Millennium Summit in New York in 2000 (United Nations, 2003). In fact, the name Right To Play should alert us to this mutually beneficial relationship between particular sport-related NGOs and the UN.

Such quotations are also meant to inspire, as are the oft-publicized success stories associated with the work of SDP practitioners. Such a story was told by Benjamin Nzobonankira—a former child refugee from Burundi who was introduced to Right To Play's programs while living in a refugee camp in Northern Tanzania—at a panel discussion about Sport, Peace, and Development that took place during the Vancouver 2010 Olympics:

In 2001, while at school in this refugee camp, I was introduced to sport activities by Right To Play. Right To Play arrived at a sensitive time. Youth in the camp were facing many political problems. Many of them were being recruited to follow rebel groups fighting in Burundi. Right To Play programs gave them an alternative. Some youth, including myself, chose to be involved in sport and play activities instead of fighting. Looking back, I believe this was a very wise decision. Sport was the only thing that gave me relief and allowed me to relax. When I played sport, things felt normal again. The stress, anxiety and depression which affected me were reduced. By playing sport, my friends and I were able to laugh and have fun and to live peacefully together. Working as a community volunteer, I participated in many Right To Play activities. From this, I learned about tolerance. Before being introduced to sport, I could not make sense of the hell of exile that deprived me of my education and all the essentials of life for almost 15 years. But, by the power of sport, I was able to overcome these difficulties. I learned how to accept people's differences and I acquired key life skills that gave me the confidence to set future goals.[1]

Such portrayals of SDP work are useful for both articulating how programs like Right To Play, at their best, can support peace-related goals, and for 'selling' the movement to potential donors and others who may want to get involved. Speaking to the latter point, if we remember back to discussions about social movements in chapter 5, we can see how such stories help create a master narrative that draws together a basic logic (that sport promotes peace) and a set of emotions (about the hope that sport can provide in dire circumstances). Such a narrative, when constructed in such a way, is powerful and difficult to deny.

Of course, and although these stories are commonly based around an uncritical functionalist understanding of sport, it is not as though there are not well-founded reasons why sport is commonly associated with the sorts of positive outcomes described by Nzobonankira. In fact, for practitioners and researchers interested in why this is, sociological theories and concepts have been quite helpful.

Social Capital and the Mathare Youth Sports Association

Among the most powerful concepts that sociologists and others use to inform sport-related development work (international work and otherwise) is **social capital**. Although prominent sociologists James Coleman (1988), Robert Putnam (2000), and Pierre Bourdieu (1986) each have their own unique take on social capital, a basic and uncontroversial definition of the concept is offered by Fred Coalter (2008), who describes the concept as comprising: 'social networks based on social and group norms, which enable people to trust one another and via which individuals or groups can obtain certain types of advantage' (p. 44). In their study of social capital and sport, Harvey et al. (2007, drawing on Putnam, 2000) described three central elements of social capital: (1) *bonding* social capital, which refers to relationships between individuals within homogenous groups (e.g., a sport team or a club); (2) *bridging* social capital, which refers to relationships 'across horizontal social divisions, such as those across teams within a league'; and (3) *linking* social capital, 'referring to ties between different social groups of society; for example, citizens from all social groups who are fans of their local professional football club' (Harvey et al., 2007, p. 208).

Working from this definition, many scholars and practitioners see sport as a forum where the social networks so integral to building social capital can be developed. When strong networks exist, so the argument goes, there is also likely to be: (a) a heightened level of trust between individuals in these networks; (b) a greater sense of reciprocity; and (c) a greater capacity to collectively support and offer resources to one another. Put simply, when people begin to work together in an efficient and effective manner—a process enabled by connection and trust—people are better supported on a number of fronts. According to Putnam's model, such associations with trusted others will likely motivate people to volunteer their time in the community out of a sense of reciprocity and interest in the collective good.

Coalter (2008, 2009) makes the case that certain sport-related programs are especially effective at building social capital within particular communities. To demonstrate this, he refers to one of the most celebrated sport for development and peace programs, the Mathare Youth Sports Association (MYSA) run out of Mathare, a slum area in northeast Nairobi, Kenya. The program, initiated by Canadian-born United Nations officer Bob Munroe in 1987 and currently based around a set of soccer leagues with over 17,000 members (aged 10–18) on 1,000 teams, is 'the largest youth organization in Africa' (Hognestad and Tollisen, 2004, p. 211). It is a 'sport plus' program, as the development work emerges from the playing of and skill development in sport, although this program has particular features that are intended to foster social capital. For example, the program:

1. links sport with community service—as members of all teams are required to commit to community service, which often includes litter cleanup in the local area (teams earn league points for completed cleanup projects).
2. positions youth as key decision-makers, coaches, and organizational leaders in the league.
3. offers leadership awards and educational scholarships to those in the league who make major volunteer contributions to MYSA (adapted from Coalter, 2008).

The program was also designed to offer young women a chance to participate, which is notable in a social and cultural context where they are commonly isolated from experiences in the public sphere. Coalter (2008) explains the thinking behind the use of soccer for this sensitive task:

> Although the subordinate economic and social positioning [of young women] (reinforced via often strong parental and community opposition to their participation) presents ongoing recruitment and retention difficulties, flexible programming and other measures are adopted to enable participation as players and, even more importantly, as peer leaders and coaches within the organization . . . The concentration on soccer can be regarded both as pragmatic and as an attempt to use a presumed male preserve to challenge gender stereotypes. (p. 49)

The various activities noted above are attempts to build social capital in the sense that they are about creating investments not only in the SDP organization, but also in the community. In a similar way, by promoting the idea that participation in the soccer league goes along with an obligation to give something back (through volunteer work in the league *and* the community), a sense of reciprocity is being fostered. At the same time, and by recipro-cally rewarding young volunteers with educational scholarships and valu-able socialization experiences in a safe and supportive community, MYSA is 'capacity building' and 'producing citizens', as Coalter (2008, p. 49) puts it. Some of the arguments here might remind you of the communitarian per-spective outlined in chapter 4, as that perspective is based around these very ideas—of building trust, encouraging reciprocity, and fostering capacity in communities.

Reflections on Theory and Practice around MYSA

We have begun to see how a theoretical understanding of ways that social capital is built within and through sport might inform SDP work, like that conducted by MYSA. Despite this optimism, Coalter and others are also quick to acknowledge the problems with and ambiguities around the social capital concept, and reasons to be cautious about the success of programs like MYSA. The most notable limitation is that such interventions that are meant to 'include' people, always, at the same time, exclude some. In fact, influential sociologist Pierre Bourdieu (1984, 1986) identified ways that the social capital concept is always tied to other forms of capital (e.g., economic capital and cultural capital) and thus the benefits accrued from certain asso-ciations—and the access one has to such associations—are never guaranteed or equal. Supporting this view, Harvey et al. (2007) found in their study of sport volunteers in Canada that boys and men have greater access to cer-tain forms of social capital through sport than do girls and women. With this in mind, we might ask 'Who benefits most from programs like MYSA, and do these programs create or exacerbate existing forms of exclusion or inequality?'

Pursuing these sorts of questions, Priscilla Wamucii (2007), in her research on perceptions of MYSA by program participants and their parents, notes that despite creative efforts to include young women in MYSA, only so much can be done by this one program. That is to say, MYSA exists in a context where women are more socially isolated than men, are disadvantaged economically and socially, and face barriers related to safety (e.g., travelling from MYSA programs after dark). They also negotiate their participation in MYSA in a sit-uation where long-standing and traditional belief systems lead some parents and others to discourage female sport involvement more generally (cf., Brady and Kahn, 2002; Coalter, 2009; Wamucii, 2007). In this way, possessing lower of levels of capital in non-sport contexts is constraining for young women, and explains why many remain excluded from MYSA (cf., Hayhurst, Frisby, and MacNeill, 2011; Kay, 2011; Saavedra, 2009).

Others question whether an incentive system for giving back to the com-munity (like the one favoured by MYSA) actually promotes trust and altruism, as Putnam (2000) would suggest, or whether participants are working in their own self-interest, doing what is necessary to attain access to MYSA and the resources that go along with it. This latter view aligns with Coleman's (1988) understanding of social capital as being based around a rational choice model that emphasizes the *extrinsic* rewards that come with particular behaviours. Although this distinction might seem unimportant, I would emphasize here that if the citizens that are 'produced' through a program like MYSA are driven largely by self-interest, then the kinds of volunteer associations that are fostered might not continue through adulthood for graduates of the program/intervention.

With these sorts of concerns in mind, development scholars like Levermore and Beacom (2009) point out that little is known about the long-term impact of programs like MYSA on the participants and volunteers who have moved on. Of course, and understanding that these programs commonly rely on competitive funding from external sources, it should perhaps be unsurprising that such organizations might not risk doing assessments (or reporting findings from such assessments) that might be unflattering, since assessments like these could make the program a less desirable investment for a donor. Counting the number of people involved in programs is the most straightforward and predictable way to assess exposure while the apparent impacts can be publicized through favourable success stories and anecdotes. In such instances though, little is really known about the lasting impacts of these programs on its many participants since more rigorous, in-depth, and longitudinal research is required to properly assess effectiveness.

In a similar way, Nicholls et al. (2011) are concerned that the program assessments that do take place seldom include the voices and perspectives of the SDP practitioners working in the field. They argue that this omission is notable because conventional impact measurement tools (such as evaluation forms that are filled out by practitioners) often do not pick up on the subtle but important day-to-day impacts of these programs—impacts that practitioners themselves could (and do) describe when asked to recount in-depth stories about their experiences with their programs and in the community. The underlying problem here is that these experiences rarely 'count' as program evaluation data, despite their obvious and inherent value for assessing something as incredibly nuanced as the impacts of SDP programs on participants, and on a marginalized community more generally. Nicholls et al. (2011) go on to suggest that a top-down, hierarchical relationship between more powerful groups (e.g., donors, policy-makers, and NGO leadership) and community members is perpetuated when these stories and perspectives are not accounted for. As noted above, there are practical and strategic reasons that some NGOs might want to maintain control over how data about their SDP programs is collected and reported—although many other NGOs are simply following what has historically been the accepted approach to assessing programs (i.e., an approach that is based around measurements, instead of perceptions and experiences), without intending to perpetuate unequal power relationships.

The point here is not to be overly or unfairly critical of those who are unwilling to risk their funding and livelihoods by doing more rigorous assessments, assessments which might lead to ongoing programmatic improvements. The point is, however, to identify an apparent flaw in a (neo-liberal) system of funding and accountability that is based on competition amongst NGOs for limited funds that are available from, in many cases, profit-driven sponsors—sponsors who only benefit from these associations when they are able to maximize exposure and enhance their image (Wilson and Hayhurst, 2009).

Football 4 Peace: A Sociological Imagination and a Sport for Peace Intervention

Although many other programs thought to embody best practices deserve attention along with MYSA (e.g., Armstrong, 2004; Gasser and Levinsen, 2006; Keim, 2003; Richards, 1997), I highlight one in particular that is described in a series of thoughtful articles by University of Brighton professor John Sugden. I feature Sugden here because he is uniquely positioned as both a critical sociologist of sport *and* a key organizer of the Football 4 Peace (F4P) program that is run out of the University of Brighton in the United Kingdom. Football 4 Peace is a reconciliation and community building intervention designed to foster positive relationships between youth living in Jewish and Arab areas in Israel. A football development camp is used as a forum for promoting these relationships, as integrated teams of Jewish and Arab youth work together in preparation for a capstone tournament that takes place at the end of the camp. Sugden (2010b) summarizes other features of the program's operations:

> F4P's fourfold aims are to provide opportunities for social contact across community boundaries; promote mutual understanding; engender in participants a desire for and commitment to peaceful coexistence; and enhance sports skills and technical knowledge about sport. In order to achieve these goals, a dedicated values-based teaching curriculum has been developed along with a coaching style through the modelling of which participants are encouraged to demonstrate appreciation of the basic qualities of good citizenship: respect, trust, responsibility, equality and inclusivity. In summary, a series of Cross-Community Sports Partnerships (CCSPs) have been established, involving small clusters of Jewish and Arab towns and villages. In these CCSPs, over six consecutive days at alternative Jewish and Arab community venues, children are coached in mixed groups (Arab and Jewish) growing into teams and taking part in end-of-project football and multi-activity festivals. Parallel to the football training there is an off-pitch program of trust-building, recreational and cultural activities. In respect for local traditions and customs, one project is for girls only and is staffed entirely by female coaches. (p. 44)

Sugden's work is rare in the sport for development and peace area because he actively links current understandings of best practices for conducting intervention work in divided societies with an attempt to inform these practices with layers of contextual information and pertinent sociological research. Put another way, Sugden's on-the-ground intervention work is informed (and iteratively 're-informed') through his use of a sociological imagination—imagining how the youths' experiences within the Football for Peace intervention are impacted by what is taking place in other contexts, and what researchers have learned about these contexts.

For example, Sugden (2010a) describes how the young people in the program maneuver within a set of contexts that begins with their families and local communities as well as the local and international volunteers who run the F4P program. The children/youth, their families, and the program workers, in turn, exist within 'a network of institutional partners [like the University of Brighton, where Sugden and the Football 4 Peace program is based] through whom ideas and findings emanating from the project can be articulated within the wider policy community for sport' (Sugden, 2010a, p. 269) The broadest context is the 'transcending social and political context,' where the activities of organizations like F4P are ultimately guided and impacted by the various United Nations–related charters that offer guidelines for and goals underlying intervention. As Donnelly and Kidd (2000) and others note, these charters speak to, among many others, human rights, the right to peace, and the right to participate in sport, physical activity, physical education, and play. This level also includes any negotiations that are taking place for peace amongst Arab and Jewish political leaders and international mediators. Sugden considers how the F4P program both 'impacts and is impacted by' these contexts, using the metaphor of the 'ripple effect' to emphasize how extremely positive experiences in F4P could influence all of these other contexts.

This ripple effect metaphor refers to the idea of a stone being dropped in water, where the impacts of the pebble (i.e., the intervention) are greatest at the core (e.g., in the local community, with the young people), then move outward across the various levels—though, granted, with decreasing effect. With this in mind, Sugden suggests that 'success of any endeavour will depend on the animation and agency provided by key actors operating across and between each level of activity' (2010a, p. 271).

Reflections on Theory and Practice around Football 4 Peace

You may have noticed here that Sugden's approach is akin to the one advocated throughout this book. In fact, he explicitly mentions praxis—discussed in chapter 5—as a term that aptly describes his attempts at theory-informed practice. His work is also guided by what he calls a 'new left realism', borrowing from work developed initially in the field of criminology. According to Sugden (2010a), new left realism allows for:

. . . the mobilization of a radical and critical sociological imagination in deter-mining strategies for progressive and pragmatic engagement with social problems with a view to influencing local policies and interventions that could improve the conditions of society's most vulnerable groups. (p. 267)

For our purposes, Sugden's writing is pertinent because it demonstrates ways that a sociological imagination can be used to inform decisions about the design and implementation of sport-related interventions.

What is also admirable here is Sugden's willingness and ability to implement a program like F4P while remaining acutely aware the program's limitations. This is evident in Sugden's (2007) conclusion to the edited book *Football for Peace: The Challenges of Using Sport for Co-Existence in Israel*, where he offers a set of lessons learned through his theory-based, sport-related interventionist work. These lessons include: that 'culturally focused peace initiatives [like those related to sport] work best within maturing peace processes'; that 'complex political and social problems are usually unresponsive to simplistic solutions', and that 'adopting a stance of impartiality/neutrality is difficult to sustain when a context of injustice prevails and intensifies' (Sugden, 2007, p. 174).

In the end, Sugden and his colleagues in F4P are an excellent example of a group that remains cognizant of the challenges associated with the develop-ment and reconciliation work they are undertaking, yet see value in trying to make a difference anyway.

Remaining Cautious about SDP Work

There are many other reasons to be cautious about SDP interventions. Even the interventions described above—that are considered by many to be best practices (cf., Kidd, 2007; Coalter, 2008)—are not immune to serious prob-lems. The Football 4 Peace program, for example, temporarily closed down in 2006 because of major conflict that had broken out in the Gaza strip and on the border with Lebanon, not too far from where F4P programs are carried out. Researchers who have examined other programs considered successful commonly offer the same sorts of reservations and warnings that Sugden ex-pressed about F4P. A recent study of ways that a sporting event was used to promote reconciliation between Sinhalese, Tamil, and Muslim sportspeople in war-torn Sri Lanka is an excellent example of this, as the author of the study concluded that:

. . . inter-community sport events can provide a starting point, booster and cata-lyst for social development and inclusive social change, and as such should be encouraged and expanded as part of an active and dynamic social development process. However, it is too much to expect sport events to have a major impact on overall community relations in the absence of a political settlement in divided societies. Taken alone, they stand little prospect of achieving lasting social outcomes beyond the events' borders. Therefore, they should be integrated into a larger agenda of social and political support to make a modest contribution to reconciliation and positive social change between disparate communities. (Schulenkorf, 2010, p. 291)

The point here is that although these interventions may be effective in promoting (at least temporary) forms of reconciliation and positive social change—and should therefore be continued and/or pursued under the right circumstances—the durability of their contributions should not be overstated. The broader issue is whether the increasingly competitive sport for international development environment encourages unrealistic and overly positive portrayals of sport's contributions—portrayals that could be detrimental to a peace-process if deceivingly optimistic assessments of sport's contributions lead to complacency among those who could/should be continuing work on other levels.

Other problems that are more program-based are outlined by sociologist and development scholar Simon Darnell (2010a). Based on his interviews with volunteer interns who have done sport-related international development work, he argues that many who work in the field continue to overestimate the contributions of sport to character development and upward mobility, while failing to recognize the many potential problems that commonly exist and are perpetuated within sport contexts. Giulianotti (2006) has similarly expressed concern that interventions (like the one Darnell examined), which are shown to have serious flaws when implemented in Western contexts, are sometimes uncritically implemented by SDP groups in international development work. With this critique in mind, the types of questions that might be asked about international SDP intervention work include: 'Are issues of child safety accounted for in SDP work?'; 'Are the interests of girls and women and older people accounted for in these programs?'; and 'Are programs sensitive to local interests and cultural traditions (cf., Giulianotti, 2006)?'

The dominant functionalist orientation detected by Darnell should be unsurprising according to Sugden (2010a), who suggests that many of those doing SDP work have had positive experiences with sport themselves, and commonly work with the assumption that 'because sport was good for me, it must be good for others'. Having said this, Darnell acknowledges that some of his interviewees—especially those who have had more diverse experiences with sport, or those who had been exposed to more critical thinking about sport in their postsecondary training—were more balanced in their view of sport's benefits and limitations. While this finding offers some hope for a more balanced and reflexive SDP movement, at their core Darnell's findings affirm the idea that more needs to be done to promote critically informed thinking about ways that sport is integrated into international development work.

Sport, Race, and Colonization

Other sport scholars are concerned about the tendency for some SDP programs to push Western values through sport (Guest, 2009). Giulianotti (2006), for example, is concerned about the level of dialogue that exists between Western-based donors to SDP programs and recipients of sports-related aid in countries of the Global South, and is distressed by situations where the donor takes the dominant role of authority and expert. All of this takes place, of course, in a context where approaches to dealing with social problems around the world are increasingly driven by a borderless neo-liberal agenda, itself a form of colonization.

With this last point in mind, some scholars also point to ways that stereotypical and derogatory understandings of race and ethnicity are sometimes articulated and perpetuated through the discourses of SDP work. Consider the following quotation from a 1923 essay by Pierre de Coubertin, founder of the Modern Olympics.

> Perhaps it may appear premature to introduce the principle of sports competitions into a continent [Africa] that is behind the times and among peoples still without elementary culture—and particularly presumptuous to expect this expansion to lead to a speeding up of the march of civilization in these countries. Let us think however, for a moment, of what is troubling the African soul. Untapped forces—individual laziness and a sort of collective need for action—a thousand resentments, and a thousand jealousies of the white man and yet, at the same time, the wish to imitate him and thus share his privileges—the conflict between wishing to submit to discipline and to escape from it—and, in the midst of an innocent gentleness that is not without its charm, the sudden outburst of ancestral violence . . . these are just some features of these races to which the younger generation, which has in fact derived great benefit from sport, is turning its attention. Sport has hardened them. It has given them a healthy taste for muscular relaxation and a little of that reasonable fatalism possessed by energetic beings, once their efforts have been accomplished. But while sport builds up, it also calms down. Provided it remains accessory and does not become a goal in itself, it helps create order and clarify thought. Let us not hesitate therefore to help Africa join in. (quoted in Guest, 2009, p. 1340)

These words are evidence of ways that sport-related, and especially Olympic-related international development work, was often justified in the early twentieth century. Guest (2009) notes how de Coubertin's 'perspective on Africa manages to simultaneously display a clearly deprecating colonial attitude and a sense of good will and hope' (p. 1340). In doing so, the 'well-meaning' de Coubertin was clearly drawing on and perpetuating long-standing derogatory stereotypes about (Black) Africans.

What is particularly troubling and unfortunate is that many of these same themes emerge, albeit more subtly, in the materials and practices of at least some SDP organizations today. This is evident from Darnell's (2007) analysis of published (online) testimonials from volunteers working for Right To Play, which were focused in large part on development work taking place in Africa. Darnell found that volunteers consistently framed their work as 'the benevolent deliverance of aid, goods and expertise from the North, First World to the southern, Third World' (p. 560). He also described the fascination volunteers expressed about their encounters with the 'racialized other' (i.e., the grateful, smiling, dancing African children). Darnell (2007) argues that such portrayals position the White, Western volunteer in 'a subject position of benevolence, rationality and expertise', and in opposition to the 'marginalized, unsophisticated and appreciative bodies of colour' (p. 560), represented by the Africans.

While Darnell acknowledges that the volunteers writing on RTP's website are not necessarily uncritical or unreflective about their work, he remains firm in his view that such portrayals reinforce long-standing stereotypes about 'natives'. He notes, for example, the perpetuation of the stereotype that the always-troubled natives are 'grateful for material means that provide respite from his/her marginalization' (p. 570). Darnell's concerns here include: that this portrayal of the 'native African' exists without the historical context that is necessary to explain the processes through which *some* groups (in any country or context) experience extreme forms of poverty and require aid. It also fails to acknowledge that 'native groups' or 'Africans' (like 'North Americans' or 'Whites'), are far more complex than any kind essentialized portrayals would indicate. In the end, according to Darnell, we are left with a set of often demeaning and usually oversimplified images of those being supported through SDP work.

In a not unrelated way, many scholars in this context also recognize that the 'human rights perspective' that underlies interventionist work in the name of peace and development comes from a Western, 'individual-focused' perspective. That is to say, Human Rights charters and legislations privilege individual rights, which means that the collective rights associated with ethnic and cultural groups are deemphasized. Giulianotti (2006) is more pointed in his critique, as he notes the 'grim irony' around the need for such a Declaration of Human Rights in the first place:

The Western powers 'discovered' these other cultures, enslaved the peoples, expropriated their natural and human resources, and then, once colonization had proved too exhausting to maintain, the colonists introduced the colonized to notions of nationhood, political independence, free-market international trading, and human rights. Such hopeful guarantees would have been perfectly unnecessary if this cycle of colonization and decolonization had never started in the first place. (Giulianotti , 2006, p. 66)

Giulianotti's point should not be taken to suggest that the 1948 Declaration of Human Rights, and subsequent amendments, are not incredibly important and progressive pieces of legislation. As Donnelly and Kidd (2000) note, 'the use of charters, declarations and covenants that enshrine codes of entitlement and conduct' is a crucial way to follow a commitment to humane sport and physical activity when the goal is to work across religious and cultural divides. It is to suggest, however, that such declarations are not entirely neutral and, as Sugden (2010a) points out, such charters and declarations are only useful if action (like certain forms of SDP work) is taken to pursue the goals and sustain the rights enshrined therein.

To Intervene or Not to Intervene?

This chapter highlights ways that different sociological theories and concepts could be linked with on-the-ground interventions. It also demonstrates how a concept like social capital can guide and be used to illustrate the benefits of sport for building trust, reciprocity, community capacity, and effectively functioning networks within and outside sport. At the same time I show how the often inspirational and commonly praised interventionist work of international NGOs like Right To Play may be (inadvertently) implicated in generating consent for a particular form of intervention that is driven by neo-liberal principles.

I also looked to the work of John Sugden, whose work is instructive for showing how a sociological imagination can be used to illuminate the contradictions and problems that underlie SDP work and to guide important decisions about the need for intervention in the first place. With such decisions in mind, Sugden is known to conclude his writing and presentations on his SDP work with the following maxim from Edmund Burke, which is, that 'the only thing necessary for the triumph of evil is for good men [and I'll insert women] to do nothing' (Sugden, 2007, p. 175). While Burke's statement should not be taken to mean that balanced and theoretically informed reflection on the value of interventions is unnecessary, what he (and Sugden) highlight is the need to avoid 'analysis paralysis'—to be sensitive to the idea that linking theory and practical action requires a willingness to, at some point, act. Questions will always remain, of course, about the kinds of contradictions we can live with when designing and doing an intervention, the need for a particular intervention at a particular moment, and what can be learned from previous experiences so that next time will be better. Put another way, SDP interventions may have particular benefits, at particular moments, in particular contexts, and we can learn from past experience when designing and revising programs. However, to be clear, there are no guarantees that an intervention is going to be entirely successful, and certainly not for all participants. For this sort of work, living with some contradictions and complexities is a requirement.

Note

1. From www.righttoplay.com/International/the-team/Pages/Coaches/
   NzobonankiraBenjamin.aspx.

Discussion Questions

1. Does it matter if our contributions to sporting communities are driven by self-interest more than altruism? Why or why not?

2. What does it mean to bring a sociological imagination to a sport for development and peace intervention? How is context relevant when assessing these interventions?

3. How is a functionalist perspective relevant to sport for development and peace interventions? How is a functionalist-only understanding of sport for development and peace interventions problematic?

4. What different types of information could (and should) be gathered when doing an evaluation of a sport for development and peace intervention? What challenges are likely faced by those who conduct these evaluations?

5. How do you interpret Edmund Burke's statement 'the only thing necessary for the triumph of evil is for good men [and women] to do nothing'? Are there circumstances where sport for development and peace practitioners should 'do nothing'? If yes, what are these circumstances?

Suggested Readings

Cornelissen, S. (2009). A delicate balance: Major sport events and development. In R. Levermore & A. Beacom (Eds.), *Sport and international development* (pp. 76–97). New York: Palgrave MacMillan. A thoughtful reflection on ways that mega–sporting events can be thought of as forms of international development.

Darnell, S. (2007). Playing with race: Right To Play and the production of whiteness in 'development through sport'. *Sport in Society*, 10(4), 560–79. A provocative and important study of ways that sport for development and peace is represented by those in the field and ways that derogatory and stereotypical race-related portrayals are prevalent.

Darnell, S. (2010). Power, politics and 'sport for development and peace': Investigating the utility of sport for international development. *Sociology of Sport Journal*, 27(1), 54–75. An excellent and recent interview-based study of those who worked in sport for development and peace programs.

Gasser, P. & Levinsen, A. (2006). Breaking post-war ice: Open fun football schools in Bosnia and Herzegovina. In R. Giulianotti & D. McCardle (Eds.), *Sport, civil liberties and human rights* (pp. 165–80). New York: Routledge. Reflections on the benefits and limitations of a sport program intended to promote reconciliation.

Kidd, B. (2007). Peace, sport and development. In Sport for Development and Peace International Working Group (SDPIWG) Secretariat (Commissioned) *Literature reviews on sport for development and peace* (pp. 158–94). University of Toronto, Faculty of Physical Education and Health. This paper includes a succinct overview of the sport for peace field and includes references to some best practices.

Levermore, R. (2011). Sport in international development: Facilitating improved standard of living? In B. Houlihan & M. Green (Eds.), *Routledge handbook of sports development* (pp. 285–307). New York: Routledge. A comprehensive overview of the benefits of and problems with SDP work, with a particular focus on whether interventions 'facilitate an improved standard of living'.

Sugden, J. (2006). Teaching and playing sport for conflict resolution and co-existence in Israel. *International Review of the Sociology of Sport*, 41(2), 221–40. Another excellent example of a set of reflections by sociologist-activist Sugden on the benefits and limitations of a sport program intended to promote reconciliation.

Sugden, J. (2010). Critical left-realism and sport interventions in divided societies. *International Review for the Sociology of Sport*, 45(3), 258–72. Sugden's article includes important suggestions for thinking about how sociological theories are useful for guiding a sport for development and peace intervention/program.

Relevant Websites

International Platform on Sport and Development
www.sportanddev.org
This is the major platform for information sharing and networking for international sport for development and peace groups.

Right To Play
www.righttoplay.com/International/Pages/Home.aspx

Mathare Youth Sports Association (MYSA)
www.MYSAkenya.org

Football 4 Peace
www.football4peace.eu

Key Terms

'plus sport' programs These are sport for development and peace programs that promote various forms of social development, with sport simply being a tool to assist in the achievement of other outcomes/goals, like disease prevention or conflict resolution.

social capital refers to the kind of currency that is held when one develops and has access to social networks—networks that 'enable people to trust one another and via which individuals or group can obtain certain types of advantage' (Coalter, 2008, p. 44). Types of social capital include: bonding social capital, which refers to relationships between individuals within homogenous groups;

bridging social capital, which refers to relationships across social divisions; and linking social capital, which refers to ties between groups from different sectors and with distinct backgrounds (Putnam, 2000; cf., Harvey et al., 2007).

sport for (international) development When sport is used as part of an organized intervention process intended to improve life chances and living standards 'throughout the world but particularly in countries considered to be low income' (Levermore and Beacom, 2009, p. 7). 'Development' here can be 'large scale and top-down' and/or 'small scale and bottom-up'. 'Large-scale and top-down' interventionist work is commonly initiated by Western-based agencies for countries believed to be in need of development. 'Small scale and bottom-up' development projects are grassroots projects that are initiated in underserved areas to address any number of issues as identified by those in a local community.

'sport plus' programs These are sport for development and peace programs that are driven by the idea that promoting skill development and excellence in sport is linked with positive social and economic outcomes outside the sporting realm.

8 Sport, the Environment, and Peace: Debates and Myths About Carbon-Neutral Sport

Questions to Consider

- In what ways does sport impact the environment?
- How are recreational peace parks and conservationism used to promote reconciliation and relationship building?
- What are the social inequalities associated with environmental degradation?
- How do the terms 'ecological modernism', the 'treadmill of production', and 'neo-liberalism' relate to thinking about sport and the environment?
- What does it mean to be carbon neutral? Should we be concerned about industry-led responses to environmental problems?
- What are the strengths of and problems with an ecological modernist response to environmental problems? What other responses are possible? Why might these other responses receive less attention?

Introduction: Sport and Green Business

In 1994, environmentalist and management specialist David Chernushenko released *Greening Our Games*, a groundbreaking examination of and response to environmental problems associated with sport. Although the book was important for a number of reasons, one of its key contributions was, quite simply, raising awareness about sport-related environmental problems—problems that received little or no attention in the years leading up to the book's publication, and *problems that remain centrally relevant to this day*. These include:

- building sport venues, hosting sport events, and producing sport apparel/equipment more generally are associated with pollution hazards and carbon emissions;
- wetland areas are being altered or reduced because of modifications to rivers and lakes for water sports like paddling and canoeing;
- natural vegetation is being destroyed and soil eroded due to alpine skiing; and
- golf course construction and the chemicals commonly used to maintain golf courses impact natural habitats and put the health of wildlife and humans at risk.

More than just identifying problems, Chernushenko went on to explain why some of these problems have arisen—noting how the single-minded focus on economic gain by certain sport-related corporations is a driving force behind sport's sometimes exploitative relationship with the environment. He pointed out how attempts by some sport organizations to be sustainable may be disingenuous or ineffective when economic progress is prioritized over environmental concerns, when 'appearing green' is prioritized over doing the strategic and challenging work that is necessary to practice environmentally friendly sport. Chernushenko expressed particular concern about the influence that sponsors of professional and amateur sporting events have over the staging and goals of these events and about the ways that the priorities of sponsors may inhibit efforts of those who are genuinely interested in sustainable sport.

Chernushenko's book has become a classic in sport management circles because, as well as offering observations about relationships between sport and the environment, he offers clear guidelines for organizing and running sustainable sport events and makes a convincing argument that sustainable sport management can be good for business. Chernushenko was an innovator here in recognizing that sustainable practices would be money-saving in the long run, while also noting that as consumers of sport become more concerned about the environment, businesses will *need* to respond. Perhaps not surprisingly, since the release of his book, Chernushenko has become a leading Canadian political figure on green issues generally, and in sustainable sport management especially. Over the years, for example, his consulting firm Green and Gold advised a variety of sport-related clients—including Nike, the International Waterski Federation, the European Golf Association that organizes the Ryder Cup, and the 2008 Toronto Olympic Bid Committee—on a variety of pro-environmental efforts. Unquestionably, Chernushenko was a forerunner in a still-emerging sport and **sustainability** movement—a movement that is beginning to address the problems mentioned earlier, and various others.

Given these credentials, you might be surprised to learn that Chernushenko's work has sparked some controversy in the sociology for sport field, as scholars like University of Toronto professor Helen Lenskyj (1998) have taken Chernushenko to task for what is ultimately a business-friendly (or what is commonly termed a 'light green') approach to dealing with environmental problems. Critics like Lenskyj are not so much arguing that businesses should not be involved in an effort to deal with environmental problems, but instead suggest that a business-*led* strategy has many dangers and flaws (although, to be fair to Chernushenko, he does not explicitly advocate this approach). These critics argue, for example, that **corporate environmentalist** practices—and especially industry-driven voluntary eco-guidelines and activities intended to promote sustainability—are in many cases hypocritical attempts by businesses to postpone or prevent efforts by government to regulate their industries (Gibbons, 1999). Others are more direct in their critique of businesses that market their pro-environment attitudes without fully embracing eco-friendly practices, what some authors term '**greenwashing**' (cf., Lubbers, 2002).

At the same time, though, and on the other side of the debate, proponents of this business-led approach argue that competition amongst (sport-related) organizations is key if pro-environment innovations are to take place. In this model, it is consumers who will ultimately drive profit-sensitive businesses to find solutions to environment-related problems. Inspired by these principles, many sport managers and some researchers outline the potential benefits of greener practices for businesses aiming to succeed in a marketplace that is, as Chernushenko predicted, increasingly requiring sensitivity to the sustainability concerns of consumers (Poncelet, 2004). Underlying many of these measures is a belief that economic growth and progress on environmental issues are truly compatible and can be mutually reinforcing.

Sport, Environmental Issues, and Peace: An Overview

With these debates in mind, I spend this chapter outlining relationships between sport, peace, and the environment, and discussing ways that sociologists of sport have approached these issues. In doing so, I illuminate tensions around the 'ecological modernist' response to sport-related environmental problems—the dominant and taken-for-granted approach of many sport managers and event organizers. These tensions are further highlighted through an assessment of the claims and assumptions of managers and organizers who claim to have hosted carbon-neutral sporting mega-events.

Throughout this chapter I raise questions about whose interests are being served by privileging particular solutions to sport-related environmental problems, whose voices are privileged when decisions are made, and how consent is being sought and secured for a particular solution. I go on to suggest that when the 'only' solution commonly offered is one that is driven by the interests of corporate and governmental elites—who are responding to the interests of consumers who buy their products, not citizens (i.e., voters) who are from all segments of society—then democratic principles are compromised (Wilson and Millington, in press).

So what do issues around sport and the environment have to do with peace (and conflict)? On the broadest level, it is important to keep in mind that fairly obvious links have been made between problems like scarcity of water and food—and related health problems—and human-driven changes in the environment (e.g., climate change). These sorts of problems are understandably considered threats to human security, which are of course relevant for those concerned with promoting positive peace.

Others have argued that when resources are scarce—which is, as above, sometimes attributed to the (hyper)consumption behaviours of humans—then conflict over these resources may arise (Diehl and Gleditsch, 2001). Although this argument is controversial—as some note that having an abundance of resources is also a reason used to explain conflict and war (Gleditsch and Urdal, 2004)—the potential relationship between environmental degradation and conflict is one that continues to occupy researchers in this field. Either way, the main point here is that environmental degradation is ultimately a global issue, and for this reason, *any* industry that negatively impacts the environment is an accomplice in these developments. In this way, the environmental impacts of sport can be tied to these forms of conflict and human security issues.

Since environmental problems also tend to impact more vulnerable and marginalized groups to a greater degree than more privileged ones, issues around social inequality are pertinent here as well. With this in mind, Maguire et al. (2002, pp. 84–85) identify a series of inequities that are commonly associated with environmental problems. These are:

- **intergenerational inequity**—referring to ways that future generations may be negatively impacted by the environment-related activities of current generations
- **transfrontier inequity**—referring to ways that environment-related activities taking place in local contexts may have a negative impact on those living in other places
- **intra-generational inequity**—referring here to the need to account for existing social inequalities of all kinds (e.g., around class, gender, ethnicity) when devising sustainability projects and considering the impacts of environmentally damaging behaviours

More optimistically, environmental issues have also been shown to bring groups together, to inspire cooperative relationships that are driven by shared concerns for the environment (Ali, 2007). In a rare and innovative book entitled *Peace Parks: Conservation and Conflict Resolution*, editor Saleem Ali (2007) assembled a set of chapters by authors who describe the possibilities for and challenges surrounding the use of park spaces that cross borders as a means of either maintaining or promoting peaceful relationships between sharing countries.

Authors throughout the book refer to the first recognized peace park, the Waterton-Glacier International Peace Park that links the southwest corner of Alberta and the southeast corner of British Columbia (both in Canada) with northern Montana in the US. The Parks Canada website offers the following synopsis of the peace-promoting recreational practices that take place in the park:

Originally, the International Peace Park commemorated the peace and goodwill that exists along the world's longest undefended border (8,892 km/ 5,525 miles). Today, the united parks represent the need for cooperation and stewardship in a world of shared resources. Cooperation within the Peace Park [between government employees in Canada and the US] is reflected in wildlife and vegetation management and in search and rescue programs. The parks also share interpretive efforts including joint hikes, programs and exhibits.

On December 6, 1995 UNESCO designated the Waterton-Glacier International Peace Park as a World Heritage Site because it has a distinctive climate, physiographic setting, mountain-prairie interface, and tri-ocean hydrographical divide. It is an area of significant scenic values with abundant and diverse flora and fauna.[1]

As you might expect, the authors in *Peace Parks* are cautious in their claims about the potential of such parks, recognizing that such collaborations are never entirely equal or devoid of political wrangling. Still, the idea of a transborder peace park is, in principle, based around the idea that humans, animals, and the natural environment are interrelated in ways that transcend borders. Moreover, these spaces are ripe with opportunities to educate about respectful and environmentally friendly forms of physical activity and recreation.

The Sociology of Sport and Environmental Issues

Although sociologists of sport seldom explicitly identify ways that the peace concept is relevant to thinking about the environmental issues, there is an emerging and pertinent tradition of research and writing on sport and environmental issues. Environmental activism, for example, has been featured in research by sociologists of sport who study:

- the Surfers Against Sewage movement (Wheaton, 2007, 2008);
- the *parkour* subculture that resists (over)development in urban spaces (Atkinson and Young, 2008; Atkinson, 2009);
- anti-Olympic movements that are based around concerns about the impacts of holding mega–sporting events on the environment (Lenskyj, 2002); and
- the anti-golf movement that emerged in response to concerns about habitat alteration and destruction associated with the building of golf courses, as well as the impacts of chemicals and excessive water usage in the maintenance of courses. These issues are especially pronounced in some areas of the Global South where access to fresh water is a notable concern in (cf., Briassoulis, 2010; Maguire et al., 2002; Stolle-McAllister, 2004; Wheeler and Nauright, 2006).

Other studies that speak to issues around sport, power relations, and environmental issues include: Lenskyj's (1998) and Beder's (2002) exploration of ways that some sport-related organizations disingenuously brand themselves as green in their attempts to attract environmentally conscious consumers; Kearins and Pavlovich's (2002) study of the greening of the 2000 Sydney Olympic Games; and Pitter's (2009) examination of the political maneuvering that took place between interest groups concerned with a proposed development of an off-highway vehicle trail system in Nova Scotia, Canada.

In their introduction to a two-volume special issue of the *Journal of Sport and Social Issues* focused on sport and the environment, Mincyte et al. (2009) note that while sociologists of sport are beginning to address environment-related concerns like those outlined above, those in the world of professional and amateur sport are also paying attention. Mincyte et al. refer to a March 2007 *Sports Illustrated* cover story by Alexander Wolff (2007) that outlines concerns about shortened ski seasons due to global warming; the threat that the expansion of the ash borer beetle habitat may have on timber that is commonly used to produce baseball bats; and rising water levels that could leave 13 major stadiums—including Orange Bowl in Miami and Monster Park in San Francisco—under water by the year 2100 (cf., Mincyte et al., 2009).

Note here how Wolff's view on environmental problems is distinct from the perspective taken by many sociologists of sport, who acknowledge the impacts of environmental problems *on sport*, but are most concerned with sport's impact *on the environment*. In fact, implicit in Wolff's perspective on ways that global warming may require humans to alter their leisure and consumption activities is the assumption that humans and nature are separate, not interrelated, that nature is somehow 'external to human endeavors' (Mincyte et al., 2009, p. 105). This is unlike other perspectives on the environment, where interrelationships (not separations) between human activity and nature are emphasized.

Modernism, Sport, and Perspectives on the 'Human and Non-human' Relationship

This view of humans and nature as separate is a central feature of what is commonly termed a modernist perspective on the world—a perspective that sociologists of sport have highlighted and critiqued in work on sport and environmental issues over time. John Bale (2001, first published in 1993), for example, in his foundational book *Sport, Space and the City*, refers to modernism in his discussion of how sport managers and entrepreneurs feel pressure to develop sporting environments and playing conditions that are uniform across contexts—with *the quest for uniformity and standardization* being a key characteristic of modernism. Although Bale's point was particularly evident in the wave of domed stadiums that were built through the 1980s and early 1990s that allowed sporting events to take place regardless of weather, the more recent trend toward the (re)creation of outdoor baseball parks that are throwbacks to the stadiums of the early twentieth century also reflects this trend. That is to say, these venues are in most cases (uniformly) corporate-sponsored, outfitted with corporate boxes, and contain equipment needed to support the most advanced televised coverage of the event (Belanger, 2000). Scholars like Belanger (2000) and Hannigan (1998) note how the development of such 'generically spectacular' facilities emerged in response to the need for world-class spectator-sport facilities that are considered essential for attracting transnational businesses to major cities.

While some of these developments may not seem pertinent to the environmental issues described earlier, it is important to recognize how the modernizing processes that Bale is describing are associated with the taken-for-granted view that the environment is a resource to be manipulated, used, reshaped, and ultimately mastered by humans to suit our consumption preferences and profit motives. Of particular relevance here is Bale's (2001, p. 41) recognition of the link between the creation of uniform consumption options and the focus on attracting tourists to always familiar sport- and leisure-related sites. Evident also from Bale's observations is the assumed link between 'mastery' of the environment and human 'progress'—with this search for and belief in progress being another underlying goal and tenet of the modernizing project.

Sociologist Brian Stoddart (1990) offered similar (but more critical) observations of modernizing processes and the environment in his early study of the internationalization of golf. He describes how the economic concerns that inspired developers/entrepreneurs to build luxury golf courses and golf-related holiday resorts are inseparable from the environmentally dangerous practices that are sometimes associated with constructing and maintaining new courses—new courses designed to attract golfer-tourists expecting a predictable experience in pristine conditions (Palmer, 2004). Extending this point, Wheeler and Nauright (2006) explain the desire to have idyllic (often pesticide-induced) turf conditions on golf courses with their use of the term **'Augusta National Syndrome'**. The term refers to Augusta National Golf Club, where the widely televised Masters PGA event is played, and to the unrealistic expectations that courses like the highly manicured Augusta—which are sometimes closed for several months to prepare for major events—place on others in the industry. The point is that some golf course managers will do (and are mandated to do) whatever it takes to satisfy 'Augusta-influenced' consumers/tourists/golfers. With this goal in mind, Stoddart (1990) argues that to it is not uncommon to see environmentally sensitive land reshaped and hazardous chemicals used to keep fairways and greens consistent and unspoiled.

Sustainability and the Ecological Modernist Response

In the years since Stoddart's 1990 article, many sport managers (especially golf course superintendents!), developers, politicians, and others have positioned themselves as supporters of a sustainable sport movement. The term 'sustainable', or 'sustainability', refers here to an integrated strategy for addressing economic, social, and environmental issues—what is commonly known as the 'triple bottom line' (Chernushenko et al. 2001, p. 10). The classic definition for sustainability, offered in the 1986 report *Our Common Future* (produced for the World Commission on Environment and Development), refers to our society's capacity to '[meet the] needs of the present without compromising the ability of future generations to meet their own needs' (see Brundtland, 1987). Chernushenko et al. (2001) is more specific in his definition of sustainable sport:

> Sport is sustainable when it meets the needs of today's sporting communities while contributing to the improvement of future sport opportunities for all and the improvement of the integrity of the natural and social environment on which it depends. (p. 10)

Sustainability—and **ecological modernization**, the term more commonly used by environmental sociologists—share many characteristics and are based on the common assumption that economic and environment progress are compatible. In fact, Gibbs (2000, p. 11, drawing on Hajer, 1995) argues that sustainability is the '"central story line" of the policy discourse of ecological modernization', which is to say, the more developed and nuanced ecological modernization concept (described below) is commonly translated into the more marketable and accessible language associated with sustainability. Either way, critiques of sustainability as a concept that is commonly adopted to promote sustained *economic* development (sometimes, unfortunately, at the expense of the environment) are similar to those commonly aimed at ecological modernization, a point I elaborate on below.

What Is Ecological Modernization?

So what is ecological modernization, and why is it so appealing to sport-related industries as an approach for dealing with environmental problems? As with many concepts, there is some disagreement about what the term means and what consequences are associated with an ecological modernist (EM) response to environmental problems. Advocates of the term subscribe to the idea that industries can switch from practices that are more harmful to the environment to ones that are sustainable (Spaargaren and Mol, 1992; Hannigan, 2006). An early proponent of this perspective was German sociologist

Joseph Huber (1985), who argued that processes of industrialization in modern societies progress from: (a) an initial industrial breakthrough; to (b) the construction of an industrial society; to (c) the development of a super-industrial society characterized by the development of environment-friendly technologies (Hannigan, 2006, p. 27).

Although most ecological modernist thinkers agree on these basic principles, there are different strands of the approach. Advocates for a 'strong' version of the theory are more sensitive to the need for public consultation, and for ongoing reflections on the intended and unintended consequences of the new and greener technologies—the technologies that will help us advance to a super-industrial society. They also recognize the need for government and (non-industry based) regulators/overseers to support and monitor attempts by industry to be more sustainable. 'Weaker' versions, on the other hand, are based around the assumption that the market (i.e., consumer demand) and industry itself, through internal and often voluntary regulations, will drive environmental change.

It is not difficult to see why this perspective, weaker versions in particular, would be favoured by for-profit industries expected to adopt more environmentally friendly practices. In fact, it is well known that this approach at least implicitly guides the activities of governments attempting to intermingle economic and environmental progress, while at the same time promote industry–NGO–consumer relationships that will support these developments. The assumption that industry can develop technologies necessary to be cleaner and greener is a key aspect of the ecological modernist narrative. Advocates of EM in sport management (like Chernushenko) commonly cite examples like Coca Cola's development of more energy-efficient coolers that use hydrocarbon or HC cooling systems, a green innovation that allowed the company to stop using coolers reliant on environmentally damaging hydro fluorocarbons (HFCs). This particular innovation—a response to criticisms from Greenpeace before the Sydney Olympics in 2000—is commonly cited by EM advocates because it fits the theory so well. That is to say, an NGO (like Greenpeace) and consumers inspired an innovation by a corporation, a corporation that continues to make profit (i.e., selling cola) to consumers who now desire greener products.

What's Wrong with Ecological Modernization?

Despite these much-publicized success stories, sociologists have critiqued strong and weaker versions of ecological modernism. Perhaps the most potent critique is that relationships that exist between different stakeholders on environmental issues—relationships promoted by 'strong' EM advocates—are, according to many researchers, unequal and often contentious. For example, Kearins and Pavlovich's (2002) study of the role played by stakeholders in the greening of the Sydney Olympics explored the undesirable compromises that are sometimes required of environmental groups when they are the less powerful member of a collaboration (cf., Lenskyj, 1998, 2002). What this sort of finding means for critics of ecological modernism is that an unfettered belief in the power of public consultation amongst corporate, governmental, and activist/NGO is naïve, and that those attempting to develop a more environmentally friendly system need to find ways to account for (and deal with) the inordinate influence that corporate stakeholders tend to have over environment-related decisions.

Ecological modernism is also not useful for explaining or dealing with the greenwashing practices of some businesses intent on maximizing profit by enhancing their image without (significantly) altering their environment-impacting practices (Beder, 1996, 2002; Lubbers, 2002). That is to say, the 'weak' ecological modernist view that consumer demand for more environmentally friendly products and services will drive the market to be greener does not account for the perverse responses that some businesses will have when their primary goal is profit.

With these issues in mind, renowned environmental sociologist Allan Schnaiberg (1980; Schnaiberg and Gould 2000) offered a powerful response to ecological modernism when he introduced the '**treadmill of production**' metaphor. The metaphor emerges from Schnaiberg's observation that environmental damage is the result of a self-reinforcing process, where government policies that support economic growth—and environmental damage—are continually revised to encourage more economic growth, and thus more environmental damage. That is to say, the response to resource shortages is always the pursuit of new areas to exploit, not the reduction of consumption or modification of lifestyles. The treadmill argument is founded on long-standing critiques of consumer culture that speak to the myriad ways that consumer demand is created and reinforced in order to meet the underlying goal of a hyper-capitalist culture—economic growth.

The actions of governments in their dual role as an initiator of economic growth and a regulator of environment-impacting activity are intriguing in this context because, of course, these actions will, in a neo-liberal era, favour market-driven activity. Hannigan (2006) speaks to this issue:

> . . . governments often engage in a process of 'environmental managerialism' in which they attempt to legislate a limited degree of protection sufficient to deflect criticism [e.g., about environmental concerns] but not significant enough to derail the engine of economic growth. By enacting environmental policies that are complex, ambiguous and open to exploitation by the forces of production and accumulations the state reaffirms its commitments to strategies for promoting economic development. (p. 21)

Sport, the Environment, and Neo-liberalism

With these sorts of critiques in mind, sociologists of sport like Barnes (2009), Mansfield (2009), Schaffner (2009), Trantor and Lowes (2009), and Pitter (2009) describe how responses to sport-related environmental issues are commonly framed in ways that privilege economic interests over environmental ones. Barnes, for example, in her recent study of adventure sports, recognized ways that deceptive associations between environmentalism and outdoor/wilderness sports are commonly promoted, noting that promoting these associations is good for business in the outdoor tourism industry. She notes that the environmentalist mountain bikers she studied:

> . . . were taken by surprise at the damage outdoor tourism, especially mountain bikes, could inflict on the land…Though mountain biking initially seemed preferable to cattle ranching, uranium mining, and gas/oil exploration [activities historically associated with the wilderness areas in Utah that Barnes was writing about], it quickly came to be viewed as a primary threat to the very existence of the landscape…According to educational campaigns designed by the NPS [National Park Service] and environmental organizations, once damaged by footprint or bike tread, soil structure regeneration can take up to 250 years. (Barnes, 2009, pp. 245–46).

Tranter and Lowes (2009) made a similar point in their research on the development of urban spaces in the name of 'public good', describing how such developments are commonly done to serve 'the interests of hegemonic groups in society' (p. 155). With this in mind, the authors note how the development of sport facilities in the 'most expensive and "spectacular" spaces of a city'—common practice in the Australian cities studied by the authors—undermines and contradicts 'the values of environmental and public health through the promotion of [potentially environmentally unfriendly forms of] conspicuous consumption' (p. 155).

Mansfield's (2009) study of health and fitness industries that market their products and activities as 'natural', 'green', and/or environmentally friendly is especially pertinent here as she notes the emphasis on the (mass-marketed) idea that it is a consumer's 'moral and ethical responsibility' to consume green products. The assumption, in this context, is that individuals negatively or positively impact the societies they live in primarily through the decisions they make *when it comes to buying products or services*. Of course, in this (neo-liberal) system, people with more economic or cultural resources have a 'stronger voice' (and those with fewer resources have a weaker voice)—since the only choices in this system are *consumer* choices.

A Closer Look at Ecological Modernization and Sport: The Case of 'Carbon-Neutral' Sporting Events

In this section I summarize key ideas from an article that I wrote on sport and the popular carbon credit system (Wilson, in press). I was inspired to write the article when I kept coming across the terms 'carbon offsetting' and 'carbon neutrality' when studying the environmental work of sport managers and event organizers. I felt it was important to better understand the assumptions that underlay these concepts, and especially the claims that these managers/organizers were making about their use of 'offsets' to help 'neutralize' the impacts of sporting events.

As I came to find out, carbon offsetting and the system for measuring and promoting carbon neutrality is based almost exclusively around ecological modernist principles. What will also become evident in the following sections is that this system, while innovative and progressive in many respects, is based on some problematic assumptions, and has some disconcerting limitations.

The Carbon Credit System and Sport

In recent years it is likely that you have seen sporting event promoters publicizing their successes in running carbon-neutral mega-events. There are many such examples, including the FIFA 2006 World Cup in Germany; the 2007 Super Bowl in Miami; the 2006 Commonwealth Games in Melbourne, Australia; and the 2006 Winter Olympics in Turin, Italy. Event promoters who run carbon-neutral events use a variety of initiatives to reduce emissions, including waste reduction through disposable materials; bottle-recycling stations throughout event venues; attempts to reduce electricity use; and trash reduction strategies, including sorting stations and education around waste reduction for event attendees. The Vancouver 2010 Olympics, for example promoted many of these sorts of initiatives, including:

- The use of hydrogen fuel cell buses to transport visitors to ski resort venues in Whistler.
- The construction of the Richmond Olympic Oval, a structure that is outfitted with an impressive rainwater collection system on its wooden roof— rainwater used for irrigation and toilet flushing.
- The newly constructed Vancouver Convention Centre, home to the Games' media centre, has: (a) a 'living roof' 'made up of 400,000 native plants that capture and reuse rainwater'; b) seawater heating and cooling; and (c) on-site water treatment.

- Employees of Coca-Cola, official sponsor of the Games, wore uniforms at the Games made from recycled plastic bottles, as part of their attempt to be achieve carbon-neutral status in their own right (from Justas, 2010).

Other examples of such innovations include the use of renewable energy technologies like the solar energy panels used in Dolphin Stadium at the 2007 Super Bowl in Miami, and emission friendly fuel used at the 2007 Indy 500 (Davidson, 2007).

The final step, however, for event organizers striving to run carbon-neutral events is to purchase **carbon offset credits**. Buying a credit involves making a contribution to a carbon-reducing initiative, like a renewable energy project. These projects are commonly based in developing countries because, generally speaking, it is much less expensive to fund offset projects in these contexts. The following excerpt from a press release by the United Nations Environment Programme (UNEP) includes an overview of some offset projects funded through the FIFA 2006 World Cup offset program:

> The Organizers [of the World Cup] . . . purchased 500,000 Euros-worth of carbon offsets in India where 900 farmers and their families in Tamil Nadu are getting bio-gas cooking fuel from cow dung instead of using fuel wood or fossil fuels. Offsets also came from investments in South Africa with financing from FIFA, Deutsche Telecom and PlasticsEurope in a sewage gas project in Sebokeng Township near Johannesburg and a sawdust-fuelled fruit drying furnace in Letaba, northern South Africa. These offsets saved an estimated 100,000 tonnes of carbon dioxide entering the global atmosphere. Christian Hockfeld of the Oeko Institute said: 'That means that at the end we over-compensated the additional emissions in Germany by 8,000 tonnes. It means that the Green Goal actually went further than we had planned by also compensating for the estimated 5,100 tonnes as a result of international travel by teams and officials.' (UNEP, 2006)

Event organizers work with independent experts who verify the carbon emissions of an event. Vancouver 2010, for example, worked with Offsetters, a Vancouver-based company that promotes themselves as being 'Canada's premier provider of high quality solutions for individuals and organizations seeking to reduce their climate impact'.[2] It is becoming common practice, and in some cases an expectation, that those organizing major sporting events use offset programs and strive for carbon-neutral status. For example, a 2007 UNEP report that evaluated the progress of the Beijing Organizing Committee for the Olympic Games (BOCOG) on environmental issues—a report that was largely complimentary of BOCOG's progress—was critical of the organization for excluding carbon offsetting as an eco-friendly practice (UNEP, 2007). Ultimately, and considering also the positive coverage that such events receive when they achieve 'carbon-neutral' status, it would seem that Chernushenko was right to suggest that that 'going green' is good for business.

Too Good To Be Green?

There are a number of reasons to be wary of unqualified claims about the carbon-neutral status of a sport event. To demonstrate some of these reasons, I outline (below) three claims about advances that have taken place because of offsetting and about carbon neutrality in sport in general—and concerns about their veracity. As you will see, concerns about carbon neutrality will also tell us something about the problems with an (exclusively) ecological modernist response to environmental issues.

> **Claim #1: The impacts of sport events can be offset through emissions reductions projects.** For example, in a report prepared by Öko-Institut in Berlin (which works with FIFA's environment program), the claim was made that '92,000 tonnes of unavoidable greenhouse gas emissions that were brought about by the 2006 FIFA World Cup in Germany will be more than offset by three climate protection projects' (*Green Goal – Legacy Report*, Stahl, Hochfeld, and Schmied, 2006, p. 93).

The problem with a claim like this one—a problem acknowledged by those who generally support the use of a carbon offset system—is that it is virtually impossible to implement an offset system in a fully standardized manner. For example, one cannot know for sure if a project that is being funded through a carbon offset program would have taken place anyway, even without the funding provided by organizations providing offset donations. As Gillenwater et al. (2007) note:

> There is no correct technique for determining additionality [the term that refers to the ability of a project to 'add' an emission offset that would not have taken place otherwise]. No test for additionality can provide certainty about what would have happened otherwise.

Others critics note that some projects funded through carbon credit purchases are never actually completed, which, of course, means that the promised emissions-savings will not take place. Although certification programs like Canadian-based Offsetters claim that they will 'confirm that [their] projects take place as promised',[3] it is unclear whether all certification programs can offer the same guarantee, and it is not obvious what happens when projects supervised by Offsetters are not carried out.

Still others point to the challenges experienced by those hired to calculate the carbon emissions of mega-events, who try to distinguish between 'avoidable' and 'unavoidable' emissions. An emissions-trading expert from Öko-Insitut in Berlin—the same organization, interestingly, that is responsible for the earlier claim about the successful greening of the 2006 FIFA World Cup—made this point in an article by Schiermeier (2006) in the journal *Nature*:

> ... 'it's almost impossible for big companies and events to decide which activities to include and where to draw the line between necessary and avoidable emissions,' says Martin Cames, an emissions-trading expert with the Öko-Institut in Berlin. This means that extra emissions are often under estimated. For example, the Öko-Institut worked out the carbon footprint of the World Cup for FIFA, but simplified the calculation by counting only the extra flights caused by the event. (Schiermeier, 2006, p. 976)

It is also well known that aforestation and reforestation projects, which are sometimes used for offsets, are problematic because 'there is no guarantee that a forest will be permanent...[and] when trees die, they release all the CO_2 they absorbed during their lives' (Schiermeier, 2006, p. 977). For this reason, several offset programs, including Offsetters, claim to 'avoid' or refuse to certify such projects, although other certification programs continue to include them.

Claim #2: Olympic Games Organizing Committees 'have the ability to utilize the latest in innovations and technology to promote Games of the highest standards of sustainability and legacy' (from Vancouver Declaration of the 8th World Conference on Sport and the Environment, 2009)

Underlying this claim is a profound faith in technology, and a related faith in the idea that economic growth and progress on environmental issues are compatible. What is assumed here, according to critics of ecological modernism, is that researchers will need to be effective and timely in their attempts to solve the various and unanticipated environment problems that may arise because of mega–sporting events, so as to avoid any long-term consequences. The idea that scientists may not always be able to 'keep up' is raised by political scientist Thomas Homer-Dixon (2000) in *The Ingenuity Gap: Can We Solve the Problems of the Future?*. In his book, Homer-Dixon refers to the 'time-gap' between 'a problem arising' and scientists actually 'solving the problem'. Robertson (2004) makes a similar argument when he notes that approaches to dealing with environmental problems leave 'no room for a view of science as a shifting and constructed set of knowledges' (p. 118). The idea here is that if societies are overly dependent on scientific advancements to support a way of life (i.e., one that requires ongoing and uninhibited forms of consumption), then there are risks involved. Critics argue that societies that do not require the same levels of growth and high levels of consumption are less at risk.

Other critics question the assumption that the development of new technologies that allow for more efficient uses of energy will necessarily lead to less consumption, and thus enhance sustainability. For example, scholars like Foster et al. (2010) refer to the 'rebound effect' that sometimes takes place following the development of a more efficient fuel-consumption technology—meaning that the overall consumption of a fuel sometimes *increases* following these oft-celebrated technological advancements. This theory is commonly called the '**Jevons Paradox**', referring to nineteenth-century economist Williams Stanley Jevons who argued that overall coal consumption (the dominant source of energy at that time) increased when coal consumption technologies (i.e., the steam engine) became more efficient. The reason for this rebound, according to Jevons and others, is that the technologies that allowed for more efficient forms of consumption often, at the same time, make consumption itself more desirable, and—in Jevons's case— made the coal-driven steam engine an attractive option for industries that did not previously use it. Although most scholars are clear to note that the Jevons Paradox only sometimes applies to post-innovation consumption patterns, and that increases in efficient consumption also, in other cases, lead to less overall consumption— the important point here is that there is no *necessary* relationship between increases in efficiency and less overall consumption.

From this argument emerges a key question for this chapter: How might the Jevons Paradox be relevant to the development of innovative and more efficient technologies intended to make sporting events of all kinds more efficient (e.g., innovative technologies that led to the development of more sustainable sport stadiums, or to the decreased emissions of Formula One race cars)? Does the development of these energy-conserving and efficient technologies mean that people are less likely to question the environmental impacts of major sporting events, which could mean that more events are held overall, leading to more *overall* emissions, despite pro-environment advancements? Although this is a new idea for sociologists of sport, these sorts of questions are important for unsettling the taken-for-granted assumptions that underlie claims about how new innovations and technologies will, as a matter of course, lead to a greener sporting landscape.

Claim # 3: (Sport-related) Environmental damage in one place is 'equivalent' to an environmentally friendly project in another place. That is to say, when emissions or damage take place in an Olympic city (for example), they can be 'offset' or neutralized by supporting an offset project somewhere else in the world.

This claim and assumption is central to the idea that carbon-neutral events are actually 'neutral'. What is overlooked or underemphasized here is the idea that carbon offsetting around mega–sporting events is a form of abstraction.

That is to say, by measuring and documenting the emission levels associated with, for example, the destruction of trees to build a highway to an event venue, *the distinctiveness of the tree and that particular ecosystem (and the air that will be impacted by increased traffic), is lost—even if more trees are planted in another location.* In this way, the (destroyed) tree or (polluted) air is 'abstracted' when the carbon emissions measure that is associated with it is considered to be 'equivalent to' emissions-saving efforts in another part of the world (cf., Castree, 2003).

As noted earlier, this way of thinking about natural, living phenomena through a series of calculations about carbon emissions is insensitive to the *interrelationships* that societies and individuals have with nature. Dryzek (2005) describes the discourse that presumes a separation between humans and nature—and positions nature as an inert resource to be manipulated by humans—as the 'Promethean' discourse. The assumption underlying this discourse is that unlimited forms of consumption are acceptable as long as resources are available.

Responding to this shortcoming, theorist Bruno Latour (1993, 1999) has come to prominence because of his insightful and provocative descriptions of ways that humans and nature's non-human 'actants' are *co-creators/co-constructors* of the world's environments (and that all environments are products of the social and biophysical). Sociologist Mark Stoddart (2008), in his study of eco-politics, skiing, and the environment, describes (drawing on Latour) person–nature 'collectives' on ski hills, and identifies interrelationships between skiers, snow, mountains, and animals. Drawing on Donna Haraway's (2003) work, Stoddart also illustrates the role of animals as 'companion species' or 'significant others' on ski hills, indicating how, 'beyond the symbolic bears or caribou that are recruited into skiing discourse, there are actual animals that share the skiing landscape...that may be negatively affected by human activity within that landscape' (Stoddart, 2008, pp. 108–09). These negative effects on animals can be seen as yet another inequality that is perpetuated when nature is seen to be a commodity to be mastered and manipulated by humans.

Reflections on Sport, the Environment, Power, and Privilege

Two main arguments underlie this chapter. The first is that many (often unacknowledged) inequalities are embedded in and sometimes perpetuated because of sport's relationship with the environment. For example, when sport is implicated in various forms of environmental damage, it is negatively impacting future generations who must live in the conditions our generation has created. At the same time, current generations that are most vulnerable to environment-related problems are more harshly impacted than others—a point made starkly by commentators around Hurricane Katrina who noted the heightened difficulties faced by lower-income people following the environmental disaster.

At the same time, sport-related activities also impact animals, plants, and other non-human inhabitants of the world. Since it is usual to consider these non-human inhabitants as commodities for our exploitation (especially by those subscribing to a modernist view)—instead of co-inhabitants of the planet—these impacts are rarely considered. Of course, within a carbon offsetting system where equivalency is drawn between the destruction of natural environments and carbon-saving activities 'somewhere else in the world', such interspecies inequalities are missing from the equation.

This point is akin to one made by critics of the sustainability concept who argue that the term can be used to promote the idea that progress on economic, social, and environmental matters can be attained by paying 'equal' attention to each of these 'lines' of the 'triple bottom line'. The problem here, of course, is that sustaining a capitalist system that is designed to promote economic growth and high standards of living (and in many cases, living beyond our needs) is sometimes seen to be 'as important as' (i.e., 'equivalent to') preserving a fragile natural environment. Many see the environment-related compromises that are sometimes made to maintain 'acceptance levels' of economic growth as short-sighted and mercenary (Williams, 2010). As you might expect, debates persist about what constitutes an acceptable level of growth, and about the ethics of promoting the hyper-consumption lifestyles that drive this growth.

The second and related argument is that the ecological modernist approach to resolving environmental problems—while a progressive and important response to one of the pressing societal issues of our time (i.e., global warming and associated environmental problems)—is commonly presented as the 'only solution' to sport-related environmental problems (Wilson and Millington, in press). This is apparent from the unqualified claims that are commonly made about the benefits of the carbon offset system, and the accolades and recognition sport mangers receive when they are able to claim carbon-neutral status for an event they organized.

Noting that carbon neutrality is a success by some measures, one is still left to ask: If carbon-neutral status is achieved, what is left to say about the environmental destruction that did take place during an event?; Is the destruction meaningless, invisible, or irrelevant as it was offset using the carbon credit system?; In what ways is a carbon-saving emissions project in another part of the world *not* equivalent to the carbon produced during, for example, the Vancouver 2010 Olympics? Perhaps most importantly, we are left to wonder why these sorts of questions are so rarely featured in mainstream discussions about the environmental impacts of mega–sporting events.

To be clear, the argument here is *not* that ecological modernist approaches to dealing with (sport-related) environmental problems should be avoided. In fact, it is crucial that the various tools and strategies that are available should be considered or adopted as part of a broader response to environmental problems. What I am arguing is that ecological modernist approaches—based around the idea that economic growth and high levels of consumption do not need to be compromised if new technologies and innovative strategies are developed—should be considered *alongside other approaches to dealing with environmental problems*, approaches that might mean less consumption and less growth. While such approaches would compromise the hegemonic power of the groups who benefit from the unquestioned need to host resource-draining and (inevitably) environmentally destructive sporting events 'at all costs', it would certainly be more democratic to feature a palette of strategies and options for dealing with environmental problems.

For example, and responding to the common argument that sporting mega-events can be used to leverage pro-environment developments in cities that host these events—we might consider how some of these same developments might be achieved *without* hosting mega-events, especially in cities that have failed in their bids for these events, but have a long-term, pro-environment plan already in place. Such a response would undermine the taken-for-granted idea that sporting mega-events are *necessary* political tools for inspiring pro-environment changes, noting that these positive changes must always be weighed against the negative impacts of these events. At the same time, it would also reestablish the idea that communities and cities can, and do, make pro-environment decisions that are not driven by the demands of organizations like the IOC—organizations that are not accountable to the people who live in these cities, but are always accountable to their corporate sponsors.

By way of conclusion, it is also important to highlight that the mega-event–sponsored, carbon offsetting projects that take place in developing countries are forms of international development and are driven by processes associated with economic globalization—and should therefore be assessed according to the principles introduced in chapters 4 and 7. For example, it is not only important to ask questions about how offsetting projects allow some businesses and mega-event organizers to achieve carbon neutrality—achievements that should, in themselves, be questioned for reasons outlined in this chapter—but questions should also be posed about the types of relationships that exist between project sponsors and those working on the projects (and those living in the communities where these projects are taking place), labour conditions for those working on these projects, and the extent to which these projects allow some sporting event organizers to continue doing business as usual in the areas where mega-events are taking place, while relying on payments to these offset projects in developing countries to 'neutralize' their impacts. With these issues in mind, it becomes easier to see how the sport and peace–related topics that are commonly dealt with separately—like sport's relationship to economic globalization, to international development, and to environmental issues—are always interrelated, and how a sociological imagination can help us see these important connections.

Notes

1. Available from: www.pc.gc.ca/eng/pn-np/ab/waterton/natcul/inter.aspx
2. Retrieved from: www.offsetters.ca/learn-more
3. Retrieved from: www.offsetters.ca/learn-more

Discussion Questions

1. Should sport's response to environmental problems be based on an assumption that economic growth and environmental progress are compatible? Where do you stand and why?

2. How might the Jevons Paradox be relevant to the development of innovative and more efficient technologies intended to make sporting events of all kinds more efficient?

3. How is carbon offsetting around mega–sporting events a form of abstraction?

4. What relationships exist between sport, the environment, and peace? Do you see any contradictions? What are they?

Suggested Readings

Chernushenko, D., van der Kamp, A. & Stubbs, D. (2001). Sustainable sport management: Running an environmentally, socially and economically responsible organization. Nairobi, Kenya: United Nations Environment Programme. This updated version of Chernushenko's classic *Greening Our Games* offers an accessible and practical approach to environmental issues, with a target audience of sport managers.

Hannigan, J. (2006). *Environmental sociology* (2nd ed.). New York, NY: Routledge. This is an outstanding overview of the field of environmental sociology, and offers more depth and background on the main topics and theories discussed here (minus the sport focus).

Lenskyj, H. (1998). Sport and corporate environmentalism: The case of the Sydney 2000 Olympics. *International Review for the Sociology of Sport*, 33(4), 341–54. An early but provocative article examining and critiquing sport-related corporate environmentalism.

Wheaton, B. (2007). Identity, politics, and the beach. Environmental activism in Surfers Against Sewage. *Leisure Studies* 26, 279–302. An original study of a sport-related social movement focused around environmental issues.

Relevant Websites

United Nations Environment Programme—Sport and the Environment
www.unep.org/sport_env
> This section of the United Nations Environment Programme website features a variety of initiatives and information related to sport's role in responding to environmental concerns.

The Globe and Mail Series on Sport and Society
www.theglobeandmail.com/intellectual-muscle/the-talks/article1312702
> This webpage includes a series of podcasts about sport and society that were posted during the 2010 Vancouver Olympic Games. Recommended listening for this chapter is the talks by and panel discussion with James Tansy, Derek Wyatt, Bruce Kidd, and Sid Katz. The session is entitled 'Sport, Legacy and Sustainability: Is it Worth It?'.

Global Forum for Sports and the Environment
http://en.g-forse.com
> The Global Forum for Sports and the Environment, the 'largest database on environmental action in sports', 'highlights a broad spectrum of environmental action in sports from around the world in order to educate and promote these activities', promoting the activities of 'sports federations, sporting goods manufactures, event producers and sports enthusiasts'.

Key Terms

Augusta National Syndrome refers to Augusta National Golf Club, where the widely televised 'Masters' Professional Golf Association (PGA) event is played, and to the unrealistic expectations that highly manicured courses like Augusta—which are sometimes closed for several months to prepare for major events—place on other golf course managers in the industry.

carbon offset credit represents a 'unit' or amount of carbon emission that is being 'offset' through a monetary contribution by a person or organization. Buying a credit is like making a contribution to a carbon-reducing initiative, like a renewable energy project. For a contribution to count as an offset credit, approval for the carbon-reducing/saving project receiving the contribution is generally required from a recognized certifier.

corporate environmentalism industry-led techniques and strategies for dealing with environmental issues.

ecological modernization a theoretical approach to understanding the relationship between humans and environmental issues that is focused around ways that humans can continue to 'progress' (e.g., economically) without long-term negative impacts on the environment because humans will also progress in their development of 'green' or 'superindustrial' technologies that will minimize or eliminate these impacts.

greenwashing the term used to describe disingenuous attempts to promote pro-environment work and attitudes, attempts that are not accompanied by eco-friendly practices. It also refers to situations where the eco-friendliness of pro-environment work is overstated, such that 'appearing green' is prioritized over 'being green'.

intergenerational inequity referring here to ways that future generations may be negatively impacted by the environment-related activities of current generations.

intra-generational inequity referring here to the need to account for existing social inequalities of all kinds (e.g., around class, gender, ethnicity, and 'race') when devising sustainability projects and considering the impacts of environmentally damaging behaviours.

Jevons Paradox referring to nineteenth-century economist Williams Stanley Jevons, who argued that overall coal consumption (a dominant source of energy at that time) increased when coal consumption technologies, especially the steam engine, became more efficient. The paradox has been referred to by environmental sociologists who highlight why we should not assume that technological innovations that are intended to promote sustainability will inevitably do so, as people may choose to consume more because of the new technology (and the increase in consumption might offset the efficiency gains).

sustainability refers here to an integrated strategy for addressing economic, social, and environmental issues—what is commonly known as the 'triple bottom line'. The classic definition for sustainability, offered in the 1986 report *Our Common Future* (produced for the World Commission on Environment and Development), refers to our society's capacity to '[meet the needs] needs of the present without compromising ability of future generations to meet their own needs' (see Brundtland, 1987).

transfrontier inequity referring to ways that environment-related activities taking place in 'local' contexts may have a negative impact on those living in other places.

treadmill of production This theoretical approach and metaphor is based around the view that environmental damage is the result of a self-reinforcing process, where government policies that support economic growth—and environmental damage—are continually revised to encourage more economic growth, and thus more environmental damage (Schnaiberg and Gould 2000).

9 Towards a Sport-for-Peace Journalism? Problems and Possibilities in Sport Media

Questions to Consider

⊛ In what ways can sports coverage and commentary promote and endorse violence, conflict, war, and militarism?

⊛ What is the 'hierarchy of influences' model and how is it useful for describing the various pressures journalists face in their day-to-day work and explaining why journalists make the decisions they do about what to include and exclude in their stories?

⊛ What are the differences between conflict journalism and peace journalism and how can an understanding of these differences be helpful for sociologists who study sport media, and the journalists responsible for it?

⊛ What are the possibilities for a sport-for-peace journalism?

Introduction: A Challenge for (Sport) Journalists and Introducing Peace Journalism

In their 2005 book *Peace Journalism*, BBC journalists Jake Lynch and Annabel McGoldrick offer a provocative and thoughtful reflection on ways that the 2003 invasion of Iraq by the US, Britain, and other participating countries was covered in the news. In an expression of regret and embarrassment— and with the goal of preventing future oversights and shortfalls—the authors admit that their coverage and the coverage of their many usually competent peers was inadequate and uncritical. Their admission was not an isolated one. Editors at the *New York Times* also published their own mea culpa for what was retrospectively perceived to be (at times) poor coverage of the events leading up to and during the invasion. The apology appears below:

> Editors at several levels who should have been challenging reporters and press-ing for more skepticism were perhaps too intent on rushing scoops into the paper . . . Articles based on dire claims about Iraq tended to get prominent display, while follow-up articles that called the original ones into question were sometimes buried. In some cases, there was no follow-up at all. (published May 26, 2004, www.nytimes.com/2004/05/26/international/middleeast/26FTE_NOTE.html, also quoted in Lynch and McGoldrick, 2005, p. 3)

While the *Times* editorial refers to the uncritical and sometimes unsubstantiated claims that were published in the newspaper, Lynch and McGoldrick and other media analysts are more straightforward in their argument that much of the coverage was biased, and more accurately, *patriotic*. What this means from a sociological perspective is that readers and viewers of news were offered narratives about the war effort that were collectively generating consent for a particular way of understanding the effort, for a particular side.

I open this chapter with Lynch and McGoldrick's reflections not only because they highlight one of the many important ways that mass media can influence ways of seeing peace and conflict–related events, a point which has particular pertinence to sport (as I will show), but also because their work includes commentary about the role that journalists *could play* in peace promotion. That is to say, these journalists challenged their peers to offer coverage of conflict that includes the voices of vulnerable groups, emphasizes roots causes for conflicts, and humanizes both sides of a conflict—all features of what has come to be known as **peace journalism** (cf., Lynch and Galtung, 2010).

Using observations by Lynch and McGoldrick as a departure point, I describe and assess the rich body of sociological research that illuminates ways that themes of war, conflict, and terrorism are embedded in and sometimes perpetuated through sport media. Since little has been written about the principles that might guide a 'sport-for-peace journalism', I also consider how journalists and media commentators could draw on principles of peace journalism to cover sport. I go on to argue that sociologists who study sport journalism would benefit from attention to heuristic devices that allow them to see opportunities for and barriers to sport-for-peace journalism. By attending to these particular opportunities and barriers, so the argument goes, sociologists of sport will be in a better position to offer practical recommendations to those interested in undermining the violence and conflict–focused culture of mainstream sport coverage.

Sport Media, Peace, and Conflict: Themes in the Sociology of Sport

Sociologists of sport have identified a range of connections between sport, conflict, and war—and the media's role in making such connections a taken-for-granted part of popular culture. One of the more obvious and oft-discussed relationships is in the shared vocabularies of sport commentators and those who report on war and conflict in mainstream news. As S. King (2008), Jansen and Sabo (1994), and others note, broadcasters, coaches, players, and others—especially those associated with gridiron football—have always drawn heavily on the argot of the military, with common references to victories, defeats, and casualties, and the frequent use of words like 'attack, blitz, bombs, ground and air assaults, offense, defense, penetrations, flanks, conflicts, and battles for territory' (Jansen and Sabo, 1994, p. 3). At the same time, language used by military and government officials in commentary about war and conflict is similarly peppered with sport metaphors. Jansen and Sabo (1994) offer one of the more powerful summaries of this sort of 'sportspeak' in their reflections on the Persian Gulf War of 1991:

> One of the most compelling and widely quoted examples of sport/war imagery during the Persian Gulf War was provided by General Norman Schwartzkopf when he characterized the strategic plan of the ground war as 'the Hail Mary play in football.' . . . The first pilots returning from bombing raids on Baghdad described the action to reporters as 'like a big football game', 'like a football game where the defense never showed up'. The general and his pilots, moreover, were echoing their Commander-in-Chief, George Bush, who had accused Saddam Hussein of 'stiff-arming' the pre-war diplomatic negotiations. (p. 3)

King (2008) notes also how the use of sport metaphors by George W. Bush were so prominent during the occupations of Iraq and Afghanistan that foreign interpreters, who were unfamiliar with such metaphors, complained about the difficulty Bush posed in their translation work. Along the same lines, sociologists of sport have noted ways that sport is sometimes positioned as a 'surrogate' for war (King, 2008, p. 529), a point represented well in Ronald Reagan's famous suggestion that 'sport is the human activity closest to war that isn't lethal' (quoted in Burstyn, 1999, p. 65). Even as the National Football League (NFL) has made efforts in recent years to reduce their use of war metaphors (Carpenter, 2009), King points out that these efforts in no way diminish the league's overt endorsements of, and implicit associations with, the military (King, 2008)—a point I pick up later in this chapter.

As a way of encapsulating these interrelationships between forms of mass entertainment (like professional sport and video games) and coverage of war and military action, the term '**militainment**' has emerged (Stahl, 2010). Interviewed in a documentary on the topic entitled *Militainment Inc.: Military and Popular Culture* (Stahl, 2007), communications professor Roger Stahl of the University of Georgia offers a provocative example of a relationship that exists between the military and professional football through his discussion of an NFL pre-game segment called 'Tough Guys'. The segment, hosted by NFL commentator and former linebacker Howie Long, is sponsored by the Pentagon as well as the Ford Motor Company. Through these associations, according to Stahl, 'a synergistic infomercial' is created for the military, Ford trucks, and NFL football. The segment itself features Long on a search across America for the toughest NFL players, a journey that is interspersed with visits to each branch of the military—so that Long can 'take a ride' in the various military vehicles. After awarding a Ford truck to the winning tough guy, Long offers these parting words to the audience: 'I'd like to thank the Department of Defense and everyone who made "Tough Guys" possible. I'm Howie Long, stay tough' (quoted in Stahl, 2007).

Certainly the military and the NFL benefit from this form of cross-promotion. The military strengthens its links with a more sanitized form of violence (i.e., sport violence) and with the other forms of positive imagery (excitement, athleticism) that the league provides. It also receives ongoing 'exposure by association' through the mass audience that the NFL attracts each week of its season. At the same time, the NFL benefits by attracting fans who see their allegiance to the NFL as patriotic and who are positioned to consume NFL-related products or donate to the NFL's charity fund as a way of 'doing good' (King, 2008). Such a strategy is, of course, embedded in a neo-liberal sensibility whereby citizenship and volunteerism is equated with consuming the goods of those considered to be the best 'corporate citizens'.

As marketers have known for years, creating many and varied associations between brands like the NFL and the US military fuels what Wernick (1991) has called a '**vortex of publicity**'—as these brands begin to automatically refer to each other in a cycle of associations. Scholars like Dewhirst and Hunter (2002) note that these links are especially powerful for consumer-audiences when the two products are 'complementary'—meaning that they share key characteristics (the way, for example, that tobacco and auto racing have had a longstanding relationship as brands associated with 'risk-takers'). All this to say, the NFL and certain other sports are clearly part of a powerful pro-military relationship and marketing scheme.

What Are the Implications of Sport–War Connections?

Violence Is Normalized

There are various intended and unintended consequences of such widespread sport–war connections—beyond the promotional benefits certain sport leagues and the military accrue. One of the most notable consequences is the *normalization* of military and war-related language and imagery.

The problem with this, according to authors like Butterworth and Moskal (2009), is that forceful and violent (i.e., 'shock and awe'–style) responses to international conflicts come to be seen as natural, rational, and (above all) expected. Such an argument could equally apply on a more micro level, as the normalized idea that conflicts of any kind are best solved through intimidation and force would seem to be reinforced here—and exacerbated in the messaging provided in the world of mixed martial arts (MMA) and professional wrestling. Pertinent here is Atkinson and Young's (2008, pp. 190–91) work on criminal violence in sport, that includes a discussion of ways that certain forms of violence become sanctioned within particular cultures and how violent behaviours which many would consider abnormal or pathological are actually 'normal' and expected in particular sporting contexts (as Robinson [1998] has argued about junior hockey in Canada).

Sport Is Implicated in Extreme Displays of Patriotism and 'Othering'

Although there is a tradition of work in the sociology of sport field that speaks to ways that patriotism and nationalist sentiments are promoted through sport media coverage (Delgado, 2003; Jansen and Sabo, 1994), research in this area has accelerated since the terrorist attacks of September 11, 2001. Falcous and Silk (2005), for example, demonstrate how Fox Network's coverage of the Super Bowl and NBC's coverage of the Salt Lake City Olympics appeared to 'manufacture consent' for a view of the US as being united in a 'common vision of defeating terror' and for articulating 'who were friends and who were foes' when it came to the war against terror (p. 63, following Herman and Chomsky, 1988). To illustrate this, Falcous and Silk (2005) provide readers with excerpts of commentary from the opening ceremonies, where countries that were clearly aligned with the US were lauded by announcers, while ambivalent responses were offered to welcome those with more questionable allegiances (see Box 9.1 for an example of this in the Canadian context). Atkinson and Young (2008) similarly argue in their study of the same Olympics that by consenting to extreme displays of patriotism at the Games the IOC and members of the international community were implicated in the dissemination of 'American political views on terrorists or enemies of the state' to 'sport audiences around the world' (p. 212).

There are several issues here that are especially troubling for those concerned with issues around peace and democracy. First, and although the critics noted above are sensitive to the reasons why a horrific incident like 9/11 would incite particular reactions and inspire an assertive, action-oriented position by those in leadership, they are clear in their argument that some of these reactions are in no way aligned with peace promotion. That is to

---

BOX 9.1 ❄ SPORT, MILITARISM, AND *HOCKEY NIGHT IN CANADA*:
          CANADA'S GAME AND A CONSERVATIVE AGENDA?

As you are beginning to see, hyper-patriotic and pro-military messages are, according to many sociologists of sport, prominent and common in media coverage of professional sporting events in the US especially (e.g., Butterworth, 2005; Falcous and Silk, 2005, 2006: S. King, 2008; McDonald, 2005). Although few recent studies exist on this topic in the Canadian context, Jay Scherer and Jordan Koch's (2010) article 'Living With War: Sport, Citizenship, and the Cultural Politics of Post-9/11 Canadian Identity' is an important exception. These researchers describe how coverage of hockey—and especially a recent broadcast of CBC's renowned *Hockey Night in Canada*—is strikingly similar to coverage of events in US. The broadcast they examined, known colloquially as *Tickets for Troops*, took place at Rexall Place in Edmonton, Alberta in November 2007 as part of an NHL game between the Edmonton Oilers and the Chicago Blackhawks. As Scherer and Koch (2010) describe:

[the game] was the culmination of a philanthropic campaign spearheaded by the Edmonton Oilers hockey club and Rexall (Canadian Retail Pharmacy) to honour and support the Canadian Forces, whose presence in Afghanistan remains one of the most pressing political debates in Canada. Local season ticket holders were called upon to perform their neo-liberal citizenship duties, and donate tickets to this specific game to military personnel garrisoned at Canadian Forces Base Edmonton in exchange for a tax receipt for the ticket's face value. (p. 2)

Scherer and Koch raise many issues about the event that are reminiscent of findings described in other areas of this chapter. For example, they note that this sort of broadcast acts an endorsement of Canada's efforts in Afghanistan—efforts that appear from this broadcast to be uncontested across the nation. In this way, according to Scherer and Koch, the pro-military stance commonly associated with Canada's Conservative Party is taken for granted in the midst of the celebrations and fund-raising, all the while the CBC is offering an open and unchallenged 'platform to speak to a national audience and promote Canada's role in Afghanistan' (p. 18). Of course, all this takes place against a background where Canada's involvement in Afghanistan remains a subject of much debate within and outside the House of Commons.

Scherer and Koch also note that although several interviews with soldiers took place throughout the game, not a single female soldier was interviewed (although several were in attendance at the game). In fact, the 'only women who appeared regularly were the soldiers' wives who were positioned as vulnerable and responsible for maintaining the domestic "front"' (p. 19), portrayals thought to reinforce stereotypes about the role that men and women should play in a world that 'requires' masculine protectors and feminine homemakers.

Although much more research is needed to investigate the types of messages that circulate in Canadian media about military and sport, Scherer and Koch's study alerts readers to the role that sport media can play in diffusing particular political and social messages.

say, although the promotion of a military-oriented culture and disposition is sometimes equated with 'protecting democracy', there are good reasons to suggest that it does quite the opposite. King (2008), for example, notes how actively questioning a culture that is highly militarized is often actively discouraged—and may be seen as unpatriotic.

There are still other ways that sport is implicated in this process of encouraging passivity. For example, Butterworth and Moscal (2009, p. 414) suggest that sport's close and often taken-for-granted link with the military may 'cultivate a nation of complicit citizens' who may be unaware of ways that their support of certain commercial sports may implicitly promote militarization, and how these taken-for-granted and 'complementary ties' between the sports and the military may discourage critical and reflective thought about militarization. Butterworth (2005) summarizes these concerns in his study of post-9/11 tributes at ballparks across America:

> [while these tributes initially] promised comfort to millions in shock . . . [they] soon developed into rituals of victimization that affirmed the Bush administration's politics of war, discouraged the expression of dissenting opinions, and burdened the nation with yet another disincentive to reflect constructively on its response to terrorism. (p. 107)

King (2008) notes also the irony that African-Americans (usually men)—who are highly represented in professional sports and in the US military—are common reference points in the promotion of nationalism in the US. The irony here is that although African-Americans and other marginalized groups receive (comparatively speaking) few benefits within a highly neo-liberalized system of governance, they are ubiquitous in sport and military-related campaigns intended to promote consent for this system.

It is also important to note here that the economic security offered to athletes and soldiers more generally is limited, as their work is most often short-term (King, 2008). King's point is that 'the prominence of men of color in [the military and sport] masquerades as evidence of the egalitarian character of US society rather than the effect of highly limited opportunities for upward mobility in a racialized, capitalist formation' (2008, p. 532). For King, this is an excellent example of ways that consent is attained for a mythical view of the US—which is to say, this an excellent example of ways that the media is implicated in the promotion and perpetuation of a hegemonic relationship.

A Hypermasculine Version of Sport Is Privileged

According to scholars like McDonald (2005), Stempel (2006), and Jansen and Sabo (1994), the links that are commonly made between 'sport and patriotism' and 'sport and militarism' work together to privilege a particular form of sport—a hypermasculine version. That is to say, the men that play sports such as professional football, basketball, hockey, and baseball are commonly held up as exemplars of powerful and aggressive forms of masculinity. Since the form of masculinity embodied by these athletes—a form of hegemonic masculinity (cf., Messner et al., 2000)—is also valued in soldiers, there is a clear link (in mass media coverage and elsewhere) between the military and *hypermasculine* sports in particular. Indeed, and as Trujillo (2000) notes, 'perhaps no single institution in American culture has influenced our sense of masculinity more than sport', as 'dominant groups have successfully persuaded many Americans to believe that sport builds manly character' and 'even prepares young men for war' (p. 1). Scherer and Koch (2010) and Wilson (2005) speak to this in their work on links between sport and the military in Canada, where they remind readers that during the First World War, hockey players were considered ideal candidates for military service because the violent sport was a 'reliable and necessary guardian of masculinity and military preparedness' (Wilson, 2005, p. 315; cf., Scherer and Koch, 2010, p. 3).

The implications of this are important if we consider how these athletes have, especially following 9/11, been positioned in mass media and elsewhere as emblems of freedom, or as 'symbolic soldiers' (McDonald, 2005, p. 135). In McDonald's essay on the topic, she highlights how sport journalists and others looked to Major League Baseball players—and the New York Yankees especially—as leaders who could help bring stability back to the US by 'lifting their citizens,' and 'helping the city [of New York] heal' in the aftermath of the terrorist attacks (McDonald, 2005, pp. 135–36).

This is not to suggest of course that there is not value in the escape and enjoyment that one can attain from spectator sport. However, there is something ironic about promoting a form of 'healing and normalcy' through the consumption of hypermasculine sports—sports where particular forms of sanctioned and unsanctioned violence are normalized (see also chapter 6). It is also ironic that some government officials and others see the athletes in these hypermasculine sports as figures who will lead us away from problems of fear and insecurity, especially when many would reasonably argue that the culture perpetuated within and around these sports *should itself generate fear and insecurity* (again, see chapter 6). I acknowledge here that many athletes in these sports are excellent role models who speak out on and are leaders around key social issues; however, research within the sociology of sport area should lead us to ask questions about blanket endorsements of commercial sport athletes as leaders in moments of tragedy, conflict, and war.

There is also a long history of relying on masculine metaphors to promote feelings of security and power, noting that 'weak' countries that are dominated in war tend to be feminized in media discourses (McDonald, 2005). For those interested in peace-promotion of all kinds, interrupting these cycles of promoting violent masculinities as a form of security and comfort is an important step towards addressing violence of all kinds.

A Nuanced Sport Media: Some Reflections and Warnings, and a Way Forward

The title of this section—'a nuanced sport media'—is meant to have two meanings. On one hand, it refers to the need for a more nuanced media approach to sport—more balanced, self-reflexive, critical, and progressive. Later in this section I describe some guiding principles with this in mind.

On the other hand, it is meant to highlight ways that (sport) media is sometimes more nuanced than it would appear from the studies I have featured above. For example, it is well known that it is usual to portray sport in ways that support and promote conflict and military, which is to say, this is the dominant framing of sport in the studies noted above. However, there are other framings as well, although these are seldom featured in research reports because they are far less common.

Delgado (2003), for example, in his study of media representations of a contentious soccer match between the US and Iran in 1998 describes a dominant frame and a set of alternative frames. One of the frames focused on historical political tensions between the US and Iran, and highlighted the symbolic political import of the match for each country. An alternative frame focused on President Bill Clinton's attempts to use the sporting event as an opportunity to break down political barriers between the countries. Yet another frame highlighted the idea that politics should have nothing to do with the event.

Delgado's analysis is notable here because, while emphasizing that the 'political tension' frame is dominant, the possibilities for sport as a tool for reconciliation are also featured. Even the 'denial of politics frame' Delgado identifies was based around a set of viewpoints offered by players, coaches, and fans from Iran and the US who suggested that the match could be an opportunity to demonstrate good sportsmanship, to focus on ways to 'get past' old tensions. Indeed, reports in this frame emphasized the camaraderie that was evident between fans and players of both countries. For example:

> Iranians and Americans, in full party mode, tied together the tips of their national flags and danced the linked colors through the streets of Lyon as they headed for the soccer showdown. (Botchford, 1998, p. 5, quoted in Delgado, 2003, p. 299)

> . . . both sides exhibited extraordinarily good sportsmanship on the playing field. Their respective fans, some of whom found themselves seated in adjacent sections in the stadium, got along famously, even exchanging hats and souvenirs as the game unfolded. (Curtiss, 1998, pp. 3, 4, quoted in Delgado, 2003, p. 299)

While there are of course issues with underplaying ways that power rela-tions and inequalities are embedded in and perpetuated through sport (i.e., saying an event is apolitical is a great way to disguise real social problems and tensions), it is important to be cognizant also of ways that these alterna-tive frames go against the grain of the hyper-patriotic and conflict-oriented frames featured in so many studies on the topic. At a minimum, this gives us a glimpse into what journalists and commentators working in sport-related media can do with issues around conflict (even if they tend not to do it), and what alternative viewpoints might look like in mainstream sport media.

Explaining Journalist Practices: The 'Propaganda Model' and the 'Hierarchy of Influences Model'

If there is evidence that journalists can, and sometimes do, report sport in ways that deemphasize conflict and the military, why don't they do it more often? Why have sociologists of sport come to expect that such reporting and coverage will be hyper-patriotic, hyper-masculinist, and contribute to the nor-malization of violence?

There are various and somewhat diverse explanations for this, some of which underlie the arguments made by the sociologists of sport cited above. Falcous and Silk (2005) in their article 'Manufacturing Consent: Mediated Sporting Spectacle and the Cultural Politics of the "War on Terror"', explic-itly draw on the '**propaganda model**' proposed by Herman and Chomsky to explain dominant patterns of media coverage. This model emphasizes the in-fluence of corporate and government elites on what becomes news, and how it is reported. They also outline a set of institutionalized reasons that particular viewpoints tend to be privileged, referring to the reliance of mainstream news media outlets on corporate advertising, and the need for journalists to remain on good terms with members of government and other 'official sources' of in-formation. All of these influences/pressures apparently reflect and contribute to what is presently an ideological orientation toward free-market principles in the news media industry (Hackett, 2006).

Although this propaganda model is extremely useful for highlighting the various pressures that impact what becomes news and how events are covered in the media, there are important shortcomings. For example, it is well known that although there are pressures on journalists to produce news in particular ways, critics suggest that it is not nearly as straightforward as many who use the propaganda model would suggest. In particular, it says little about the agency of journalists to make independent decisions that impact how news is reported (Hackett, 2006). It also assumes that relationships between cor-porate and political elites and those working in newsrooms and other spaces of (sport) media production are direct and uncomplicated. Finally, and ac-knowledging that Herman and Chomsky are aware of the potential of 'the audience' to make sense of media messages in sometimes unintended ways, the propaganda approach is generally thought to downplay the agency of readers/viewers in its emphasis on the impacts of elites (Klaehn, 2002).

A more responsible and balanced heuristic for analyzing media according to Hackett (2007) (and I agree) is to use what Shoemaker and Reese (1996) call a '**hierarchy of influences**' model. This model was designed to highlight the various levels (from micro to macro) at which media is produced and influenced. It allows commentators/sociologists to more easily recognize the different players in and processes at work in media production, and to highlight the indirect paths through which the influences of corporate and government elites make their way into a complex organizational field. Guided by Hackett (2007) and Shoemaker and Reese (1996), I summarize the model below:

Hierarchy of Influences

Level 1: At this level, the influence of *media workers themselves* on how news is delivered is highlighted. Hackett (2007) notes how the 'professionally-related roles and ethics' of those in the industry appear to directly influence content. The socio-demographic backgrounds and personal and political beliefs of journalists/editors 'shape news indirectly, especially when individuals are in a position to override institutional pressures or organizational routines' (Hackett, 2007, cf., Shoemaker and Reese, 1996, p. 65).

Level 2: According to Hackett (2007), *daily work routines* within the newsroom 'structure journalists' output independently of their personal backgrounds and values'. That is to say, 'converting raw materials (information) garnered from suppliers (sources) and delivering it to customers (audiences and advertisers) results in standardized and recurring patterns of content' (Hackett, 2007, cf., Shoemaker and Reese, 1996. p. 109).

Level 3: The *broader organizational imperatives* of media institutions are the next level of influence. In this context, Hackett (2007) describes how the 'commercial systems, the profit orientation shared by private media companies, combined with their hierarchical structure . . . shape content in accordance with ownership's interests'.

Level 4: It is also commonly argued that *extra-media influences* impact how events are reported and news stories constructed. These influences include the 'sources' that feed information to journalists, along with the 'advertisers, the political power of governments, market structures, and technology' (Hackett, 2007).

Level 5: The final and most encompassing level is based around the influence of the dominant *ideologies and cultural narratives* that circulate within and around media. The dominant ideologies and narratives refer in this case to 'a system of values and beliefs that governs what audiences, journalists and other players in the news system see as "natural" or "obvious" and that furthermore serves in part to maintain prevailing relations of power' (Hackett, 2007, cf., Shoemaker and Reese, 1996, pp. 221–24).

This final level—the ideological—is the level most often referred to in the critiques of sport-related media noted in the first part of this chapter (and throughout this book). Ideology, which Hackett suggests is responsible not only for shaping the news but also for shaping, and reproducing, how we see the world through a variety of intertextual means, is integrally associated with (for example) neo-liberalism, since neo-liberalism is both a policy (at a governmental level) and a perspective (at a personal level) on how society operates most effectively. Of course, ideology, which by definition refers to (among other things) a 'set of ideas', a particular perspective, and a 'front' for a particular agenda (Eagleton, 1991), is always part of media production, as the perspectives of the different players associated with media are never absent.

This model also helps analysts see the more and less deterministic aspects of media culture—focusing attention on the agency of journalists and on other 'fissures in the system' where change can take place. This is one of the reasons that the model is so appealing for those interested in promoting a change from 'war/violence journalism' to 'peace journalism', as war/violence journalism is thought to already be woven into the various levels noted above. Looking for ways to interrupt cycles of production at particular places—especially at the level of the journalist (the least 'determined' of the levels)—is a goal here, with the belief that change on one level may begin to radiate to other levels.

Is a Sport-for-Peace Journalism (SPJ) Possible?

Using these models for understanding why the media industry and those working within it operate the way they do, media scholars have in recent years debated whether more peace-promoting journalistic practices are viable. The term 'peace journalism' itself was originally introduced by renowned peace studies scholar Johan Galtung (1998), who drew a set of clear distinctions between what he termed 'war' or 'violence' journalism and 'peace/conflict journalism'. In doing so, he proposed a set of distinctions between these two types of journalism. I outline these distinctions below in an adaptation of ideas offered by Johan Galtung:

War/Violence Journalism Is:
I. War/violence oriented
- Meaning that there are two parties and one goal of winning
- There is an 'us and them' orientation, and the voice expressed is for 'us'
- 'They' are the problem, and the focus is on who prevails in war
- 'They' are dehumanized in war/violence coverage
- It is reactive: it emerges as a response to violence

II. Propaganda-oriented
- It intends to expose 'their' untruths and help 'our' spin on the conflict

III. Elite-oriented
- Meaning there is a focus on 'our' suffering
- Able-bodied elite males are the spokespeople
- A label (often pejorative) is given to the opposing side

IV: Victory-Oriented
- Peace=victory plus ceasefire (and there is a winner and loser)

Peace/Conflict Journalism Is:
I. Peace/conflict-oriented
- Gives voice to all parties; empathy, understanding
- Sees conflict/war as problem, and there is a focus on creative ways to avoid/end conflict
- Humanization of all sides
- Focuses on the invisible effects of violence (trauma, damage to structure/culture)

II. Truth-oriented
- Exposes untruths on all sides / uncovers all cover-ups

III. People-oriented
- Focuses on suffering in general; civilians, women, the aged, children; giving voice to voiceless

IV. Solution-oriented
- Peace = non-violence + creativity
- Focuses on structure, culture, the peaceful society
- Highlights the peace initiative, looks to prevent more war
- Aftermath: resolution, reconstruction, and reconciliation

Authors like Lee and Maslog (2005) and Shinar (2009) revised Galtung's list, suggesting also that '**war journalism**' includes military language, an emphasis on elite or official sources, an emphasis on here-and-now events, partisanship, and the labelling of people as good or bad. Peace journalism, on the other hand, is characterized by an absence of military vocabulary and good–bad taggings, an emphasis on the context for and history of events that led to a particular conflict or incident, and the inclusion of stories of various people associated with a issue in an attempt to humanize various parties (Shinar, 2009, p. 12). It also focuses on the types of relationships that exist between conflicting groups (at various levels, not just an elite level) instead of concentrating on who is winning a tug of war for power. It means being sensitive to ways that marginalized groups are portrayed in media, since stereotyping and negative and partial depictions of these groups is, in itself, a form of cultural violence. It also means raising awareness about the structural forms of violence (e.g., poverty) that exist alongside physical forms that are commonly the focus in coverage of conflict and war (Shinar, 2009). The peace journalist also provides a deep and historical consideration of the context when covering conflict and an awareness of the range of stakeholders that are impacted by various forms of violence. Finally, a peace journalist highlights voices working for creative and non-violent forms of change, and engages challenges around and suggestions for transforming conflict situations.

As you might expect, there have been many and diverse concerns expressed about the guiding principles Galtung and others propose for peace-promoting journalism. Most notably, the idea that peace journalists seek the 'truth' (noted in Galtung's original formulation) while war journalists promote propaganda is controversial, as many analysts suggest that all news stories reflect a particular/partial perspective. Many journalists would see the ideas underlying a pro-peace journalism as a threat to principles of objectivity that are thought to guide their practices. Still others are concerned about the viability of—and likely impact of—peace journalism in the contemporary media environment (Shinar, 2009).

Despite these issues, Galtung's proposal has influenced a range of journalists and scholars who have in many cases updated or adapted aspects of the model as a way of exploring the possibilities for more progressive and democratic forms of journalism that break the cycle of violence/war journalism. As Shinar (2009) notes, Galtung's original dichotomy has inspired a range of ideas from scholars about what alternative framings and representations of violence and conflict might look like. Others, like Lynch and McGoldrick (2005), are concerned with raising awareness about and developing skills in peace journalism—holding seminars in areas of conflict around the world.

The challenge remains, of course, to influence journalistic practices in light of (and in spite of) the hierarchy of influences that Hackett (2006) and Shoemaker and Reese (2006) outline.

Examples of Sport-for-Peace Journalism

With this background then, the question remains—is a sport-for-peace journalism possible? On one level, the answer is a resounding yes! Sport could be—and has been—reported in ways that are better aligned with some of the pro-peace principles outlined by Galtung and others. Prominent American sport journalist and commentator Dave Zirin is a prominent example and a leader in this area. Zirin is a regular contributor to *The Nation* magazine and the *Los Angeles Times*, a columnist for *SLAM Magazine*, the *Progressive*, and the

Philadelphia Weekly, and is author of *What's My Name, Fool?* (Zirin, 2005), *Welcome to the Terrordome* (Zirin, 2007a), *The Muhammad Ali Handbook* (Zirin, 2007b), and *A People's History of Sports in the United States* (Zirin, 2008) (cf., C.R. King, 2008). As C. Richard King notes (2008):

> The politics of sport center Zirin's work. He concerns himself with labor relations and the corporatization of sport; the prejudices and biases of fans and sportswriters, especially racism, homophobia, and sexism; and the spectacles of nationalism. Whereas the mainstream media castigate athletes, often inciting moral panics and social outrage, Zirin champions the humanness and potential of players. In fact, Zirin often focuses on the athletes who resist, transgress, or reject prevailing norms and dominant ideologies. He takes hope in the resistance of past and present players, often calling out superstars who remain silent or compliant, while complicating the comfortable declarations of others. (p. 334)

It is notable here that Zirin's work has drawn interest and praise from sociologists of sport, like C. Richard King, who interviewed Zirin for an article in the *Journal of Sport and Social Issues*, a premiere journal in the field. In fact, the great interest that sociologists of sport have in Zirin's work is likely attributable—at least in part—to the reciprocal interest that Zirin has shown in the sociology of sport! Of course, the interest in Zirin's work can also be explained by the quality and accessibility of his writing, as he models what it means to be a 'critically oriented' or 'radical' sport journalist. In fact, Zirin has reciprocally challenged sociologists of sport to 'get off the bench', to make sure their work is relevant and widely read. As he states:

> [the sociology of sport is] too ghettoized and too coded in academic language presented for other academics. I'm not saying there isn't a place for academic writing, but every [sports sociologist] should also...have a sports and society column in their college paper. Every sports and sociology student should try to intern in their athletic departments. Let's get the ideas out there in the oxygen. There are way too many brilliant trees falling quietly in the forest. (Zirin, quoted in interview with C.R. King—C.R. King, 2008, p. 343)

Canadian journalist Laura Robinson is also significant in this context, as the author of the books *Black Tights: Women, Sport and Sexuality* (2002b), *Crossing the Line: Violence and Sexual Assault in Canada's National Sport* (1998), and various critically oriented examples of sport journalism in newspapers. Robinson was also a key contributor to the award-winning documentary on the Canadian news program *The Fifth Estate* that dealt with issues around athlete violence and sexual assault in Canada's minor hockey league system. Zirin himself recognizes other journalists who historically examined social issues and sport referring to a 'proud tradition [in] . . . the Black Press in the first half of the twentieth century confronting racism and sport, [with] writers like Christine Brennan and Sally Jenkins calling out sexism, [and] Lester Red Rodney of the *Daily Worker*' (Zirin, quoted in interview with C.R. King—C.R. King, 2008, p. 342).

SPJ, the Internet, and the Future

Despite these examples, however, questions remain about the viability of being a sport-for-peace journalist in the context of a corporatized Western media. As with any profession, those who go against the grain risk marginalization, and journalists are no different. *However,* there are reasons to be optimistic—especially in an age of Internet communication—an age when alternative forms of media receive unprecedented forms of attention. Dave Zirin, with his own successful blog edgeofsports.com, notes these possibilities and the challenges they pose to more traditional sport journalists and their practices:

> What infuriates old-school sportswriters is that people on the web are calling them on their privilege, isolation and celebrity. In sharp contrast, bloggers, with their messy passion and sharp interaction with readers, sometimes sound far more authentic . . . the future of sportswriting won't be defined by bloggers but by all writers who care for the craft, whether they write in the newsroom or the basement. It's a bold new world, and traditional sportswriters, with all their puffery and pretension, should step back from the team-sponsored buffet and open bar and get their hands dirty in the virtual sporting scrum taking place online. They may just find they like it. (Zirin, quoted in interview with C.R. King—C.R. King, 2008, pp. 335–36)

At the same time, and as Hackett (2006) notes, if we see (sport) media audiences as having more agency than Herman and Chomsky's propaganda would suggest, then there are reasons to remain open to the emergence of more critically oriented readers/viewers who may demand sport-for-peace journalism—and will certainly consume it if available. Zirin confirms this possibility when he observes: 'If I've found out anything, it's that the angry sports fan is an underserved market' (quoted in interview with C.R. King—C.R. King, 2008, p. 341).

Again, the emergence of new media offers further possibilities, as Internet-based alternative media outlets offer opportunities not just for new forms of consumption, but also renewed forms of citizenship and community. In an article I wrote in the *Sociology of Sport Journal* in 2007 entitled 'New Media, Social Movements, and Global Sport Studies: A Revolutionary Moment and the Sociology of Sport', I spoke to these possibilities—to the potential for collective action around sport-related social issues, for a sport-related 'globalization from below' (Wilson, 2007a). Along with Zirin, sociologists of sport like

Sean Smith, with his thoughtful blog www.sportsbabel.net, are beginning to tap into these Internet-driven possibilities.

Peace Studies, Journalism, and the Sociology of Sport: A Way Forward

This chapter is intended to inspire reflection on ways that critical approaches to understanding sport media might be complemented by the work and ideas of those working in peace studies. In this context, I attempted to show how the 'peace journalism' model, while limited in some respects, offers a template for doing sport-for-peace journalism, instead of the conventional war/violence journalism that is reflected in most sport coverage. Recognizing that constraints on the activities of sport journalists remain in place, the work of people like Dave Zirin can be used to inspire thinking about how more people could simultaneously 'take on and revel in sport' like Zirin has. As Zirin himself put it: 'By speaking out for the political soul of the sports we love, we do more than just build a fighting left that stands for social justice. We also begin to impose our own ideas on the world of sports—a counter morality to compete with the rank hypocrisy of the pro leagues' (quoted in interview with C.R. King—C.R. King, 2008, p. 337). With this in mind, sociologists of sport—who continue to do outstanding work identifying ways that sport media reflect and perpetuate a pro-military culture—can also begin to emphasize fissures in the system, and exploit opportunities for change in an age where alternative forms of media have an extraordinary and global presence.

Discussion Questions

1. How can we explain the prevalence of sport–military linkages?

2. What media venues do you know of that are more likely to promote connections between sport and war/violence? Why these venues?

3. What media venues do you know of that are more likely to provide alternative, critically oriented, and/or peace-promoting coverage of sport? Why these venues?

4. What would need to happen for a 'sport-for-peace journalism' to become the norm?

Suggested Readings

Atkinson, M. & Young, K. (2003). Terror Games: media treatment of security issues at the 2002 Winter Olympic Games. *OLYMPIKA* 11, 53–78. A provocative study of the various media framings of terrorism and security issues in coverage of the 2002 Salt Lake City Olympic Games.

Delgado, F. (2003). The fusing of sport and politics: Media constructions of U.S. versus Iran at France '98. *Journal of Sport and Social Issues*, 27(3), 293–307. An intriguing study that shows how different media 'frames' emerged in coverage of a politically significant sport event.

Scherer, J. & Koch, J. (2010). Living with war: Sport, citizenship, and the cultural politics of post-9/11 Canadian identity. *Sociology of Sport Journal*, 27(1), 1–29. An excellent example of ways that media in Canada and NHL hockey are implicated in the promotion of a 'sport-military' complex.

Stahl, R. (2010). *Militainment, Inc.: War, Media, and Popular Culture*. New York: Routledge. A thought-provoking examination of and reflection on the existence and meaning of relationships between the military, media, and popular culture.

Relevant Websites

The Edge of Sports
www.edgeofsports.com
> This is the website of Dave Zirin, a sports journalist renowned for his proactive stances on peace and justice-related issues.

United States Institute of Peace Media
http://peacemedia.usip.org/frontpage
> This joint project between the US Institute of Peace's Media, Conflict and Peacebuilding Center of Innovation and Georgetown University's Conflict Resolution Program was set up as a site for the collection of media resources that the site moderators believe help promote peace. The 'about' page states 'Our database is extensive, and continues to grow every day. Within seconds, you might find a heartfelt documentary on Afghan and Iraq war veterans saved by flyfishing, poignant and telling photos of conflicts across the world, or a challenging game that places you in the role of African subsistence farmer.'

Media Awareness Network
www.media-awareness.ca/english/index.cfm
> This is a Canadian non-profit organization that develops and delivers media literacy programs. Their website includes information that identifies and describes issues around portrayals of masculinity and femininity in sport.

Peace Journalism
www.peacejournalism.org/Welcome.html
> A webpage with links to an array of articles on peace journalism.

Key Terms

hierarchy of influences model a model designed to highlight the various levels (from micro to macro) at which media is produced and influenced. The model allows sociologists to more easily recognize the different players in and processes at work in media production, and to highlight the 'indirect paths' through which the influences of corporate and government elites make their way into a complex organizational field, like the field of journalism.

militainment a term that has come to be used to encapsulate interrelationships between forms of mass entertainment (like professional sport and video games) and coverage of war and military action.

peace journalism an approach to doing journalism that is characterized by what are thought to be peace-promoting qualities, including an absence of military vocabulary and 'good-bad' taggings, an emphasis on the context for and history of events that led to a particular conflict or incident, the inclusion of stories of various people associated with a issue in an attempt to humanize various parties, a focus on the types of relationships that exist between conflicting groups (at various levels, not just an elite level), being sensitive to ways that marginalized groups are portrayed in media, and highlighting voices working for creative and non-violent forms of change (Galtung, 1998; Shinar, 2009).

propaganda model a model proposed by Herman and Chomsky (1988) to explain dominant patterns of media coverage. This model emphasizes the influence of corporate and government elites on what becomes news and how it is reported. They outline a set of institutionalized reasons that particular viewpoints tend to be privileged, referring to reliance on corporate advertising and on members of government and other 'official sources' information.

vortex of publicity when different brands/symbols/terms (like those associated with the military and NFL football) begin to automatically 'refer to' the each other in a cycle of associations, so that thinking of one brand/symbolic/term is automatically associated with the other brand/symbol/term (Wernick, 1991).

war journalism an approach to doing journalism that is based around the use of military language, emphasizes elite or official sources, emphasizes 'here-and-now' events, and tags people as 'good or bad'. It is also characterized by its coverage of conflict such that there is an 'us and them' orientation (and they are dehumanized) (Galtung, 1998; Shinar, 2009).

PART V

Conclusion

10 Six Summary Arguments and a Minor Utopian Vision

The role of the peace and conflict researcher means...recognizing the tension between theory and practice. Where peoples' lives are at stake there is little more that can be done than try, learn, and try again, aware, but unaware, enlightened but still blind. The conflict researcher cannot reconcile the intellectual discussion of conflict and peace with often devastating experiences in the field other than being true to the goal of emancipation, while also being aware that the emancipator discourse of peace treads a fine line between emancipation and domination.

—excerpt from *The Transformation of Peace*
by Oliver Richmond (Richmond, 2007, p. 204)

In this quotation, Oliver Richmond captures the essence of the tension between theory and practice in peace-related work—a tension that is inescapable for those who study links between sport and peace using a sociological imagination. While lives aren't at stake in most of the work described in this book (although in some cases they may be), the tension between the role of sport as a tool for peace and as a cultural practice that is implicated in so many forms of structural and cultural violence is palpable.

With this tension in mind, I spend this final chapter reviewing key arguments and observations that are woven into the different chapters of this book—arguments and observations that in many cases embody the tensions around theory meeting practice that Richmond speaks to. In doing so, I note also how the use of different sociological lenses and perspectives helps us see these tensions, see instances where sport supports peace promotion, and see other instances where sport does quite the opposite.

I also outline arguments for ways that a more democratic and inclusive sport can be pursued, and how the sociology of sport can help with this. In doing so, I return to the peace concept, and consider how a bridge between peace studies and the sociology of sport might be useful. I also consider here what a critical peace studies of sport could look like in the future, and how by identifying, imagining, and pursuing 'minor utopias' of democratic and inclusive sport, along with more conventional sport-related reforms, a cultural and structural renewal of sport and society can take place.

I have structured the remainder of this chapter into two parts. The first part is a series of six arguments that speak to the ideas noted above. The second part of the chapter includes a commentary about how hope for change in and around sport can be found despite the limitations and impossibilities associated with the pursuit of peace.

Themes in Sport, Sociology, and Peace: A Set of Concluding Arguments

Argument #1: *The complexity of social problems in and around sport must be accounted for. If responses to such problems are oversimplified, it is unlikely that responses to these problems will be effective or lasting.*

In his 2005 book *The Moral Imagination: The Art and Soul of Building Peace*, peace-building and reconciliation expert John Paul Lederach argues that without sensitivity to the experiences of those living in the areas of deep-rooted conflict, peace-building efforts are likely to fail. With this in mind, Lederach (2005) informs readers early on in his treatise that the people he works with in these settings commonly give the following warning—'if the proposed changes [offered by those who are attempting to intervene in and deal with conflict situations] lack a serious account of *complexity* . . . then the proposed changes are dangerous' (p. 55, emphasis added). Put another way, 'if simple answers are reached as though the complexity of the situation does not exist, then . . . they are not worth a fig' (p. 55).

This observation aligns well with arguments I made in the previous chapters for being sensitive to complexity. Although Lederach's example speaks to the kind of work that is done in conflict situations, it applies equally to sport-related solutions that are proposed to any number of economic and social problems. For example, the idea that hosting the Olympic Games or another mega–sporting event is a solution to problems as diffuse as a social housing shortage, or economic woes, or inactivity levels in a city or country, obviously requires attention to the complexity of situations where these events are being held.

This is not to say that these events cannot have positive impacts. What I am arguing, however, is that when (sport-related) solutions are presented in simple terms, when sport is described as a panacea and 'headline' for the development and regeneration of cities, then there are good reasons to be suspicious. In chapters throughout this book I offered a number of examples of situations where claims about sport's contributions to society were shown to be un-nuanced and oversimplified and, as Lederach's contacts suggest, potentially dangerous. Here are some:

- The view that sport unites nations and people only stands up if we ignore the experiences of marginalized populations whose sport experiences frequently reinforce divisions within countries. At the same time, claims that international sport competitions create bonds and promote peaceful relations between rivals is also too simplistic, as there are numerous examples where sport competitions have been little more than metaphors for war, forums where persistent tensions were exacerbated, not overcome.

- The argument that increased economic ties between nations promote peace presumes a very narrow definition of peace. That is to say, although there is evidence that countries linked by their shared interest in supporting (sport-related) global economic integration may be less likely to go to war with one another, this says little about the forms of structural violence that may exist because of the neo-liberal system.

- NGOs like Right To Play, or the Susan G. Komen Race for the Cure, both respected for their work providing a range of peace-promoting services for young people in developing contexts (in the case of Right To Play) or raising money for breast cancer research and offering forums for community building and empowerment (in the case of the Susan B. Komen Foundation), are also participants in a (neo-liberal) system of governance that is thought by many to (ironically) perpetuate social inequalities, and to undermine the health-promoting and peace-promoting goals on which these organizations are founded.

- In a similar way, the pro-environment work of many sport-related organizations has two sides. On the one hand, the focus on the development of innovative 'clean' technologies and the promotion of 'green' business practices by these organizations are commonly celebrated. On the other hand, there are many reasons to question whether these organizations are motivated to *be* environmentally friendly or to *appear* environmentally friendly, because these organizations exist in a profit-based incentive system where appearing green may be most lucrative.

Reflecting on the above examples and many others offered throughout this book, we can begin to see how analyses of sport that focus only on ways that sport can contribute to society and not on ways that sport is both enabling and constraining, could lead researchers and practitioners to some problematic (and potentially dangerous) conclusions. This point leads me to the second and third arguments.

Argument #2: *Critical sociological theories can help us see how sport and society are complex and multi-faceted and help us be sensitive and responsive to ways that sport: (a) contributes to peace-promotion, and (b) can, often at the same time, perpetuate and reinforce inequalities and social problems.*

and

Argument #3: *By using a sociological imagination in particular—along with the many lenses provided by critical theorists that help magnify the mechanisms underlying the existence and perpetuation of social inequalities—sociologists of sport are best positioned to understand and thus make recommendations for dealing with these inequalities as they exist within and around sport.*

Put another way, for those interested in pursuing more 'peaceful' societies where overt and underlying forms of oppression and structural inequalities are minimized, and where inclusivity and democratic forms of participation are prioritized and privileged, the appropriate tools/theories are needed to support this pursuit. Since critical theories were developed to help people see and understand these inequalities, it makes sense that these would be the theories that would be particularly useful in this situation. This is also why, in this book, I have featured a contextual cultural studies approach that highlights how what is happening at one level of social life is interconnected with happenings at all other levels. This is also why I have returned over and over to Mills's (1959) vision of a sociological imagination, which is perhaps a more straightforward but equally useful tool for revealing and understanding interconnections and context. Either way, the main idea is this—since a contribution that sport is making to peace on one level may actually be connected to (and possibly perpetuating) a broader problem that exists on another level, it is important to be able to see and be sensitive to all levels.

Argument #4: *A sociological imagination can also be useful for guiding interventionist work by sport for development and peace practitioners. It is especially useful when used in combination with micro-sociological theories and models that speak to the best practices of those who have worked in peace-promoting interventions and programs.*

Implicit here is the view that those guided by a functionalist perspective, whose research questions tend to focus around ways that sport can contribute to society, may have a great deal to contribute to thinking about 'best practices' for designing and implementing specific peace-promoting programs. The best practices of sport for development and peace programs referred to in chapter 7 (and discussed in more detail in Kidd, 2007) are excellent examples of this. *However*, and at the same time, those working in a functionalist tradition are not positioned to ask questions about, for example, how it is that some programs (especially those sustained through high levels of corporate funding) might be implicated in a neo-liberal system that is, in part, responsible for the very problems these programs are designed to resolve. If the goal is to get to the root of the problems sport-related interventions are designed to deal with, functionalism is limited.

More compatible with the cultural studies approach to understanding sport are micro-sociological or 'interpretive' theories like those that informed chapter 5's discussion of ways that the Mentors in Violence Prevention anti-violence program was designed. These theories, referred to in chapter 2, can be especially helpful for those interested in designing programs that account for the lived experiences and group dynamics of those involved. In fact, there is a long history of what has been termed 'critical interpretivist' thinking that is based around the idea that the lived experiences of people in social settings—and the status hierarchies, power relationships, cultural norms, group perspectives, and so on—can and should be understood 'in context' (Denzin, 1992; Willis, 1977; Wilson, 2006b).

In the peace studies field, conceptualizations of violence and reconciliation offered by Johan Galtung, the 'nested paradigm' approach offered by Marie Duggan, the 'web approach' offered by Lederach, and the accompanying 'ripple' effect metaphor offered by John Sugden have been useful for sport practitioners intent on better understanding how to support the creation of resilient relationships between conflicting groups, the multiple levels at which these relationships need to be built and maintained, and the relationships between these levels (cf., Kidd, 2007). Such models are built around an understanding of the social processes through which relationships are created and maintained, and the social contexts these relationships take place within, which aligns them in some respects with the critical interpretivist approaches outlined above.

Lynch and McGoldrick's arguments for the adoption of peace-promoting journalistic practices are similarly based on an understanding of the micro-processes associated with the construction of news and also of the profit- and corporate-driven priorities of the multinational corporations that own most media outlets. Such an understanding of the nuances of the newsroom and relationships between the newsroom and broader political and economic drivers is akin to a contextual cultural studies approach to thinking not only about how news is produced, but also about how it could be produced with peace-promoting principles in mind.

Argument #5: *Sociologists of sport have something to offer those working in peace studies*

Throughout this book I referred to ways that the peace concept and selective work from the peace studies discipline can inform work in the sociology of sport. Since this book is designed first and foremost to inform thinking about sport and peace from a critical sociological perspective, this approach made sense. Still, my hope is that this book—with its emphasis on ways that peace-related issues can be constructively addressed using various critical (i.e., context-sensitive and change-oriented) theoretical lenses, and how the study of sport, as a cultural practice, can provide a window into broader peace-related issues—offers something to peace studies.

There is some evidence that such contributions would be important for the peace studies field. This evidence is featured in a provocative essay by Jutila, Pehkonen, and Väyrynen (2008), who explored the possibility of what they call a 'critical peace research'. Reflecting on the history of the peace studies discipline—a discipline that evolved following the Second World War as scholars attempted to better understand how to prevent war-related horrors from taking place again—these authors observed a series of limitations and problems. The authors note, for example, that at points in time the peace studies field has been viewed as a 'tool of the establishment', producing oversimplified studies that are easily fed to politicians interested in justifying a particular intervention. A less damning (but not unrelated) critique is that the field is unreflexive and unresponsive, meaning that the major peace studies journals (the *Journal of Peace Research* [JPR] and the *Journal of Conflict Resolution* [JCR]) include few articles that offer reflections on the state of the field, or on ways it can and should evolve and improve. With this in mind, Jutila, Pehkonen, and Väyrynen (2008) are clear in their view that the field has in many ways failed to take up and respond to important theoretical developments in other disciplines.

Specifically, they suggest that many in the field have been especially unresponsive to the evolution of theories that describe the nuances and complexities of power relations. Instead, according to Jutila, Pehkonen, and Väyrynen (2008), work has focused on the effects of certain kinds of interventions without understanding contexts for these interventions or ways that success or failure may be less straightforward. They explain:

> The lack of critical theorising in mainstream PR [peace research] can be demonstrated with one example. Maybe the most influential theory of peace at the moment is the 'democratic peace theory' according to which democracies do not fight each other. This theory has become one part of the common sense of contemporary world politics. During the past decade there have been plenty of articles in JPR and JCR dealing with this theory. Most of them try to falsify or support the theory using various forms of quantitative data. In quantitative articles [the] sole technical criticism is levelled against the methodological choices. In JCR almost all articles on democratic peace use quantitative methods, whereas half of the articles published in JPR use some form of qualitative analysis (e.g. policy analysis, historical research, history of ideas). Yet none of these articles uses any form of critical theory to analyse the conceptual choices defining the theory. (Jutila, Pehkonen, and Väyrynen, 2009, p. 633)

If we take Jutila, Pehkonen, and Väyrynen's (2008) summary of the field at their word, we have a situation in peace studies where a theory like the Golden Arches Theory of Conflict Prevention described in chapter 3 would be either affirmed or dismissed based on assessments of whether conflict or unrest has been present or absent in countries where there is a McDonald's restaurant (or more reasonably, where capitalist principles associated with free trade are evident). What would not be taken into account are the ways that a system of power relations associated with the uninhibited spread of multinational organizations is advantageous in some ways, *for some people*, and not for others. My discussion of this topic in chapter 4 speaks to ways that a critical approach to thinking about international relations and peace promotion through sport— the kind of approach Jutila, Pehkonen, and Väyrynen suggest is missing in the peace studies literature—is necessary in contexts like these.

Speaking more generally, the attention paid in this book to the work conducted by sociologists of sport on the role sport can play and does play in conflict transformation could inform thinking about other ways that unofficial forms of diplomacy (i.e., driven by private citizens, NGOs, and/or businesses) are utilized. Specifically, this would contribute to thinking about what is commonly referred to as track-two diplomacy—unlike track-one diplomacy, which is based around interactions between state officials.

At the same time, this book's emphasis on the vast body of work in the sociology of sport field that speaks to ways that sport can (if often inadvertently) reinforce taken-for-granted forms of inequality would seem to be pertinent to the peace studies field, that is increasingly attentive to ways that the pursuit of positive peace is undermined, and how forms of cultural violence are carried out.

Of course, it is unfair to use such broad strokes to sketch a field like peace studies and the arguments offered by Jutila, Pehkonen, and Väyrynen include several caveats and references to researchers like Richmond (2007), Galtung, and others who are at times extremely reflexive and theoretically progressive in their work. Still, I hope that my attempt to examine relationships between sport and peace in this book, which were guided by various critical sociological tools and with a cultural studies sensibility, might be a small but helpful contribution to the peace studies field.

Argument #6: *The term 'peace', at present, is a rallying concept. It is part of a 'collective action frame' for the sociologists of sport and sport practitioners who are inspired by what it represents. That is to say, those interested in making a difference in and around sport can (and often do) benefit from the popular and positive associations between sport and peace that presently exist. History also tells us that this 'sport for peace' moment is temporary, and that new rallying concepts will be needed. All this to say—now is a moment for 'praxis through peace and sport'.*

Some words have meanings. Other words, however, also have a 'feel' (Bauman, 2001, p. 1)

Although I argued in chapter 1 that there are good reasons to be careful about investing too much in any particular definition of peace, there are also reasons to be optimistic about the ways that the term has been a symbol, a rallying point for many sociologists and sport practitioners and activists alike who are concerned with issues around inequality, and are driven to address problems with sport-related violence and conflict. Put another way, although the meaning of terms like 'peace' 'float', they are relatively anchored in particular contexts and at moments in time.

It seems that, in the current historical moment, sociologists of sport and many others share a 'feeling' about the term 'peace', a feeling that Bauman refers to in the opening quotation (although Bauman was talking about the term 'community'). I noted earlier in this book how important emotion is when rallying and inspiring people around an idea, a goal. I also noted how social movement groups commonly use a collective action frame to inspire people to be part of a social movement. In this case, peace— and the positive feelings it seems to represent for people—is integral to this frame for many involved in sport-related activist work. While the optimism the term presently inspires will need to be renewed over time (and perhaps a different concept 'with feeling' will emerge), at present peace is a concept that serves this purpose. Let's go with it.

And Where Do We Go From Here?
Reflections on Social Change and Strategies to Achieve It

Other sociology of sport books offer impressive sets of recommendation for ways that sociologists of sport can be part of creating change. Such recommendations would be useful for those interested in some of the arguments offered in this book—one ultimately driven by an interest in promoting peace in and through sport. Although previous discussions of 'sport, social movements, and social change', and 'sport and peace education' include in-depth examinations of strategies for change, there is certainly value in noting ways that others have summarized suggestions for making a difference. Coakley and Donnelly (2009) provide one of the more comprehensive lists of strategies, outlining (following Hall et al., 1991) four vantage points through which change can be initiated:

- by working within the system of sport and attempting to initiate and carry out reforms;
- by joining an opposition group that lobbies for change;

- by creating alternative sports that are based around the rejection of 'dominant power and performance sports and the organizations that sponsor them and develop news sports grounded in the values and experiences of a wide array of different groups of people'(Coakley and Donnelly, 2009, p. 510); and
- by focusing on transforming culture and social relations, which may include changing the values of sport organizations or challenging producers of mass-mediated sport violence, or managers of sport leagues that do not have anti-violence training for coaches and players.

Other sociologists of sport, like Atkinson and Young (2008) and Carrington (2007, following the work of Burawoy, 2004) argue that the 'detachment' that many sociologists maintain in their research can be problematic if it means that the important issues and problems that are uncovered in research are dealt with and addressed on a more public level. With this in mind, these authors argue for a 'public sociology' of sport—a point I elaborate on in chapter 6's discussion of peace education. In a similar way, sociologists of sport like Andrews and Giardina (2008) and many others are driven by a commitment to praxis and conscientization—to using research and commentary in ways that continue to reveal how power operates and how oppression and social inequalities are reinforced and perpetuated within and through sport.

Final Thoughts: Imagining and Pursuing Minor Utopias and Structural Renewal in and around Sport

The term Utopia means 'no place', not to be found on the map . . . The term is easily (and intentionally confused) with the term 'Eutopia', the place of happiness. The homonym suggests something about what utopia is, and also the playfulness of its inventors . . . (p. 2)

Utopia is a discourse in two contradictory parts. First, it is a story through which men and women imagine a radical act of disjunction, enabling people, acting freely and in concert with others, to realize the creative potential imprisoned by the way we live now. But secondly, since the narrative is written by men and women rooted in contemporary conditions and language.

Utopias force us to face the fact that we do not live there; we live here . . . Utopia, in sum, is a fantasy about the limits of the possible, a staging of what we take for granted, what is left unsaid about our current social conventions and political culture. Those who expose these silences, often playfully, begin to disturb the contradictions in the way we live. (p. 3)

Jay Winter, from *Dreams of Peace and Freedom: Utopian Moments in the 20th Century* (2006)

I read these quotations as I was beginning to write this book and never quite shook the somewhat haunting and certainly provocative thoughts that Jay Winter offered the reader about a term so pertinent to 'the pursuit of peace in and around sport'—a utopian project for sure. The reason I found it haunting is that Winter articulates, through his discussion of utopia, the 'unsaid' reality—that we will never actually 'get there'. In the context of this book, what this means is that a wholly inclusive, democratic, positively peaceful sport will never be fully attained. The link between a nicely visualized theory of change and what actually happens on the ground, in practice, will always be imperfect—a point akin to the one made by Oliver Richmond in the opening quotation of this chapter. As Winter suggests, such 'perfect' links are fantasies, dreams.

Fortunately, Winter 'bails out' those who do not like to be reminded of this by distinguishing between two types of utopian projects. 'Major' utopian projects, on one hand, are universalizing projects that become failed dreams (at best), and ideological rhetoric disguised in utopian clothes (at worst). According to Winter, these utopias are only realized in science fiction novels like Margaret Atwood's *The Handmaid's Tale* or Aldus Huxley's *Brave New World* (or, of course, William Harrison's screenplay *Rollerball*, referred to in chapter 4). Of course, these fictionalized utopias, as those who have read these sci-fi classics know, are often cautionary tales, revealing themselves over time to be the complete opposite, dystopias. Winter refers to Hitler's Germany as a real-life example of a utopian project gone wrong. I would argue (on a much less devastating scale, of course) that unqualified descriptions of the Olympics as a panacea are 'major utopian' visions in their own way.

On the other hand, Winter refers to 'minor' utopian projects. Minor utopian projects are simultaneously flawed, inspired, creative, and human. While always imperfect, they are in many ways—and in certain contexts—effective as attempts to transform, to, for example, democratize (instead of de-democratize), or decrease violence. He refers to the development of the Universal Declaration of Human Rights in 1948 as an example, along with the emergence of global social movements in the 1990s, and to ongoing attempts in the twentieth century to create forms of global citizenship. He also points to the various student revolts of 1968 and their impacts and goals, and to various peace exhibits and peace conferences of the early twentieth century. Winter is clear that there are contradictions and problems with all of these efforts and many were failures by most measures. But they were attempts to do something about problems that needed a response, some kind of a response—a point reminiscent of John Sugden's (2007) argument that sociologists and concerned others must do *something* in the face of tragedies, but be reflexive in doing so.

Visions of and efforts toward a more peaceful sport and society are akin to minor utopian projects. Sport-related environmental movements like Surfers

Against Sewage and sport for development and peace programs like Football 4 Peace—all small-scale and reflexive projects for social change—come to mind here. Attempts to link theory and practice for those carrying out these projects, as Richmond points out in the quotation that opens this section, are always imperfect, but this is as it should be, as it must be. The value of minor utopian visions and practices is that they can offer hope, provide (context-specific) templates for what sport could be, and inspire us to learn from what went wrong in an attempt to move a little closer to 'the limits of the possible'. Of course, what is needed to move in this direction is inspiration, understanding, and imagination—a sociological imagination.

References

Akindes, G. & Kirwin, M. (2009). Sport in international aid: Promoting under-development in sub–Saharan Africa. In R. Levermore & A. Beacom (Eds.), *Sport and international development* (pp. 219–45). New York: Palgrave MacMillan.

Ali, S. (Ed.). (2007). *Peace parks: Conservation and conflict resolution*. Cambridge: MIT Press.

Allon, S. (2004), *News culture*. Maidenhead, UK: Open University Press.

Allison, L. (2000). Sport and nationalism. In J. Coakley & E. Dunning (Eds.), *Handbook of sports studies* (pp. 344–55). London: Sage.

———. (2005). Sport and globalization: The issues. In L. Allison (Ed.), *The global politics of sport: The role of global institutions in sport* (1–4). New York: Routledge.

———. (2008, July 30). What do governments want from sport and what do they get?. *Foreign Policy In Focus*, Retrieved May 3, 2010 from: www.fpif.org/articles/what_do_governments_want_from_sport_and_what_do_they_get.

Althusser, L. (1971). *Lenin and Philosophy*. New York: Monthly Review Press.

Amenta, E. (2005). Political contexts, challenger strategies, and mobilization: Explaining the impact of the Townsend Plan. In D. Meyer, V. Jenness & H. Ingram (Eds.), *Routing the opposition: Social movements, public policy, and democracy* (pp. 29–64). Minneapolis: University of Minnesota Press.

Anderson, A. (1997). *Media culture and the environment*. London: UCL Press.

Andrews, D. (2002). Coming to terms with cultural studies. *Journal of Sport and Social Issues*, 26(1), 110–17.

———. (2006). *Sport–commerce–culture: Essays on sport in late capitalist America*. New York: Peter Lang.

———. (2008). Kinesiology's inconvenient truth and the physical cultural studies imperative. *Quest*, 60, 45–62.

Andrews, D. & M. Giardina. (2008). Sport without guarantees towards a cultural studies that matters. *Cultural Studies ↔ Critical Methodologies*, 8(4), 395–422.

Andrews, D. & Ritzer, G. (2007). The grobal in the sporting glocal. In R. Giulianotti & R. Robinson (Eds.), *Globalization and sport* (pp. 28–45). Malden, MA: Blackwell.

Andrews, D. & Wagg, S. (2007). Introduc-tion: war minus the shooting? In S. Wagg & D. Andrews (Eds.), *East plays West: Essays on sport and the Cold War* (pp. 1–9). London: Routledge.

Appadurai, A. (1996). *Modernity at large: Cultural dimensions of globalization*. Minneapolis: University of Minnesota Press.

Armstrong, G. (2004). Life, death and the biscuit: *Football and the embodiment of society in Liberia, West Africa*. In G. Armstrong. & R. Giulianotti (Eds.), *Football in Africa: Conflict, Reconciliation and Community* (pp. 183–209). New York: Palgrave Macmillan.

Armstrong, G. & Giulianotti, R. (Eds.) (2004). *Football in Africa: Conflict, reconciliation and community*. New York: Palgrave Macmillan.

Atkinson, M. (2000). Brother, can you spare a seat: Developing recipes of knowledge in the ticket scalping subculture, *Sociology of Sport Journal*, 17(2), 151–70.

———. (2009). Parkour, anarcho-environ-mentalism, and poiesis. *Journal of Sport and Social Issues*, 33(2), 169–94.

Atkinson, M. & Young, K. (2003). Terror Games: media treatment of security issues at the 2002 Winter Olympic Games. *OLYMPIKA* 11, 53–78.

——— & ———. (2008). *Deviance and social control in sport*. Champaign, IL: Human Kinetics.

Bairner, A. (2001). *Sport, nationalism, and globalization*. Albany, NY: SUNY Press.

———. (2005). Sport and the nation in the global era. In L. Allison (Ed.), *The global politics of sport: The role of global institutions in sport* (pp. 87–100). New York: Routledge.

———. (2009a). Re–appropriating Gramsci: Marxism, hegemony and sport. In B. Carrington & I. McDonald (Eds.), *Marxism, cultural studies and sport* (pp. 195–212). London: Routledge..

———. (2009b). Sport, intellectuals and public sociology: Obstacles and opportunities. *International Review for the Sociology of Sport*, 44 (3/4), 115–30.

Bairner, A. & Sugden, J. (2000). Sport in divided societies: An introduction. J. Sugden & A. Bairner (Eds.), *Sport in Divided Societies*. (pp. 1–11). Oxford: Meyer and Meyer.

Bale, J. (2001). *Sport, space, and the city*. West Caldwell, NJ: Blackburn.

Barash, D. & Webel, C. (2002). *Peace and conflict studies*. Thousand Oaks, CA: Sage.

Barnes, B. (2009). 'Everybody wants to pioneer something out here': Landscape, adventure, and biopolitics in the American Southwest. *Journal of Sport & Social Issues*, 33(3), 230–56.

Barr, S. (2003). Strategies for sustainability: Citizens and responsible environmental behaviour. *Area*, 35(3), 227–40.

Bauman, Z. (2001). *Community: Seeking safety in an insecure world*. Malden, MA: Blackwell.

Beal, B. (1995). Disqualifying the official: An exploration of social resistance through the subculture of skateboarding. *Sociology of Sport Journal*, 12, 252–67.

———. (2002). Symbolic interactionism and cultural studies: Doing critical ethnography. In J. Maguire & K. Young (Eds.), *Theory, Sport & Society* (pp. 353–73). New York: JAI.

Beamish, R. (2008). The social construction of steroid subcultures. In M. Atkinson & K. Young (Eds.), *Tribal play: Subcultural journeys through sport* (pp. 273–94). Bingley, UK: Emerald Group Publishing.

Beck, U. (1992). *The risk society: Towards a new modernity*. London: Sage.

Beder, S. (1996). Sydney's toxic green Olympics. *Current Affairs Bulletin*, 70(6), 12–18.

———. (2002). *Global spin: The corporate assault on environmentalism*. White River Junction, VT: Chelsea Green Publishing Company.

Belanger, A. (2000). Sport venues and the spectacularization of urban spaces in North America: The case of the Molson Centre in Montreal. *International Review for the Sociology of Sport*, 35(3), 378–97.

Benford R.D. (2007). The college sports reform movement: Reframing the 'Edutainment' industry. *The Sociological Quarterly*, 48(1), 1–28.

Bennett, A. (1999). Subcultures or neo-tribes? Rethinking the relationship between youth, style and musical taste. *Sociology* 33(3), 599–617.

———. (2000). *Popular music and youth culture: Music, identity and place*. New York: St. Martin's Press.

Black, D. (2008). Dreaming big: The pursuit of 'second order' games as a strategic response to globalization. *Sport in Society*, 11(4), 467–80.

———. (2010). The ambiguities of development: Implications for 'development through sport'. *Sport in Society*, 13(1), 121–29.

Blumer, H. (1969). *Symbolic interactionism: Perspective and method*. Englewood Cliffs, NJ: Prentice-Hall.

Botchford, J. (1998, June 22). Iran's fans: Loud and proud. *The Toronto Sun*, p. 5.

Bourdieu, P. (1984) *Distinction: A social critique of the judgement of taste*. London: Routledge.

———. (1986). The forms of capital. In J.G. Richardson (Ed.), *Handbook of theory and research for the sociology of education* (pp. 241–58). New York: Greenwood Press.

Brady, M. & Kahn, A. (2002). *Letting girls play: The Mathare Youth Sports Association's football programme for girls*. New York: The Population Council.

Briassoulis, H. (2010). 'Sorry golfers, this is not your spot!': Exploring public opposition to golf development. *Journal of Sport and Social Issues*, 34(3), 288–311.

Brown, W. (2006). *Edgework: Critical essays on knowledge and politics*. Princeton: Princeton University Press.

Bruce, T. & Hallinan, C. (2001). Cathy Freeman: The quest for Australian identity. In D. Andrews & S. Jackson (Eds.), *Sport stars: The cultural politics of sporting celebrity* (pp. 257–70). London: Routledge.

Bruce, T. & Wensing, E. (2009). 'She's not one of us': Cathy Freeman and the place of Aboriginal people in Australian national culture. *Australian Aboriginal Studies*, 2, 90–100.

Brundtland, G. (Ed.) (1987). *Our common future* (Report of the World Commission on Environment and Development). New York: Oxford University Press.

Burstyn, V. (1999). *The rites of men: Manhood, politics, and the culture of sport*. Toronto: University of Toronto Press.

Butler, J. (1990). *Gender trouble: Feminism and the subversion of identity*. New York: Routledge.

Butterworth, M. (2005). Ritual in the 'church of baseball': Suppressing the discourse of democracy after 9/11. *Communication and Critical/Cultural Studies*, 2(2), 107–29.

———. (2007). The politics of the pitch: Claiming and contesting democracy through the Iraqi national soccer team. *Communication and Critical/Cultural Studies*, 4(2), 184–203.

Butterworth, M. & Moskal, S. (2009). American football, flags, and 'fun': The Bell Helicopter Armed Forces Bowl and the Rhetorical Production of Militarism.

Communication, Culture & Critique, 2(4), 411–33.

Burawoy, M. (2004, August 13th). To advance sociology must not retreat. *The Chronicle of Higher Education: The Chronicle Review,* 50(49), p. B24.

Cahn, S. (1994). *Coming on strong: Gender and sexuality in twentieth-century women's sport.* New York: Free Press.

Carlin, J. (2008). *Playing the enemy: Nelson Mandela and the game that made a nation.* New York: Penguin.

Carpenter, L. (2009, February 1). NFL orders retreat from war metaphors. *Washington Post.* Retrieved March 8, 2011 from: www.washingtonpost.com/wp-dyn/content/article/2009/01/31/AR2009013100163.html?sid=ST2009013101859

Carrington, B. (2007). Merely identity: Cultural identity and the politics of sport. *Sociology of Sport Journal,* 24(1), 49–66.

Carrington, B., Andrews, D., Jackson, S., & Mazur, Z. (2001). The global Jordanscape. In D.L. Andrews (Ed.), *Michael Jordan Inc.: Corporate sport, media culture, and late modern America* (pp. 177–216). Albany: SUNY Press.

Carrington, B. & McDonald, I. (Eds.) (2009). *Marxism, cultural studies and sport.* New York: Routledge.

Castree, N. (2003). Commodifying what nature? *Progress in Human Geography* 27(3), 273–97.

Chang, H.-J. (2008). *Bad samaritans: The myth of free trade and the secret history of capitalism.* New York: Bloomsbury Press.

Chernushenko, D. (1994). *Greening our games: Running sports events and facilities that won't cost the earth.* Ottawa: Centurion.

Chernushenko, D., van der Kamp, A., & Stubbs, D. (2001). *Sustainable sport management: Running an environmentally, socially and economically responsible organization.* Nairobi, Kenya: United Nations Environment Programme.

CNN (2010, February 10). South Africa 20 years after Mandela release. Retrieved April 5, 2011 from: http://articles.cnn.com/2010-02-10/world/mandela.anniversary_1_rolihlahla-mandela-mandela-release-nelson-mandela?_s=PM:WORLD.

Coakley, J. (2002). Using sports to control deviance and violence among youths. In M. Gatz, M. Messner, & S. Ball-Rokeach (Eds.), *Paradoxes of youth and sport* (pp. 13–30). Albany: SUNY Press.

Coakley, J. & Donnelly, P. (Eds.) (1999). *Inside sports.* New York: Routledge.

——— & ———. (2009). *Sports in society: Issues and controversies* (2nd Canadian edition). Toronto: McGraw-Hill Ryerson.

Coalter, F. (2008). Sport-in-development: Development for and through sport?. In R. Hoy & M. Nicholson (Eds.), *Sport and social capital* (pp. 39–67). London: Elsevier.

———. (2009). Sport-in-development: Accountability or development. In R. Levermore & A. Beacom (Eds.), *Sport and international development* (pp. 55–75). New York: Palgrave MacMillan.

———. (2010). The politics of sport-for-development: Limited focus programmes and broad gauge problems. *International Review for the Sociology of Sport,* 45(3), 295–314.

Coleman, J. (1988). Social capital in the creation of human capital. *American Journal of Sociology,* 94, 95–120.

Connell, R. & Messerschmidt, J. (2005). Hegemonic masculinity: Rethinking the concept. *Gender and Society,* 19(6), 829–59.

Cornelissen, S. (2008). Scripting the nation: sport, mega-events, foreign policy and state-building in post-apartheid South Africa. *Sport in Society,* 11(4), 481–93.

———. (2009). A delicate balance: Major sport events and development. In R. Levermore & A. Beacom (Eds.), *Sport and international development* (pp. 76–97). New York: Palgrave MacMillan.

Cortright, D. (2008). *Peace: A history of movements and ideas.* New York: Cambridge University Press.

Coté, M., Day, J.F., & de Peuter, G. (2007). Introduction: What is utopian pedagogy? In M. Coté, J.F. Day, & G. de Peuter (Eds.), *Utopian pedagogy: Radical experiments against neoliberal globalization* (pp. 3–19). Toronto: University of Toronto Press.

Coubertin, P. (2000). *Olympism: Selected writings.* Lausanne: International Olympic Committee.

Cowie, Elizabeth. (1977). Women, representation and the image. *Screen Education,* 2–3, 15–23.

Cronin, M. & Mayall, D. (Eds.) (1998). *Sporting nationalisms: Identity, ethnicity, immigration and assimilation.* London: Frank Cass.

Crosset, T. (2007). Capturing racism: An analysis of racial projects within the Lisa Simpson vs. University of Colorado football rape case. *International Journal of the History of Sport,* 24(2), 172–96.

Crosset, T., Ptacek, J., McDonald, M., & Benedict, J. (1996). Male student-athletes and violence against women: A survey of campus judicial affairs offices. *Violence Against Women*, 2, 163–79.

Crossman, J. (2003). Sport sociology in the Canadian context. In J. Crossman (Ed.), *Canadian sport sociology* (pp. 1–21). Scarborough, ON: Nelson Press.

———. (Ed.) (2007). *Canadian sport sociology* (2nd edition). Toronto: Thomson Nelson.

Cull, N. (2008). The public diplomacy of the modern Olympic Games and China's soft power strategy. In M. Price & D. Dayan (Eds.), *Owning the Olympics: Narratives of the new China* (pp. 117–44). Ann Arbour: University of Michigan Press.

Curtiss, R. (1998, September). Iran-U.S. World Cup match: What the world saw, what Iranians saw and what participants recall. *Washington Report on Middle East Affairs*, pp. 33–34.

Darnell, S. (2007). Playing with race: Right to Play and the production of whiteness in 'development through sport'. *Sport in Society*, 10(4), 560–79.

———. (2010a). Power, politics and 'sport for development and peace': Investigating the utility of sport for international development. *Sociology of Sport Journal*, 27(1), 54–75.

———. (2010b). Sport, race, and biopolitics: Encounters with difference in "sport for development and peace" internships. *Journal of Sport & Social Issues*, 34(4), 396–417.

Darnell, S. & Wilson, B. (2006). Macho media: Unapologetic hypermasculinity in Vancouver's 'talk radio for guys'. *Journal of Broadcasting and Electronic Media*, 50(3), 444–66.

Davidson, A. (2007, January 19). Greening The Super Bowl. *Forbes.com*, retrieved July 6, 2008 from: www.forbes.com/2007/01/19/super-bowl-green-sports-biz-cz_ad_0119green.html.

Davis-Delano, L. & Crosset, T. (2008). Using social movement theory to study outcomes in sports-related social movements. *International Review for the Sociology of Sport*, 43(2), 115–34.

Day, R. (2005). *Gramsci is dead: Anarchist currents in the newest social movements*. Toronto: Between the Lines.

de Certeau, M. (1984). *The practice of everyday life*. Berkeley: University of California Press.

Delgado, F. (2003). The fusing of sport and politics: Media constructions of U.S. ver-

sus Iran at France '98. *Journal of Sport and Social Issues*, 27(3), 293–307.

Denzin, N. (1992). *Symbolic interactionism and cultural studies: The politics of interpretation*. Cambridge, MA: Blackwell.

———. (2003). *Performance ethnography: Critical pedagogy and the politics of culture*. Thousand Oaks, CA: Sage.

———. (2009). A critical performance pedagogy that matters. *Ethnography and Education*, 4(3), 255–70.

DePauw, K. & Gavron, S. (2005). *Disability sport* (2nd Ed.) Champaign, IL: Human Kinetics Publishers.

Dewhirst, T. & Hunter, A. (2002). Tobacco sponsorship of Formula One and CART auto racing: Tobacco brand exposure and enhanced imagery through co-sponsors' third party advertising. *Tobacco Control*, 11, 146–50.

Diehl, P. & Gleditsch, N. (Eds.) (2001). *Environmental conflict*. Boulder: Westview.

Dietz, M. Prus, R. & Shaffir, W. (Eds.) (1994). *Doing everyday life: Ethnography as human lived experience*. Mississauga: Copp Clark Longman Ltd.

Donnelly, P. (1996). The local and the global: Globalization in the sociology of sport. *Journal of Sport and Social Issues*, 20(3), 239–57.

———. (2000). Interpretative approaches to the sociology of sport. In J. Coakley & E. Dunning (Eds.), *Handbook of sport studies* (pp. 77–91). London: Sage Publications.

———. (2006). Who's fair game?: Sport, sexual harassment and abuse. In P. White & K. Young (Eds.), *Sport and gender in Canada* (pp. 279–301). Toronto: Oxford University Press.

———. (2007). The use of sport to foster child and youth development and education. In *Report for the Sport for Development and Peace International Working Group (SDP IWG) Secretariat* (pp. 7–47). University of Toronto, Faculty of Physical Education and Health.

———. (January 2009/December 2010). Own the podium or rent it? Canada's involvement in the global sporting arms race. *Policy Options*, 31(1), 41–44.

Donnelly, P. & Coakley, J. (2002). The role of recreation in promoting social inclusion (pp. 1–21). Paper part of Laidlaw Foundation working paper series, *Perspectives on social inclusion*. Toronto: The Laidlaw Foundation.

Donnelly P. & Kidd B. (2000). Human rights in sport. *International Review for the Sociology of Sport* 35(2), 131–48.

Donnelly, P. & Young, K. (1988). The construction and confirmation of identity in sport subcultures. *Sociology of Sport Journal*, 5(3), 223–40.

Dryzek, J. (2005). *The politics of the earth: Environmental discourse.* Cambridge University Press, Cambridge.

Duncombe, S. (1997). *Notes from the underground: Zines and the politics of alternative culture.* New York: Verso.

Eagleton, T. (1991). *Ideology: An introduction.* London: Verso.

Edwards, H. (1973). *Sociology of sport.* Homewood, IL: The Dorsey Press.

Eitzen, S. (2003). Sport is healthy, sport is destructive. In S. Eitzen (Author), *Fair and foul: Beyond the myths and paradoxes of sport* (pp. 59–78). New York: Rowman & Littlefield Publishers.

Eitzen, S. & Sage, G. (2003). *Sociology of North American sport.* Toronto: McGraw-Hill.

Engle Folchert, K. (2008). *The role of institutional discourses in the perpetuation and propagation of rape culture on an American campus.* Unpublished Masters thesis, University of British Columbia, Vancouver, Canada.

Falcous, M. & Silk, M. (2005). Manufacturing consent: Mediated sporting spectacle and the cultural politics of the 'War of Terror.' *International Journal of Media and Cultural Politics*, 1, 59–65.

———. (2006). Global regimes, local agendas: Sport, resistance and the mediation of dissent. *International Review for the Sociology of Sport* 41(3–4), 317–338.

Foer, F. (2004). *How soccer explains the world: An unlikely theory of globalization.* New York: Harper Collins.

Forsyth, J. & Wamsley, K. (2006). 'Native to native . . . we'll recapture our spirits': The World Indigenous Nations Games and North American Indigenous Games as cultural resistance. *International Journal of the History of Sport*, 23(2), 294–314.

Foster, J.B., Clark, B., & York, R. (2010). *The ecological rift: Capitalism's war on the earth.* New York: Monthly Review Press.

Foucault, M. (1980). *Power/knowledge: Selected interviews and other writings 1972–1977.* Colin Gordon (Ed.). New York: Pantheon.

———. (1990 [1978]). *The history of sexuality volume 1: An introduction.* London: Penguin Books.

Freire, P. (1970). *Pedagogy of the oppressed.* New York: Herder and Herder.

Friedman, T. (2000). *Lexus and the olive tree: Understanding globalization.* New York: Anchor Books.

Frisby, W., Alexander, T., Taylor, J., Tirone, S., Watson, C., Harvey, J. et al. (2005). *Bridging the recreation divide: Listening to youth and parents from low income families across Canada.* Ottawa: Canadian Parks and Recreation Association.

Frisby, W., Maguire, P. & Reid, C. (2009). The 'f' word has everything to do with it: How feminist theories inform action research. *Action Research*, 7(1), 13–19.

Frisby, W., Reid, C. & Ponic, P. (2007). Levelling the playing field: Promoting the health of poor women through a community development approach to recreation. In P. White & K. Young (Eds.), *Sport and gender in Canada* (pp. 121–36). Don Mills, ON: Oxford University Press.

Fuller, A. (2004). Toward an emancipatory methodology for peace research. In W. Carroll (Ed.), *Critical strategies for social research* (pp. 91–102). Toronto: Canadian Scholars' Press.

Furlong, A. & Cartmel, F. (1997). *Young people and social change: Individualization and risk in late modernity.* Buckingham, UK: Open University Press.

Galtung, J. (1971). A structural theory of imperialism. *Journal of Peace Research*, 8(2), 81–117.

———. (1996). *Peace by peaceful means: Peace, conflict, development and civilization.* Thousand Oaks, CA: Sage.

———. (1998). High road, Low road: Charting the course for peace journalism. *Track Two*, 7(4). Available at: http://ccrweb.ccr.uct.ac.za/two/7_4/p07_highroad_lowroad.html.

Gasser, P. & Levinsen, A. (2006). Breaking post-war ice: Open fun football schools in Bosnia and Herzegovina. In R. Giulianotti & D. McCardle (Eds.), *Sport, civil liberties and human rights* (pp. 165–80). New York: Routledge.

Giardina, M. (2005). *Sporting pedagogies: Performing culture and identity in the global arena.* New York: Peter Lang.

Giardina, M. & Hess, L. (2007). If not us, than who?: Performing pedagogies of hope in Post-Katrina America. *Cultural Studies ↔ Critical Methodologies*, 7(2), 169–87.

Giardina, M. & Weems, M. (2004). Not in our name! *Qualitative Inquiry*, 10(4), 481–92.

Gibbons, R. (1999). Questions about a gift horse. In R. Gibbons (Ed.), *Voluntary initiatives and the new politics of corporate greening* (pp. 3–12). Peterborough, ON: Broadview Press.

Gibbs, D. (2000). Ecological modernisation, regional economic development and regional development agencies. *Geoforum*, 31(1), 9–19.

Giddens, A. (1991). *Modernity and self-identity: Self and society in the late modern age*. Cambridge: Polity Press.

———. (1994). Living in a post-traditional society. In U. Beck, A. Giddens & S. Lash (Eds.), *Reflexive modernization: Politics, tradition, and aesthetics in the modern social order* (pp. 56–109). Cambridge: Polity Press.

Gill, D. (2007). Integration: The key to sustaining kinesiology in higher education. *Quest*, 59(3), 270–86.

Gillenwater, M., Broekhoff, D., Trexler, M., Hyman, & J. Fowler, R. (2007, October 11). Policing the voluntary carbon market: Voluntary greenhouse-gas emission offset markets are in need of government oversight. *Nature Reports Climate Change*. Retrieved July 6, 2008 from: www.nature.com/climate/2007/0711/full/climate.2007.58.html.

Giroux, H. (1981). *Ideology, culture and the process of schooling*. Philadelphia: Temple University Press.

———. (2007). Utopian thinking in dangerous times: Critical pedagogy and the project of educated hope. In M. Coté, J.F. Day & G. de Peuter (Eds.), *Utopian pedagogy: Radical experiments against neoliberal globalization* (pp. 25–42). Toronto: University of Toronto Press.

Giulianotti, R. (1999). *Football: A sociology of a global game*. Cambridge: Polity.

———. (2005). *Sport: A Critical Sociology*. Cambridge: Polity.

———. (2006). Human rights, globalization and sentimental education: The case of sport. In R. Giulianotti & D. McCardle (Eds.), *Sport, civil liberties and human rights* (pp. 63–77). New York: Routledge.

Giulianotti, R. & McCardle, D. (Eds.) (2006). *Sport, civil liberties and civil rights*. New York: Routledge.

Gleditsch, N. & Urdal, H. (2004, November 22). Roots of conflict: Don't blame environmental decay for the next war, *New York Times*. Retrieved August 26, 2010 from: www.nytimes.com/2004/11/22/opinion/22iht-ednils_ed3_.html.

Gold, J. & Gold, M. (Eds.) (2007). *Olympic cities: City agendas, planning and the World's games, 1896–2016*. New York: Routledge.

Gramsci, A. (1971). *Selections from the prison notebooks*. New York: International Publishers.

Grossberg, L. (1997). *Bringing it all back home: Essays on cultural studies*. Durham, NC: Duke University Press.

Gruneau, R. (1983). *Class, sports, and social development*. Amherst, MA: University of Massachusetts Press.

Gruneau R. & Whitson D. (1993). *Hockey night in Canada: Sport, identities, and cultural politics*. Toronto: Garamond.

Guest, A. (2009). The diffusion of development–through–sport: Analysing the history and practice of the Olympic Movement's grassroots outreach to Africa. *Sport in Society*, 12(10), 1336–52. Reprinted by permission of the publisher. Taylor & Francis Group, www.informaworld.com.

Gullette, M.M. (1997). *Declining to decline: Cultural combat and the politics of the midlife*. London: University Press of Virginia.

Hackett, R. (2006). Is peace journalism possible? Three frameworks for assessing structure and agency in news media. *Conflict and Communication Online* 5(2). Available from: www.cco.regener-online.de.

———. (2007). Journalism versus peace? Notes on a problematic relationship. *Global Media Journal*, Mediterranean Edition 2(1) (Spring). Available from: http://globalmedia.emu.edu.tr/spring2007/issues.

Hackett, R. & Gruneau, R. (2000). *The missing news: Filters and blind spots in Canada's press*. Ottawa: Garamond Press.

Hajer, M. (1995). *The politics of environmental discourse*. New York: Oxford.

Hall, A. (1996). *Feminism and sporting bodies: Essays on theory and practice*. Champaign, IL: Human Kinetics.

———. (2007). Cultural struggle and resistance: Gender, history and Canadian sport. In K. Young, & P. White (Eds.), *Sport and gender in Canada* (pp. 56–74). Toronto: Oxford University Press.

Hall, A., Slack, T., Smith, G. & Whitson, D. (1991). *Sport in Canadian Society*. Toronto: McClelland and Stewart.

Hall, S. (1985). Signification, representation, ideology: Althusser and the post–structuralist debates. *Critical Studies in Mass Communication* 2, 91–114.

———. (1986). The problem of ideology: Marxism without guarantees. *Journal of Communication Inquiry*, 10(2), 28–44.

————. & Jefferson, T. (Eds.). (1976). *Resistance through rituals: Youth sub-cultures in post-war Britain*. London: Hutchison.

Hannigan, J. (1998). *Fantasy city: Pleasure and profit in the postmodern metropolis*. London: Routledge.

————. (2006). *Environmental sociology* (2nd ed.). New York: Routledge.

Haraway, D. (2003). *The companion species manifesto: Dogs, people, and significant otherness*. Chicago: Prickly Paradigm.

Hardt, M. & Negri, V. (2000). *Empire*. Cambridge: Harvard University Press.

Hardt, M. & Negri, A. (2004). *Multitude: War and democracy in the age of empire*. New York: Penguin.

Hargreaves, J.E. (1986). *Sport, power and culture*. Cambridge: Polity Press.

Hargreaves, J.A. (1994). *Sporting females: Critical issues in the history and sociology of women's sports*. London: Routledge.

Harris, I. (2004). Peace education theory. *Journal of Peace Education*, 1(1), 5–20.

Harris, I., Fisk, L. & Rank, C. (1998). A portrait of university peace studies in North America and Western Europe at the end of the millennium. *The International Journal of Peace Studies* 3(1), 91–112.

Hartmann, D. (1996). The politics of race and sport: Resistance and domination in the 1968 African American Olympic protest movement. *Ethnic and Racial Studies*, 19(3), 548–66.

————. (2003). *Race, culture, and the revolt of the black athlete: The 1968 Olympic protests and their aftermath*. Chicago: University of Chicago Press.

Harvey, D. (2005). *A brief history of neoliberalism*. New York: Oxford University Press.

Harvey, J. (2000). Sport and Quebec Nationalism: Ethnic or Civic Identity?. In J. Sugden & A. Bairner, (Eds.) *Sport in divided societies* (pp. 31–50). Oxford: Meyer and Meyer.

Harvey, J., Horne, J. & Safai, P. (2009). Alter–globalization, global social movements and the possibility of political transformation through sport. *Sociology of Sport Journal*, 26(3), 383–403.

Harvey, J. & Houle, F. (1994). Sports, world economy, global culture and new social movements. *Sociology of Sport Journal*, 11, 337–55.

Harvey, J., Lévesque, M. & Donnelly, P. (2007). Sport Volunteerism and Social Capital. *Sociology of Sport Journal*, 24(2), 206–23.

Hayhurst, L. (2009). The power to shape policy: Charting sport for development and peace policy discourses. *International Journal of Sport Policy*, 1(2), 203–07.

Hayhurst, L. & Frisby, W. (2010). Inevitable tensions: Swiss and Canadian sport for development NGO perspectives on partnerships with high performance sport. *European Sport Management Quarterly*, 10(1), 75–96.

Hayhurst, L., Frisby, W., & MacNeill, M. (2011). A postcolonial feminist approach to gender, development and Edusport. In B. Houlihan & M. Green (Eds.), *Routledge handbook of sports development* (pp. 353–66), New York: Routledge.

Hayhurst, L., Wilson, B., & Frisby, W. (2010). Navigating neoliberal networks: Transnational internet platforms in sport for development and peace. *International Review for the Sociology of Sport* (published online first November 1, 2010 at http://irs.sagepub.com/content/early/recent).

Hebdige, D. (1979). *Subculture: The meaning of style*. London: Methuen.

Heino, R. (2000). New sports: What is so punk about snowboarding? *Journal of Sport and Social Issues* 24(1), 176–191.

Held, D. & McGrew, A. (2007). *Globalization/anti–globalization: Beyond the great divide*. Cambridge: Polity.

Hellison, D. (2003). *Teaching responsibility through physical activity*. Champaign, IL: Human Kinetics.

Hellison, D., Martinek, T. & Cutforth, N. (1996). Beyond violence prevention in inner city physical activity programs. *Peace & Conflict: Journal of Peace Psychology*, 2, 321–37.

Hellison, D. & Walsh, D. (2002). Responsibility-based youth programs evaluation: Investigating the investigations. *Quest*, 54(4), 292–307.

Henderson, B. & Crilly, R. (2010, June 4). World Cup replica balls made on less than £2 a day: The replica of the official Adidas match ball for the World Cup is being made in Pakistan by workers earning less than £2 a day, The Daily Telegraph has learned. *Daily Telegraph*. Retrieved April 3, 2011 at: www.telegraph.co.uk/sport/football/competitions/world-cup-2010/7803428/World-Cup-replica-balls-made-on-less-than-2-a-day.html.

Herman, E. & Chomsky, N. (1988). *Manufacturing consent. The political economy of the mass media*. New York: Pantheon Books.

Heywood, L. & Montgomery, M. (2008).

Ambassadors of the last wilderness?: Surfers, environmental ethics, and activism in America. In M. Atkinson & K. Young (Eds.), *Tribal play: subcultural journeys through sport* pp. 153–72). Bingley: JAI.

Hilvoorde, I., van Elling, A., & Stokvis, R. (2010). How to influence national pride? The Olympic medal index as a unifying narrative. *International Review for the Sociology of Sport* 45(1), 87–102.

Hitchens, C. (2010, February 5). Fool's gold: How the Olympics and other international competitions breed conflict and bring out the worst in human nature. *Newsweek.* Retrieved April 3, 2011 from: www.news week.com/id/233007.

Hoberman, J. (1992). *Mortal engines.* Don Mills, ON: Maxwell Macmillan.

Hobsbawm, E. (1959). *Primitive rebels: Studies in archaic forms of social movement in the 19th and 20th centuries.* Manchester: Manchester University Press.

Hognestad, H. & Tollisen, A. (2004). Playing against deprivation: Football and Development in Kenya. In G. Armstrong & R. Giulianotti, (Eds.), *Football in Africa: Conflict, Reconciliation and Community* (pp. 210–26). New York: Palgrave Macmillan.

Homer-Dixon, T. (2000). *The ingenuity gap: Can we solve the problems of the future?* New York: Knopf.

Houlihan, B. (2000). Politics and sport. In J. Coakley & E. Dunning (Eds.), *Handbook of sports studies* (pp. 213–27). Thousand Oaks, CA: Sage Publications.

———. (2006). Civil rights, doping control and the world anti-doping code. Human rights, globalization and sentimental education: The case of sport. In D. McCardle & R. Giulianotti (Eds.), *Sport, civil liberties and human rights* (pp. 128–45). New York: Routledge.

Howell, J., Andrews, D., & Jackson, S. (2002). Cultural studies and sport studies: An interventionist practice. In J. Maguire & K. Young (Eds.), *Theory, sport & society* (pp. 151–77). New York: JAI.

Huber, J. (1985). *Die Regenbogengesellschaft: Ökologie und Sozialpolitik* (The Rainbow Society. Ecology and Social Policy). Frankfurt/Main: Fischer.

Human Development Report (2006). Beyond Scarcity: Power, Poverty and the Global Water Crisis. Available from: www. hdr.undp.org/hdr2006.

Hurd Clarke, L. (2010). *Facing age: Women growing older in anti–aging culture.* Toronto: Rowman and Littlefield.

Hurd Clarke, L., Repta, R., & Griffin, M. (2007). Non-surgical cosmetic procedures: Older women's perceptions and experiences. *Journal of Women and Aging,* 19(3/4), 69–87.

Illich, I. (1971). *Deschooling society.* New York: Harper and Row.

Ingham, A. & McDonald, M. (2003). Sport and community/communitas. In R. Wilcox, D. Andrews, R. Pitter, & R. Irwin (Eds.), *Sport dystopias: The making and meaning of urban sport cultures* (pp. 17–33). Albany: SUNY.

Jackson, S. & Andrews, D. (1999). Between and beyond the global and the local. *International Review for the Sociology of Sport,* 34(1), 31–42.

Jackson, S. & Haigh, S. (2008). Between and beyond politics: Sport and foreign policy in a globalizing world. *Sport in Society,* 11(4), 349–58.

Jackson, S. & Hokowhitu, B. (2005). Sports, tribes and technology: The New Zealand All-Blacks *Haka* and the politics of identity. In M. Silk, D. Andrews, & C. Cole (Eds.), *Sport and corporate nationalisms* (pp. 1–12). Oxford: Berg.

James, C.L.R. (1993). *American civilization.* Oxford: Blackwell.

Jansen, S. & Sabo, D. (1994). The sport-war metaphor: Hegemonic masculinity, the Persian-Gulf war, and the new world order. *Sociology of Sport Journal,* 11(1), 1–17.

Jarvie, G. (2006). *Sport, culture and society: An introduction.* New York: Routledge.

Jeong, H. (2000). *Peace and conflict studies: An introduction.* Aldershot, UK: Ashgate.

Jermyn, D. (2010, July 27). Kick a ball, save the world. *Globe and Mail,* Retrieved July 27, 2010, from: www.theglobeandmail. com/report-on-business/your-business/ business-categories/leadership/kick-a-ball-save-the-world/article1652368/.

Jette, S. (2009). *Governing risk, exercising caution: Western medical knowledge, physical activity and pregnancy.* Unpublished Ph.D. dissertation, University of British Columbia, Vancouver, British Columbia.

Jhally, S. (Director). (1999). *Tough guise: Violence, media & the crisis in masculinity.* Northampton, MA: Media Education Foundation.

Joll, J. (1977). *Gramsci.* London: Fontana.

Justas, A. (2010, February 18). Vancouver 2010: Greenest Olympic Games Ever. Retrieved Sept. 16, 2010 at: www. greendiary.com/entry/vancouver-2010-greenest-olympic-games-ever/.

Jutila, M., Pehkonen, S., & Väyrynen, T. (2008). Resuscitating a discipline: An agenda for critical peace research. *Millennium: Journal of International Studies*, 36(3), 623–40.

Karetu, T. (1993). *Haka!: The dance of a noble people*. Auckland, NZ: Reed Books.

Katz, J. (2005). Reconstructing masculinity in the locker room: The mentors in violence prevention project. In P. Leistyna (Ed.), *Cultural studies: From theory to practice* (pp. 397–407). Malden, MA: Blackwell.

———. (2006). *The macho paradox: Why some men hurt women and how all men can help*. Naperville, IL: Sourcebooks.

Kay, T. (2011). Development through sport?: Sport in support of female empowerment in Delhi, India. In B. Houlihan & M. Green (Eds.), *Routledge handbook of sports development* (pp. 308–22). New York: Routledge.

Kearins, K. & Pavlovich, K. (2002). The role of stakeholders in Sydney's green games. *Corporate Social Responsibility and Environmental Management*, 9, 157–69.

Keim, M. (2003). *National building at play: Sport as a tool for re-integration in post-apartheid South Africa*. Oxford: Meyer and Meyer.

Kemple, T. & Mawani, R. (2009). The sociological imagination and its imperial shadows. *Theory, Culture & Society*, 26(7–8), 228–49.

Kennelly, J. (2008). Citizen youth: Culture, activism, and agency in an era of globalization. Unpublished Ph.D. dissertation, University of British Columbia, Vancouver, British Columbia.

Kidd, B. (2007). Peace, sport and development. In Sport for Development and Peace International Working Group (SDP IWG) Secretariat (Commissioned) *Literature reviews on sport for development and peace* (pp. 158–94). University of Toronto, Faculty of Physical Education and Health.

———. (2008). A new social movement: Sport for development and peace. *Sport in Society* 11(4), 370–80.

———. (2009/2010). Canada needs a two-track strategy for hosting international games. *Policy Options*, 31(1), 20.

———. (2010). Epilogue: the struggles must continue. *Sport in Society* 13(1), 157–65.

King, C.R. (2008). Toward a radical sport journalism: An interview with Dave Zirin. *Journal of Sport and Social Issues by ARENA: The Institute for Sport and Social Analysis*, 32 (4), 2008. Reproduced with permission of SAGE PUBLICATIONS INC. in the format Journal via Copyright Clearance Center.

King, S. (2006). *Pink Ribbons, Inc*. Minneapolis: University of Minnesota Press.

King, S. (2008). Offensive lines: Sport-state synergy in an era of perpetual war. *Cultural Studies ↔ Critical Methodologies*, 8(4), 527–39.

Kirby, S., Greaves, L., & Hankivsky, O. (2000). *The dome of silence: Sexual harassment and abuse in sport*. Halifax: Fernwood Publishing Ltd.

Kirk, D. (2002). The social construction of the body in physical education and sport. In A. Laker (Ed.), *The sociology of sport and physical education: An introductory reader* (pp. 79–91). New York: Routledge.

Klaehn, J. (2002). A critical review and assessment of Herman and Chomsky's 'propaganda model'. *European Journal of Communication* 17(2), 147–82.

Knight, G. & Greenberg, J. (2002). Promotionalism and subpolitics: Nike and its labour critics. *Management Communication Quarterly* 15(4), 541–570.

Krüger, A. (1999). Strength through joy: The culture of consent through Nazism, Fascism and Francoism. In J. Riordan & A. Krüger (Eds.), *The international politics of sport in the 20th century* (pp. 67–89). New York: Taylor & Francis.

Larkin, J. (2007). Gender, sport and development. In *Report for the Sport for Development and Peace International Working Group (SDP IWG) Secretariat* (pp. 89–123). University of Toronto, Faculty of Physical Education and Health.

Latour, B. (1993). *We have never been modern* (trans. C. Porter). Cambridge: Harvard University Press.

———. *Pandora's hope*. Cambridge: Harvard University Press.

Lederach, J. (1997). *Building peace: Sustainable reconciliation in divided societies*. Washington: United States Institute of Peace.

———. (2005). *The moral imagination: The art and soul of building peace*. New York: Oxford.

Lee, K. (2008, July 30). Beyond ping–pong diplomacy. *Foreign Policy In Focus*. Retrieved March 30, 2011 from: www.fpif.org/articles/beyond_ping-pong_diplomacy

Lee, S. & Maslog, C. (2005). War or peace journalism?: Asian newspaper coverage of conflicts. *Journal of Communication* 55(2), 311–330.

Leistyna, P. (2005). Introduction: Revitalizing the dialogue: Theory, coalition–building and social change. In P. Leistyna (Ed.), *Cultural studies: From theory to practice* (pp. 1–15). Malden, MA: Blackwell.

Lenskyj, H. (1998). Sport and corporate environmentalism: The case of the Sydney 2000 Olympics. *International Review for the Sociology of Sport*, 33(4), 341–54.

———. (2000). *Inside the Olympic industry: Power, politics and activism.* Albany: SUNY Press.

———. (2002). *The best Olympics ever: Social impacts of Sydney 2000.* Albany: SUNY Press.

———. (2006). The Olympic industry and civil liberties: the threat to free speech and freedom of assembly. In D. McCardle & R. Giulianotti (Eds.), *Sport, civil liberties and human rights* (pp. 78–92). New York: Routledge.

———. (2008). *Olympic industry resistance: Challenging Olympic power and propaganda.* Albany: SUNY Press.

Leonard, W. (1998). *A sociological perspective of sport.* Toronto: Allyn and Bacon.

Levermore, R. (2004). Sport's role in constructing the 'inter-state' worldview. In R. Levermore & A. Budd, (Eds.), *Sport and international relations: An emerging relationship* (pp. 16–30). New York: Routledge.

———. (2008). Sport-in-international development: Time to treat it seriously?. *Brown Journal of World Affairs*, 14(2), 55–66.

———. (2009). Sport-in-international development: Theoretical perspectives. In R. Levermore & A. Beacom (Eds.), *Sport and international development* (pp. 26–54). New York: Palgrave MacMillan.

Levermore, R. & Beacom, A. (2009). Sport and development: Mapping the field. In R. Levermore & A. Beacom (Eds.), *Sport and international development* (pp. 1–25). New York: Palgrave MacMillan.

Levermore, R. & Budd, A. (Eds.) (2004). *Sport and international relations: An emerging relationship.* New York: Routledge.

Lévi-Strauss, C. (1987). *Introduction to Marcel Mauss.* London: Routledge.

Lubbers, E. (Ed.) (2002). *Battling big business: Countering greenwash, infiltration and other forms of corporate bullying.* Monroe, ME: Common Courage Books.

Lynch, J. & Galtung, J. (2010). *Reporting conflict: New directions in peace journalism.* St. Lucia: University of Queensland Press.

Lynch, J. & McGoldrick, A. (2005). *Peace journalism.* Gloucestershire: Hawthorn Press.

McBride, S. & McNutt, K. (2007). Devolution and neoliberalism in the Canadian welfare State: Ideology, national and international conditioning frameworks, and policy change in British Columbia, *Global Social Policy*, 7(2), 177–201.

McCarthy, J. & Zald, M. (1977). Resource mobilization and social movements: A partial theory. *American Journal of Sociology*, 82, 1212–41.

McDonald, I. (2008, November). Brighton bandits. Screening of short film at the *North American Society for the Sociology of Sport (NASSS) Conference*, Denver, USA.

———. (2009). One–dimensional sport: Revolutionary Marxism and the critique of sport. In B. Carrington & I. McDonald (Eds.), *Marxism, cultural studies and sport* (pp. 320–47). New York: Routledge.

McDonald, M. (2005). Imagining benevolence, masculinity and nation: Tragedy, sport and the transnational marketplace. In M. Silk, D. Andrews, & C. Cole (Eds.), *Sport and corporate nationalisms* (pp. 127–41). Oxford: Berg.

Macintosh, D. & Hawes, M. (1994). *Sport and Canadian diplomacy.* Montreal and Kingston: McGill-Queen's Press.

McKay, J. (1986). Marxism as a way of seeing: Beyond the limits of current critical approaches to sport. *Sociology of Sport Journal*, 3(3), 261–72.

———. (1995). 'Just Do It': Corporate sports slogans and the political economy of enlightened racism. *Discourse: Studies in the cultural politics of education*, 16(2), 191–201.

———, J. (2002). Teaching against the grain: A learner-centered, media-based, and profeminist approach to gender and nonviolence in sport. In M. Gatz, M. Messner, & S. Ball-Rokeach (Eds.), *Paradoxes of youth and sport* (pp. 103–18). Albany: SUNY Press.

McKay, J., Mikosza, J., & Hutchins, B. (2005). 'Gentlemen, the lunchbox has landed': Representations of masculinities and men's bodies in the popular media. In M. Kimmel, J. Hearn & R. Connell (Eds.), *Handbook of studies on men and masculinities* (pp. 270–88). Thousand Oaks, CA: Sage.

MacNeill, M. (1996). Networks: Producing Olympic hockey for a national television audience. *Sociology of Sport Journal*, 13(2), 103–24.

Maguire, J. (1999). *Global sport: Identities,*

societies, civilizations. Cambridge: Polity Press.

Maguire, J., Jarvie, G., Mansfield, L. & Bradley, J. (2002). *Sport worlds: A sociological perspective.* Champaign, IL: Human Kinetics.

Majors, R. & Billson, J.M. (1992). *Cool pose: The dilemmas of Black manhood in America.* New York: Lexington Books.

Mansfield, L. (2009). Fitness Cultures and Environmental (in)Justice? *International Review for the Sociology of Sport,* 44(4), 345–62.

Manzenreiter, W. (2010). The Beijing Games in the Western imagination of China: The weak power of soft power. *Journal of Sport & Social Issues,* 34(1), 29–48.

Marglin, S. (2008). *The dismal science: How thinking like an economist undermines community.* Cambridge, MA: Harvard University Press.

Markula, P. (2006). Body–movement–change: Dance as performative qualitative research. *Journal of Sport and Social Issues* 30(4), 353–63.

Markula, P. & Pringle, R. (2006). *Foucault, sport and exercise: Power, knowledge and transforming the self.* London: Routledge

Martinek, T. & Hellison, D. (1997). Fostering resiliency in underserved youth through physical activity. *Quest,* 49(1), 34–49.

Martinek, T., Schilling, T., & Hellison, D. (2006). The development of compassionate and caring leadership among adolescents. *Physical Education & Sport Pedagogy,* 11(2),141–57

Meikle, G. (2002). *Future active: Media activism and the internet.* New York: Routledge.

Melucci, A. (1996). *Challenging codes: Collective action in the age of information.* New York: Cambridge University Press.

Messner, M. (1990). When bodies are weapons: Masculinity and violence in sport. *International Review for the Sociology of Sport* 25(3), 203–218.

——. (1992). *Power at play: Sports and the problem of masculinity.* Boston: Beacon Press.

——. (2005). The triad of violence in men's sports. In Buchwald, E., Fletcher, P. & Roth, M. (Eds.) *Transforming a rape culture* (2nd ed.) (pp. 25–46). Minneapolis: Milkweed Editions.

Messner, M., Dunbar, M., & Hunt, D. (2000). The televised sports manhood formula. *Journal of Sport and Social Issues,* 24(4), 380–94.

Messner, M. & Sabo, D. (Eds.) (1990). *Sport, men and the gender order: Critical feminist*

perspectives. Champaign, IL: Human Kinetics Publishers.

Messner, M. & Stevens, M. (2007). Scoring without consent: Confronting male athletes' violence against women. In M. Messner (Author), *Out of play: Critical essays on gender and sport* (pp. 107–19). Albany: SUNY.

Miller, T., Lawrence, G., McKay, J., & Rowe, D. (2001). *Globalization and sport.* Thousand Oaks, CA: Sage.

Millington, B. & Wilson, B. (2010a). Context masculinities: Media consumption, physical education, and youth identities. *American Behavioral Scientist,* 53(11), 1669–88.

——— & ———. (2010b). The Golf Industry and the Making of Environmental Responsibility. Presented at the *North American Society for the Sociology of Sport Conference* entitled 'Producing Knowledge, Producing Bodies: Cross–Currents in Sociologies of Sport and Physical Culture.' San Diego, CA, Nov. 3–6.

Mills, C. W. (1959). *The sociological imagination.* London. Oxford.

Mincyte, D., Casper, M.J. & Cole, C.L. (2009). Sports, environmentalism, land use, and urban development. *Journal of Sport & Social Issues,* 33(2), 103–10.

Miracle, A. & Rees, R. (1994). *Lessons of the locker room: The myth of school sports.* Amherst, NY: Prometheus Books.

Moores, S. (1993). *Interpreting audiences: The ethnography of media consumption.* Thousand Oaks, CA: Sage.

Morgan, W. (1993). *Leftist theories of sport.* Urbana: University of Illinois Press.

——. (2004). Habermas on sports. In R. Giulianotti (Ed.), *Sport and modern social theorists* (pp. 173–86). New York: Palgrave Macmillan.

Morley, D. & Robins, K. (1995). *Spaces of identity: Global media, electronic landscapes and cultural boundaries.* London: Routledge.

Morris, A. & Herring, C. (1987). Theory and research in social movements: A critical review. *Annual Review of Political Science 2,* 137–198.

Nicholls, S. (2009). On the backs of peer educators: Using theory to interrogate the role of young people in the field of sport in development. In R. Levermore & A. Beacom (Eds.), *Sport and international development* (pp. 156–75). New York: Palgrave MacMillan.

Nicholls, S., Giles, A., & Sethna, C. (2011). Perpetuating the 'lack of evidence' discourse in sport for development: Privileged voices, unheard stories and subjugated knowledge. *International Review for the Sociology of Sport*, 46(3), 249–64.

Nicholson, M. & Hoye, R. (Eds.) (2008). *Sport and social capital*. New York: Elsevier.

Norman, M. (2009). *Living in the shadow of an 'obesity epidemic': The discursive construction of boys and their bodies*. Unpublished Ph.D. dissertation, University of Toronto, Toronto, Ontario.

Palmer, C. (2004). More than just a game: The consequences of golf tourism. In B. Ritchie & D. Adair (Eds.), *Sport tourism: Interrelationships, impacts and issues* (pp. 117–34). Toronto: Channel View Publications.

Paraschak, V. (1997). Variations in race relations: Sporting events for Native peoples in Canada. *Sociology of Sport Journal* 14(1), 1–21.

Parnes, P. (2007). Sport as a means to foster inclusion, health and well-being of people with disabilities. In *Report for the Sport for Development and Peace International Working Group (SDP IWG) Secretariat* (pp. 124–57). University of Toronto, Faculty of Physical Education and Health.

Pieterse, J. (2001). *Development theory: Deconstructions/reconstructions*. London: Sage Publications.

Pitter, R. (2009). Finding the Kieran Way: A study of sport, recreation and lifestyle politics in rural Nova Scotia. *Journal of Sport and Social Issues*, 33(1), 331–51.

Poncelet, E. (2004). *Partnering for the environment: Multistakeholder collaboration in a changing world*. Toronto, ON: Rowan & Littlefield Publishers.

Price, M. (2008). Introduction. In M. Price & D. Dayan (Eds.), *Owning the Olympics: Narratives of the new China* (pp. 1–13). Ann Arbor: The University of Michigan Press.

Price, M & Dayan, D. (Eds.) (2008). *Owning the Olympics: Narratives of the new China*. Ann Arbor: The University of Michigan Press.

Pringle, R. (2005). Masculinities, sport, and power: A critical comparison of Gramscian and Foucauldian inspired theoretical tools. *Journal of Sport & Social Issues*, 29(3), 256–78.

Pronger, B. (1995). Rendering the body: The implicit lessons of gross anatomy. *Quest*, 47(4), 427–46.

Prus, R. (1996). *Symbolic interactionism and ethnographic research*. Albany: SUNY Press.

Putnam, R. (2000). *Bowling alone: The collapse and revival of the American community*. New York: Simon & Schuster.

Richards, P. (1997). Soccer and violence in war torn Africa: Soccer and social rehabilitation in Sierra Leone. In G. Armstrong and R. Giulianotti (Eds.), *Entering the field: New perspectives on world football* (pp. 141–58). New York: Berg.

Richmond, O. (2007). *The transformation of peace*. New York: Palgrave Macmillan.

Rinehart, R. E. (2010). Poetic sensibilities, humanities, and wonder: Toward an e/affective sociology of sport. *Quest*, 62(2), 184–201

Riordan, J. (1999). The worker sports movement. In J. Riordan & A. Krüger (Eds.), *International politics of sport in the twentieth century* (pp.105–120). London: E & FN Spon.

Robertson, M. (2004). The neoliberalization of ecosystem services: Wetland mitigation banking and the problem of measurement. In N. Heynan, J. McCarthy, S. Prudham, & P. Robbins (Eds.), *Neoliberal environments: False promises and unnatural consequences* (pp. 114–125). New York: Routledge.

Robertson, R. (1992). *Globalization: Social theory and global culture*. New York: Russell Sage.

Robinson, L. (1998). *Crossing the line: Violence and sexual assault in Canada's national sport*. Toronto: McClelland & Stewart.

———. (2002a). *The FrontRunners: A story of ten indigenous runners in Canada*. Available from: www.playthegame.org/knowledge–bank/articles/the–frontrunners–a–story–of–ten–indigenous–runners–in–canada–1086.html.

———. (2002b). *Black tights: Women, sport and sexuality*. Toronto: Harper Collins.

Rowe, D. (2003). Sport and the repudiation of the global. *International Review for the Sociology of Sport*, 38(3), 281– 94.

———. (2004). Antonio Gramsci: Sport, hegemony and the national–popular. In R. Giulianotti (Ed.), *Sport and modern social theorists* (pp. 97–110). New York: Palgrave MacMillan.

Rozee, P. & Koss, M. (2001). Rape: A century of resistance. *Psychology of Women Quarterly*, 25(4), 295–311.

Rugge, J. (1982). International regimes, transactions, and change: Embedded liberalism in the postwar economic order. *International Organization* 36(2), 379–415.

Saavedra, M. (2009). Dilemmas and opportunities in gender and sport-in-development. In R. Levermore & A.

Beacom (Eds.), *Sport and international development* (pp. 124–55). New York: Palgrave Macmillan.

Sabo, D. & Runfola, R. (1980). *Jock: Sports and male identity*. Englewood Cliffs, NJ: Prentice Hall.

Sage, G. (1998). *Power and ideology in American sport: A critical perspective*. Champaign, IL: Human Kinetics.

———. (1999). Justice do it! The Nike transnational advocacy network: Organization, collective action and outcomes. *Sociology of Sport Journal*, 16(3), 206–35.

Schaffner, S. (2009). Environmental sporting: Bliding at superfund sites, landfills, and sewage ponds. *Journal of Sport & Social Issues*, 33(3), 206–29.

Scherer, J., Duquette, G., & Mason, D. (2007). The Cold War and the (re)articulation of Canadian national identity: The 1972 Canada–USSR Summit Series. In S. Wagg & D. Andrews (Eds.), *East plays West: Essays on sport and the Cold War* (pp. 171–94). London: Routledge.

Scherer, J. & Jackson, S. (2010). *Globalization, sport and corporate nationalism: The new cultural economy of the New Zealand All Blacks*. New York: Peter Lang.

Scherer, J. & Koch, J. (2010). Living with war: Sport, citizenship, and the cultural politics of post-9/11 Canadian identity. *Sociology of Sport Journal*, 27(1), 1–29.

Schiermeier, Q. (2006, December 21). Climate credits. *Nature*, 444(7122), 976–977.

Schnaiberg, A. (1980). *The Environment: From Surplus to Scarcity*. New York: Oxford University Press.

Schnaiberg, A. & Gould, K. (2000). *Environment and Society: The Enduring Conflict*. West Caldwell, NJ: Blackburn Press.

Scholte, J. (2005). *Globalization: A critical introduction*. New York: Palgrave Macmillan.

Schulenkorf, N. (2010). Sport events and ethnic reconciliation: Attempting to create social change between Sinhalese, Tamil and Muslim sportspeople in war-torn Sri Lanka. *International Review for the Sociology of Sport*, 45(3), 273–94.

Shaull, R. (2000). Forward. In P. Freire (Author), *Pedagogy of the oppressed* (pp. 29–34). New York: Continuum.

Shinar, D. (2009). Why not more peace journalism?: The coverage of the 2006 Lebanon War in Canadian and Israeli media. In S. Dente Ross & M. Tehranian (Eds.), *Peace journalism in times of war* (pp. 7–30). New Brunswick, NJ: Transaction Publishers.

Shoemaker, P. & Reese, S. (1996). *Mediating the message: Theories of influences on mass media content*. White Plains, NY: Longman.

Silk, M. (2008). Mow my lawn. *Cultural Studies: Critical Methodologies*, 8(4), 477–78.

Silk, M. & Andrews, D. (2001). Beyond a boundary: Sport, transnational advertising, and the re-imagining of National Culture. *Journal of Sport & Social Issues* 25(2), 180–202.

Silk, M., Andrews, D., & Cole, C. (2005). Corporate nationalism(s)?: The spatial dimensions of sporting capital. In M. Silk, D. Andrews, & C. Cole (Eds.), *Sport and corporate nationalisms* (pp. 1–12). Oxford: Berg.

Silk, M., Bush, A., & Andrews, D. (2010) Contingent intellectual amateurism, or, the problem with evidence–based research. *Journal of Sport and Social Issues*, 34(1), 105–28.

Slack, J. (1996). The theory and method of articulation. In D. Morley & K. Chen (Eds.), *Stuart Hall: Critical dialogues in cultural studies* (pp. 112–27). London: Routledge.

Smith, B. (1999) The abyss: Exploring depression through a narrative of the self. *Qualitative Inquiry*, 5(2), 264–79.

Smith, B. & Sparkes, A.C. (2005). Men, sport, spinal cord injury and narratives of hope. *Social Science & Medicine*, 61(5), 1095–105.

Sorek, T. (2007). *Arab soccer in a Jewish state: The integrative enclave*. New York: Cambridge University Press.

Spaargaren, G. & Mol, A. (1992). Sociology, environment, and modernity: Ecological modernization as a theory of social change. *Society and Natural Resources*, 5, 323–44.

Sport for Development and Peace International Working Group (2008). *Harnessing the Power of Sport for Development and Peace: Recommendations to Governments*. Toronto: Right to Play.

Staggenborg, S. (1988). The consequences of professionalization and formalization in the pro-choice movement, *American Sociological Review* 53(4), 585–605.

———. (2008). *Social movements*. Toronto: Oxford University Press.

Stahl, R. (2007). *Militainment, Inc.: Militarism and popular culture*. Northampton, MA: Media Education Foundation.

———. (2010). *Militainment, Inc.: War, media, and popular culture*. New York: Routledge.

Stahl, H., Hochfeld, C., Schmied, M. (2006). *Green goal: Legacy report*. Frankfurt: Organizing Committee 2006 World Cup.

Stempel, Carl. (2006). Televised sports, masculinist moral capital, and support for the U.S. invasion of Iraq. *Journal of Sport and Social Issues*, 30(1), 79–106.

Stiglitz, J. (2002). *Globalization and its discontents*. New York: Penguin Books.

Stoddart, B. (1990). Wide world of golf: A research note on the interdependence of sport, culture, and economy. *Sociology of Sport Journal*, 7(4), 378–88.

Stoddart, M. (2008). *Making meaning out of mountains: Skiing, the environment and eco-politics*. Unpublished doctoral dissertation, University of British Columbia, Vancouver, British Columbia, Canada.

Stolle-McAllister, J. (2004). Contingent hybridity: The cultural politics of Tepoztlán's anti-golf movement. *Identities: Global Studies in Culture and Power*, 11, 195–213.

Sugden, J. (2006). Teaching and playing sport for conflict resolution and co-existence in Israel. *International Review of the Sociology of Sport*, 41(2), 221–40.

———. (2007). War stops peace!. In J. Sugden & J. Wallis (Eds.), *Football for peace?: The challenges of using sport for co-existence in Israel* (pp. 172–75). Oxford: Meyer & Meyer Sport.

———. (2010a). Critical left–realism and sport interventions in divided societies. *International Review for the Sociology of Sport*, 45(3), 258–72.

———. (2010b). Between idealism and fatalism: Critical realism, sport and social intervention. In Joint Research Institute for International Peace and Culture (Ed.), *Fostering peace through cultural initiatives: From the roundtable on conflict and culture* (pp. 33–53). Accessed at: www.jripec–aoyama.jp.

Sugden, J. & Bairner, A. (Eds.) (2000). *Sport in divided societies*. Oxford: Meyer & Meyer Sport.

Sugden, J. & Wallis, J. (Eds.) (2007). *Football for peace?: The challenges of using sport for co–existence in Israel*. Oxford: Meyer & Meyer Sport.

Symons, C. (2010). *The gay games: A history*. New York: Routledge.

Tarrow, S. (1980). *Power in movement: Social movements and contentious politics*. Cambridge: Cambridge University Press.

Teeple, G. (2000). *Globalization and the decline of social reform into the twentieth century*. Aurora, ON: Garamond.

Thibault, L. (2009). Globalization and sport: An inconvenient truth. *Journal of Sport Management*, 23(1), 1–20

Thomas, N. & Smith, A. (2009). *Disability, sport and society. An introduction*. New York: Routledge.

Thomas, W.I. (1923). *The unadjusted girl*. Boston: Little, Brown.

Tilly, C. (2007). *Democracy*. New York: Cambridge.

Tomlinson, A. (1999). *The game's up: Essays in the cultural analysis of sport, leisure and popular culture*. Aldershot: Arena.

Toohey. K. (2008). Terrorism, sport and public policy in the risk society. *Sport in Society*, 11(4), 429–42.

Tranter, P.J. & Lowes, M. (2009). Life in the fast lane: Environmental, economic, and public health outcomes of motorsport spectacles in Australia. *Journal of Sport & Social Issues*, 33(2), 150–68.

Trujillo, N. (2000). Hegemonic masculinity on the mound: Media representations of Nolan Ryan and American sports culture. In S. Birrell & M. McDonald (Eds.), *Reading sport: Critical essays on power and representation* (pp. 14–39). Boston: Northeastern University Press.

Tschang, Chi-Chu (2008, August 11). Olympic ambush heats up Li Ning-Adidas rivalry. *Businessweek*. Retrieved April 3, 2011 from: www.businessweek.com/global biz/content/aug2008/gb20080811_303782.htm.

Turner, V. (1969). *The ritual process: Structure and anti–structure*. Chicago: Aldine.

Tzu, Sun. (2002). *The art of war* (trans. J. Minford). New York: Viking.

UNEP (2007, October 25). Greening of 2008 Beijing Games impressive says UN Environment Programme Report. Press Release, retrieved on July, 2008 from: www.unep.org/Documents.Multilingual/Default.asp?DocumentID=519&ArticleID=5687&l=en.

United Nations (n.d.). *Achieving the objectives of the United Nations through sport*. Geneva: United Nations.

United Nations (2003). *Sport for development and peace: Towards achieving the millennium development goals*. Report from the UN Inter-Agency Task Force on Sport for Development and Peace: New York.

United Nations (2004, November 5). Universal language of sport brings people together, teaches teamwork, tolerance, secretary-general says at launch of international year. *United Nations Press Release*, SG/SM/9579.

Unruh, A. & Elvin, N. (2004). In the eye of the dragon: Women's experience of breast cancer and the occupation of dragon boat racing. *Canadian Journal of Occupational Therapy*, 71(3), 138–49.

van Hilvoorde, I., Elling, A., & Stokvis, R. (2010). How to influence national pride? The Olympic medal index as a unifying narrative. *International Review for the Sociology of Sport*, 45(1), 87–102.

Vancouver Declaration of the 8th World Conference on Sport and the Environment (2009). *Innovation and inspiration: Harnessing the power of sport for change*. Retrieved December 2, 2011 from: www.wcse2009.com/documents/final_%20declaration_eng.pdf

Vertinsky, P. (1994). *The eternally wounded woman: Doctors, women and exercise in the late nineteenth century*. Champaign, IL: University of Illinois Press.

———. (2009). Mind the gap (or mending it): Qualitative research and interdisciplinarity. *Quest*, 61(1), 39–51.

Wall, M. (2007). Social movements and email: Expressions of online identity in the globalization protests, *New Media & Society* 9(2), 258–77.

Wallace, T. (2003). NGO dilemmas: Trojan Horses for global neoliberalism?. In L. Panitch, & C. Leys (Eds.), *The new imperial challenge: Socialist register 2004* (pp. 202–19). London: Merlin Press.

Wamucii, P. (2007). *Scoring for social change: A study of the Mathare Youth Sports Association in Kenya*. Unpublished Ph.D. dissertation, Ohio University, Athens, Ohio.

Watts, R., Chioke Williams, N. & Jagers, R. (2003). Sociopolitical development. *American Journal of Community Psychology*, 31(1/2), pp. 185–94.

Webel, C. (2007). Introduction: Toward a philosophy and metapsychology of peace. In C. Webel & J. Galtung, (Eds.), *Handbook of peace and conflict studies* (3–13). New York: Routledge.

Webel, C. & Galtung, J. (Eds.) (2007). *Handbook of peace and conflict studies*. New York: Routledge.

Wedemeyer, B. (1999). Sport and terrorism. In J. Riordan & A. Krüger (Eds.), *The international politics of sport in the 20th century* (217–33). New York: Taylor & Francis.

Welch, M. (1997). Violence against women by professional football players: A gender analysis of hypermasculinity, positional status, narcissism, and entitlement. *Journal of Sport & Social Issues*, 21(4), 392–411.

Wernick, A. (1991). *Promotional culture: Advertising, ideology and symbolic expression*. London: Sage.

Wheaton, B. (Ed.) (2004). *Understanding Lifestyle Sports: Consumption, Identity and Difference*. London: Routledge.

———. (2005). Selling out? The commercialization and globalization of lifestyle sport. In L. Allison (Ed.), *The global politics of sport: The role of global institutions in sport* (pp. 140–61). New York: Routledge.

———. (2007). Identity, politics, and the beach: Environmental activism in Surfers Against Sewage. *Leisure Studies* 26, 279–302.

———. (2008). From the pavement to the beach: Politics and identity in 'Surfers Against Sewage'. In M. Atkinson & K. Young (Eds.), *Tribal play: Subcultural journeys through sport* (pp. 113–134). Bingley, UK: Emerald Group Publishing.

Wheaton, B. & Beal, B. (2003). 'Keeping it real': Subcultural media and the discourses of authenticity in alternative sport. *International Review for the Sociology of Sport*, 38(2), 155–76.

Wheeler, K. & Nauright, J. (2006). A global perspective on the environmental impact of golf. *Sport in Society*, 9(3), 427–43.

White, P. & Young, K. (2006). Gender, sport, and the injury process. In K. Young & P. White (Eds.), *Sport and gender in Canada* (pp. 259–78). Toronto: Oxford University Press.

White, P., Young, K., & Gillett, J. (1995). Body work as a moral imperative: Some critical notes on health and fitness. *Loisir and Société*, 18(1), 163–86.

Whitson, D. (1984). Sport and hegemony: On the construction of the dominant culture. *Sociology of Sport Journal*, 1(1), 64–78.

Williams, C. (2010). *Ecology and socialism: Solutions to capitalist ecological crisis*. Chicago: Haymarket Books.

Williams, R. (1977). *Marxism and literature*. London: Oxford University Press.

Willis, P. (1977). *Learning to labour: How working class kids get working class jobs*. New York: Columbia University Press.

———. (1990). *Common culture*. Milton Keynes: Open University Press.

Wilson, B. (1997). 'Good blacks' and 'bad blacks': Media constructions of African-American athletes in Canadian basketball. *International Review for the Sociology of Sport*, 32(2), 177–89.

———. (2002). The 'anti–jock' movement: Reconsidering youth resistance, masculinity and sport culture in the age of the Internet. *Sociology of Sport Journal*, 19(2), 207–34.

————. (2006a). Selective memory in a global culture: Reconsidering links between youth, hockey and Canadian identity. In R. Gruneau & D. Whitson (Eds.), *Artificial ice: Hockey, culture, and commerce* (pp. 53–70). Peterborough, ON: Broadview/Garamond Press.

————. (2006b). *Fight, flight, or chill: Subcultures, youth, and rave into the 21st century.* Montreal & Kingston: McGill-Queen's University Press.

————. (2007a). New media, social movements, and global sport studies: A revolutionary moment and the sociology of sport. *Sociology of Sport Journal,* 24(4), 457–77.

————. (2007b). Oppression is the message: Media, sport, spectacle and gender. In P. White & K. Young (Eds.), *Sport and gender in Canada* (2nd Edition) (pp. 212–33). Toronto: Oxford University Press.

————. (2008). Believe the hype? The impact of the Internet on sport-related subcultures. In M. Atkinson & K. Young (Eds.), *Tribal play: Subcultural journeys through sport* (pp. 135–152). Bingley, UK: JAI Press.

————. (in press). Growth and nature: Reflections on sport, carbon neutrality, and ecological modernization. In D. Andrews & M. Silk (Eds.), *Sport and neo-liberalism.* Philadelphia: Temple University Press.

Wilson, B. & Hayhurst, L. (2009). Digital activism: Neo-liberalism, the internet, and 'sport for development'. *Sociology of Sport Journal,* 26(1), 155–81.

Wilson, B. & Millington, B. (2011). *From Reformism to Resistance: Golf, the Environment, and Social Change.* Presented at the North American Society for the Sociology of Sport Conference, Minneapolis, MN, November 2–5.

Wilson, B. & Millington, B. (in press). The only solution? Sport, 'ecological modernization', and the production of silence. In D. Andrews & B. Carrington (Eds.), *The Blackwell companion to sport.* Malden, MA: Blackwell Publishing.

Wilson, B. & Sparks, R. (1999). Impacts of black athlete media portrayals on Canadian youth. *Canadian Journal of Communication,* 24(4), 589–627.

Wilson, B. & White, P. (2001). Tolerance rules: Identity, resistance, and negotiation in an inner city recreation/drop in center. *Journal of Sport and Social Issues,* 25(1), 73–103.

———— & ————. (2003). Urban sanctuary: Youth culture in a recreation/drop–in centre. In R. Wilcox, D. Andrews, R. Pitter, & R. Irwin (Eds.) *Sporting Dystopias: The Making and Meaning of Urban Sport and Cultures* (pp. 153–78). Albany: State University of New York Press.

Wilson, B., White, P., & Fisher, K. (2001). Multiple identities in a marginalized culture: Female youth in an 'inner city' recreation/drop-in centre. *Journal of Sport and Social Issues,* 25(3), 301–23.

Wilson, J. (2005). Skating to Armageddon: Canada, hockey and the First World War. *The International Journal of the History of Sport,* 22(3), 315–43.

Winter, J. (2006). *Dreams of peace and freedom: Utopian moments in the 20th century.* New Haven: Yale University Press.

Wolff, A. (2007, March 6). Going, going green. *Sports Illustrated.* Retrieved January 25, 2010 from: http://sportsillustrated. cnn.com/2007/more/03/06/eco0312/.

Wushanley, Y. (2004). *Playing nice and losing: The struggle for control of women's intercollegiate athletics, 1960–2000.* Syracuse: Syracuse University Press.

Young, K. (Ed.) (2004). *Sporting bodies, damaged selves: Sociological studies of sport-related injury.* Amsterdam: Elsevier Press.

Young, K. & White, P. (1995). Sport, physical danger and injury: The experiences of elite women athletes. *Journal of Sport and Social Issues,* 19(1), 45–61.

Zackus, D. (2007). The use of sport and physical activity to achieve health objectives. In Sport for Development and Peace International Working Group (SDP IWG) Secretariat (Commissioned) *Literature reviews on sport for development and peace* (pp. 48–88). University of Toronto, Faculty of Physical Education and Health.

Zirin, D. (2005). *What's my name, fool? Sports and resistance in the United States.* Chicago: Haymarket Books.

————. (2007a). *Welcome to the terrordome: The pain, promise, and politics of sport.* Chicago: Haymarket Books.

————. (2007b). *The Muhammad Ali handbook.* Minneapolis: MQ Publications.

————. (2008). *A people's history of sports in the United States.* New York: New Press.

————. (2011, January 31). Soccer clubs central to ending Egypt's 'Dictatorship of Fear'. *Sports Illustrated,* Retrieved March 9, 2011 from: http://sportsillustrated.cnn. com/2011/writers/dave_zirin/01/31/egypt. soccer/index.html#ixzz1G8BGtYnS

Index